Journey by Junk

JAPAN AFTER MACARTHUR

Books by
Willard Price

JOURNEY BY JUNK

THE AMAZING AMAZON

SOUTH SEA ADVENTURE

I CANNOT REST FROM TRAVEL

AMAZON ADVENTURE

ROVING SOUTH

KEY TO JAPAN

JAPAN AND THE SON OF HEAVEN

JAPAN'S ISLANDS OF MYSTERY

JAPAN RIDES THE TIGER

BARBARIAN (a novel)

CHILDREN OF THE RISING SUN

PACIFIC ADVENTURE

ANCIENT PEOPLES AT NEW TASKS

THE NEGRO AROUND THE WORLD

AMERICAN INFLUENCE IN THE ORIENT

Journey by Junk

JAPAN AFTER MACARTHUR

Willard Price WITH MAPS AND
PHOTOGRAPHS BY THE AUTHOR

The John Day Company NEW YORK

TO

WIDE-MARGIN-OF-SAFETY

GOOD-FORTUNE-IN-AUTUMN

AND

LITERATURE-PURSUING-SIXTH-SON

CONTENTS

7

A section of illustrations from photographs
appears following page 96

Journey by Junk

JAPAN AFTER MACARTHUR

I

TWO REASONS FOR GOING TO JAPAN

A COMPELLING REASON for a visit to Japan was the desire to see the spectacle of a transformed nation. The miracle had been eloquently described in many statements such as the following by General Douglas MacArthur during his six years as Supreme Commander for the Allied Powers in Japan:

"The greatest reformation of a people ever attempted."

"One of the great revolutions of all time."

"Probably the greatest the world has ever known."

"A spiritual revolution ensued almost overnight, tore asunder a theory and practice of life built upon two thousand years of history and tradition and legend. . . . This revolution of the spirit among the Japanese people represents no thin veneer to serve the purposes of the present. It represents an unparalleled convulsion in the social history of the world."

"The military purpose, which is to ensure that Japan will follow the ways of peace and never again be a menace, has been, I think, accomplished."

"[The Japanese] could not rearm themselves for war within one hundred years."

"Japan should be the Switzerland of the Far East."

"The new Japanese constitution is the most democratic in the world."

"History may finally point to the Japanese constitution as the Magna Charta of free Asia."

"The Emperor's function is about that of the Stars and Stripes in the United States, or the Union Jack in England."

"[Land reform in Japan] is the most successful experiment of its kind in history."

"If we moved out tomorrow and any group tried to restore the old conditions they would be hanged to the lampposts."

"I believe sincerely and absolutely that it [democracy] is here to stay."

"The Japanese have got the spirit of the Sermon on the Mount."

A fair interval having elapsed since the close of the MacArthur regime in Japan it would be interesting to see how his estimates and predictions had stood the test of time. Did the Japanese still have the spirit of the Sermon on the Mount? Could one still feel sure that democracy was there to stay? Had reactionaries tried to restore the old conditions and, if so, had they been hanged to the lampposts? Was the emperor now a mere symbol like the flag and no longer a tool in the hands of designing men? Could a spiritual revolution that took place "almost overnight" be trusted to last, or might it disappear overnight? And what of the prediction that Japan could not rearm in a hundred years and would never again be a menace? Never is a long word.

12

While a shade suspicious of the sweeping nature of the Supreme Commander's statements, I hoped to be convinced of their truth. What normal person would not welcome a spiritual revolution anywhere in this corroded world? And what greater satisfaction could an Occidental have than to know that his way of life, freely taught to a defeated enemy, had profoundly moved and improved existence on the darker side of the world? Therefore it can hardly be said that I went to Japan with an open mind. It was partially closed—biased by the hope that we had really done a great job in Japan and that the Japanese, whom I had come to know and like on many visits to Japan and during five years' residence there before World War II, were truly seeing the dawn of a new day.

Whatever the truth, I meant to report it objectively. General MacArthur's departure from Japan and the subsequent signature of the Peace Treaty had left all the work of the Occupation in the hands of history. How had those hands dealt with it? The dust of temporary emotions had had time to sift through the fingers, leaving only the hard facts.

But where find the facts? Certainly not in Tokyo. Tokyo is not typical of Japan. It comprises all nationalities and speaks more than a hundred tongues. Since the headquarters of the Occupation were in Tokyo, the city was abnormally attracted and repelled by Occupation policies. Bloody Tokyo riots were proof enough that Tokyo reactions were apt to be distortions.

What of the effect of the "spiritual revolution" in the real Japan—the farms, villages, towns, the genuinely Japanese cities? But I could not travel everywhere. I must choose a fairly typical section and concentrate on it.

I chose the Inland Sea area. This has been known historically as "the heart of Japan." It was above this point that the gods stood on the Bridge of Heaven on the day when they decided to create the Japanese islands. Evidently they paid particular attention to the portions directly beneath the Bridge, for the Inland Sea is one of the most picturesque spots on earth. Two hundred and fifty miles long and dotted with three thousand enchanted isles, it washes the shores of the three great Japanese islands, Honshu, Kyushu, and Shikoku.

The Inland Sea region is not only picturesque but important. Geographer George Cressey calls it "Japan's economic and cultural Main Street." Osaka and Kobe make it the industrial heart of Japan. Kyoto makes it the home of Japanese arts. Its score of lesser cities are so thoroughly Japanese that a foreign face is a startling novelty. Its villages are simon-pure Japanese, with visible roots reaching back two millenniums. Its farms are the oldest in Japan and long experience in tilling them has resulted in a yield per acre that cannot be matched elsewhere in the world.

Here is the focus of the fishing industry in which Japan leads the world, her annual catch exceeding three million tons. Compare with 2,600,000 for the United States, 1,200,000 for the United Kingdom, 1,100,000 for Norway. Here are the home waters of Japanese shipping, Kobe ranking third among world ports, outstripped by only New York and London.

About the Inland Sea one may find the most dynamic and progressive forces of Japan at work, while on many

14

of its secluded islands life has not changed in a thousand years. No more representative area could be found in which to study the effects of what one of the Supreme Commander's aides, out-MacArthuring MacArthur, was pleased to call "the greatest miracle since the Resurrection."

But my wife and I had another and more personal reason for choosing this area. We wanted to sail the Inland Sea. Not on a steamer, as we had frequently traversed it in the past, but in a small boat.

Viewed from the deck of a steamer, the sea of three thousand isles fully lives up to its reputation as the loveliest waterway in the world, and the voyage is an unforgettable experience. But it whets the appetite for more. As the steamer plows relentlessly ahead down the main avenue, islanded vistas open up on every side and demand exploration. One wants to follow the winding sea lanes, too narrow for a steamer, between the islands, ride the bronco of the rushing tidal currents or match strength against them, fish for octopus in the coves, land on the sunshine-yellow beaches, walk through the tucked-away fishing villages, climb the wooded mountains, probe the mysteries of pirates' caves.

Why not sail a small boat from one end to the other, following not the direct steamer track but a weaving route that would take in most of the islands? It would come to something over a thousand miles. Because of the complication of islands, reefs and currents, that would be the equivalent of perhaps ten thousand miles of travel over blank ocean, and far more interesting.

We had a little experience of the sort to go on, having sailed in like fashion the Nile, the Amazon, and China's Grand Canal. Of the fact that this trip offered obstacles quite lacking in the former ventures, we were blissfully ignorant.

2

WHIRLPOOLS AND FLOATING MINES

WE HAD NOT been in Japan an hour before we were told that we had made the 5,000-mile trip for nothing.

Although Tokyo was not to be the scene of our operations, we had come there first, and were lodged at the Imperial Hotel. Tokyo was the place to make official arrangements before proceeding to the Inland Sea.

A Ministry of Transportation official met us at the hotel. At a table in the cocktail lounge he regarded his dish of American ice cream with infinite sadness.

"It is a pity," he said, "that you have come so far only to be disappointed. Cruising on the Inland Sea is forbidden."

"Forbidden? Why?"

"It is too dangerous—because of floating mines. They were dropped by American airmen during the War."

Did I catch just a glint of satisfaction in his eye? It was a sort of poetic justice that Americans should be barred from the Inland Sea because Americans had sowed it with mines.

"But that was years ago," I objected. "Surely those mines must be dead by this time."

"There are still occasional disasters. Boats blown up, fishermen killed."

"But haven't the minesweepers swept the channels?"

"The main steamer channel, yes. If you will agree to follow only the steamer channel. . . ."

I shook my head. "You speak of fishermen being blown up. Evidently they are allowed to sail the Sea."

"They must do so in order to earn their livelihood—no matter at what risk. The restrictions do not apply to Japanese, but only to foreigners. In fact," he hurried on, sensing that I was about to object to such gross discrimination, "the restrictions were laid down by your own Army. Their purpose was to protect United Nations personnel from unfortunate accidents."

"Then I'll go see the Army."

The next morning I visited GHQ. It was true, a busy Colonel told me, Army personnel was not allowed to sail the Inland Sea except when required by official duty, and I might just as well give up the idea.

"But we are not Army personnel."

"Nevertheless, we feel responsible for you."

"You needn't. We are quite prepared to act on our own responsibility."

The Colonel's eyes sharpened. "Are you suggesting that you should be given special consideration not accorded to our own men?"

"That is correct," I said as mildly as I could. "It is only natural that Army personnel should be under strict orders. Civilians should be allowed more rope."

"Enough to hang themselves," suggested the Colonel dryly. "Now, look here. I admit there's not a thing we can

18

do about it if you want to go and commit suicide. All we can do is advise you. But let me show you some things that may change your mind."

He drew from a desk drawer an envelope of reports and clippings. He left his desk to attend to other duties while I perused the material. From it I gleaned several items of information.

Item 1: GHQ warns all personnel that Inland Sea routes are not recognized as free from danger from mines, except those limited areas specifically named as cleared by the appropriate authorities.

Item 2: The United States Navy Hydrographic Office in a supplement to its "Sailing Directions for Japan" states, "The waters outside the swept channel are dangerous to navigation."

Item 3: During the last war B-29s had strewn a total of 10,703 sensitive mines in the waters around Japan. They were so made as to explode on their own accord due to magnetism, sound waves or sudden change of aquatic pressure as ships approached them. They comprised 4,472 magnetic mines, 3,027 acoustic mines and 3,204 aquatic pressure mines. Of these, 7,182 mines were laid in the Inland Sea, especially in the waters around the Shimonoseki-Moji Straits. To date, 5,555 mines had been disposed of by minesweeping operations or by self-explosion. The acoustic and aquatic pressure mines were presumed to have become "dead" by the end of 1946. At present still dangerous are the 1,201 magnetic mines. Judging by recent investigations, authorities believe that they will continue to be alive and dangerous for several more years.

Item 4: Following the termination of hostilities no fewer

19

than 175 vessels aggregating 221,000 tons have been sunk or damaged by coming in contact with mines. In these accidents 727 lives have been lost and 377 persons injured. The cost in ships lost or damaged exceeds twenty billion yen. The task of clearing the mine-strewn channels in the Inland Sea has not been easy. In the minesweeping operations thirty-one ships were sunk or damaged and ninety crew members were killed and two hundred others injured.

Item 5: Out of the thirty thousand square kilometers of the Inland Sea, five thousand square kilometers are now declared free of mine hazards.

Item 6: The estimated daily total number of vessels, large and small, making use of Inland Sea waters is twenty thousand.

I arranged to have this item lying directly before the Colonel as he reseated himself at his desk.

"Colonel," I began defensively, "your conception of me as a wild-eyed adventurer is all wrong. I'm really a very cautious soul. But I've come a long way to do a job and I'm not going to give it up unless I must. So far as hazard is concerned, I think this item tells the story. Twenty thousand vessels use the Inland Sea every day. No accident has been reported in several weeks. Of course when there is an accident due to mines it hits the headlines—it's sensational— it makes a better story than an automobile accident. If all of one day's collisions in Tokyo streets were reported in the newspapers there wouldn't be room for anything else. It looks to me, Colonel, as if we'll be safer on the Inland Sea than on the Ginza."

The Colonel threw up his hands in mock despair.

"All right, all right. Nothing more I can say. Except—"

he added with a sudden smile as I rose to leave, "only wish I could go with you!"

And so it happened that we were the first foreigners since World War II to be accorded complete freedom of movement on the Inland Sea.

It was to prove a dubious privilege. For there were other problems that had nothing to do with mines.

What of the attitude of the Japanese in these areas beyond the direct control of Tokyo? Would they treat us as enemies, welcome us as friends, or tolerate us as necessary evils?

The Japan Travel Bureau went a long way toward solving this difficulty by providing us with five letters signed by the governors of the five *ken* (provinces or states) through which we would pass. These letters were to prove almost as valuable as one obtained long before we came to Japan, promising us "every reasonable facility," written and signed personally by the Supreme Commander. The MacArthur magic swayed many minds, the authority of a governor was potent with others, while we were to find that some recalcitrants were immune to influence from either quarter.

These latter were usually communists, the most anarchic element in Japan today. As a small lever may upset a great monument, so the communist minority may spell the downfall of Japan. In the meantime, the communists are hellbent to make Japan uncomfortable for westerners.

But it was not until we reached Osaka at the head of the Inland Sea that we encountered the most serious objections to our project. Here on the very shores of the Sea, men knew its true nature. It was lovely, they agreed, but, like some other lovely creatures, treacherous. The same thing that makes it beautiful makes it dangerous—its magnificent fling of islands.

The islands obstruct the flow of the tides. Twice a day the tide pours in from the ocean through the bottlenecks between islands at the rate of ten knots or better, forming tumultuous rapids like those of a swift Canadian river. Twice a day it pours out again.

But the turmoil is not confined to four periods a day— it is continuous, since it takes so long for the flood to penetrate the inner reaches of the Sea that before it does so it encounters the ebb on the way out. Where an in-current rubs against an out-current the water completely loses its sense of direction, and starts spinning to form whirlpools, some of them small, some as great and grim as Poe's maelstrom. Small boats are sucked down and occasionally large steamers have upended and disappeared.

Besides, we were told, the coming month, September, was the typhoon month.

But whenever we were tempted to heed the voice of caution, forget the whole thing, and go quietly back to California, we remembered that thousands of Japanese craft negotiate the perils of the Inland Sea every day of the year. This seemed to prove that the waters were reasonably safe.

We were to learn that it proved nothing of the sort.

3

CAPTAIN WIDE-MARGIN-OF-SAFETY

IT WAS A LUCKY DAY for us when we met Kunitsuna Sasaki. He knew the Inland Sea. He was passenger traffic manager of the Kansai Steamship Company which sails a fleet of smart steamers through the Inland Sea, following, of course, the prescribed mine-free lanes.

He might have preferred that we would ride on Kansai steamers and write about them—but finding us obsessed with the small-boat idea, he wholeheartedly set out to help us find a suitable craft.

"It won't be easy," he warned.

"But there are twenty thousand . . ."

"Yes, I know. There are plenty of fishing boats. But the average fishing boat never goes more than five miles from its home port. Why should it?—the fishing is as good near home as far away. Near home the men know the sea—where it's safe and where not. They won't want to risk their boat in unfamiliar waters. Anyhow, Osaka is not the place to look for a boat. This is not a fishing port. Let me take you tomorrow to Sumoto—we may find something there."

With Mr. Sasaki we journeyed on a highly recommendable Kansai steamer to Sumoto on Awaji Island. Five hundred passengers from steaming Osaka were on their way to bathe on the delectable beaches of Sumoto. The trip took four hours—the time would have been half that if we had not been required to follow a circuitous route to avoid possible minefields.

There was plenty of time for Sasaki-san to tell us about the Kansai Steamship Company. It has built nine ships since the war. It now has twenty ships plying the Inland Sea. They have comfortable cabins, good food, and a perfect safety record. They provide what is by all odds the most luxurious means of enjoying the wonders of the Inland Sea. Or, at least, some of the wonders. Needless to say, Kansai steamers do not stray into the maze of islands on either side of the great sea lanes.

At Sumoto—miracle of miracles—we found just what we were looking for. The head of the fishing cooperative took us to see Tomio Tai's boat, moored to the Sumoto wharf. Tomio was aboard. He was a rather blank-faced young giant with a mouth that habitually hung open. The boat was a nine-ton vessel with mast, sail, and ten-horsepower engine. Would he lease it for two thousand yen a day? He nodded. Would he sail it to the other end of the Inland Sea? His lower jaw dropped to full stretch but again he nodded. He stood as if mesmerized while eloquent Sasaki-san painted a glowing picture of the trip and the wealth and fame it would bring to Tomio Tai. We agreed on all details and shook hands. Tomio's hand was hot and moist.

Returning to Osaka, we drew up a written contract and sent it to Sumoto for Tomio's signature.

But he had had time to think things over and retrieve his lower jaw. The Cassandras of Sumoto had doubtless filled his ears with stories of wrecks in the far parts of the Inland Sea. His boat might be smashed on the reefs, or pulled down by the *kappa*, water goblins, that haunt the whirlpools. Instead of signing the contract he made a counterproposition—we should *buy* the boat—then any disaster would be on our shoulders, not his.

Hardly prepared to acquire permanently a white elephant in the form of a Japanese fishing junk, we looked elsewhere. Mr. Sasaki had another idea. He sent two newspaper friends to see us at our Japanese hotel. One of them took our story, the other snapped photographs. The story appeared in the *Osaka Shimbun* under the head, "I Want to See the Real Japan," with the sub-head, "I Wish to Borrow a Boat to Sail the Inland Sea." Boat owners were invited to write the paper.

This brought a handful of letters. One offered a twenty-five-ton boat. Another offered a thirty-five-ton boat. Both, of course, were far too large. A Mr. Kitano of the fishing village of Minoshima offered his twelve-ton craft along with captain, engineer and sailors, for three thousand yen a day. The most surprising offer came from Tokushima. There a public-spirited citizen offered the use of his boat free. From many other fishing hamlets offers drifted in.

But when they were traced back to their sources and the boatmen learned how far we wished to go, the offers were withdrawn.

All except one. The letter came from Kanonji, an Inland Sea port famed in Japanese history as a nest of black pirates. It was founded well over a thousand years ago by Indonesian buccaneers who proceeded to terrorize the Inland Sea, looting ships and taking their crews captive.

Their descendants are no longer black, having mixed thoroughly with other strains, nor are they pirates. But they are the most venturesome sailors of the Inland Sea. Kanonji's ships are all of a pattern—low, swift, piratical-looking, not greatly changed in appearance since buccaneer days.

We journeyed to Kanonji and met the young man who had written the letter. His name was Yasuhiro which, liberally translated, means Wide-Margin-of-Safety. That was reassuring. How could anything go wrong under a captain with so auspicious a name?

He took us to the waterfront off which some of the Kanonji fleet lay at anchor. Draped with brown nets drying, they looked like enormous bats. He pointed out one lying about a hundred yards from shore. That was his. It could be ours for six weeks, if we wished. Yes, he would take us anywhere. He had not been to other parts of the Inland Sea, but he was not afraid. His two uncles would go along as crew. He regretted that neither he nor his uncles could speak English. That was a drawback, though not too serious—we had a modest knowledge of Japanese gained through five years' residence in Japan before the war.

The little ship at once took our fancy. Riding the waves, head in the wind, it looked as if it could hardly wait to be off in quest of adventure. It was larger than our Nile craft, but that was as it should be, for we were to sail a sea, not a river. We had already learned from the captain's letter that it was a seven-ton boat, forty-five feet long, with ten-foot beam. It carried two sails and a twelve-horsepower auxiliary engine. It looked more like a schooner than any other western vessel, but it was strictly a junk, a junk being de-

26

fined as a boat with a high poop, overhanging stem, shallow draft, and lug sails.

Could I go aboard? The captain grinned doubtfully. A high sea was rolling into the roadstead, urged on by a smart wind. But it was only natural that I should want to inspect the ship—so he went for a dinghy.

When I saw it, I was tempted to change my mind. It was a cockleshell not more than eight feet long. It rolled and tossed and skipped. Beside it a Canadian canoe would look as steady as Gibraltar. Wide-Margin-of-Safety, standing in the stern manipulating the sweep, brought the boat within jumping distance of the stone steps of the mole.

Spray showered into the boat. That would not be good for a camera, so I handed my Rolleiflex to my wife to keep until my return. My color camera was in my pocket where it should be safe from spray. I watched my chance to go down the steps which were buried in water one instant, bare the next. I leaped into the boat and crouched.

The captain waggled the sweep and we zigzagged out into the roadstead. It is impossible to pursue a straight course by use of the sweep. The great blade is not removed from the water but, projecting behind the boat, presses back and forth, now to starboard, now to port. The bow, responding to this pressure, also swings from side to side. Only for a split second in each swing is the bow pointed straight for its objective. It behaves like a small dog being wagged by an over-sized tail.

But that is not the worst of it. If the oarman is vigorous, the boat light, the sweep heavy—and all these conditions applied in our case—the action of the sweep violently rocks the boat. You must brace your feet and grip the gunwales

27

firmly to avoid being tossed out. If you have been brought up in the antiquated doctrine that a boat should be held in steady equilibrium at all times, you unlearn your lessons fast in a dinghy. There, the admired boatman is he who can tip his craft farthest without filling it with water or spilling its passengers.

And so, rocking and weaving, not more than a cupful of water slapping my trousers each time the gunwale sank, we squirmed through the high waves. Coming at last alongside the ship we did not exactly scramble onto it, but allowed a wave to throw us aboard.

The drying fish nets suspended from the masts were weighted with flat stones four inches across and these tossed back and forth, giving me several decisive konks on the head before I learned to skulk beneath them.

Two towering masts marked the ship off roughly into thirds. Aft of the mainmast was the engine and crew's quarters. Beyond the foremast were the big rusty anchors and coils of line. Between the masts was a good expanse of deck that we would have to ourselves. The captain explained that an awning would be erected to keep off the sun. There was a covered tub of fresh water and we could cook on a charcoal brazier.

"But where do we sleep?"

The captain cheerfully removed a hatch and I looked down through the hole. If I had expected to see a roomy cabin I would have been sadly disappointed. What I saw was a compartment of the hold ordinarily used as a fishbin. It did not smell fishy—it had been scrubbed perfectly clean —but it was very shallow, not more than eighteen inches deep. I looked at the captain unbelievingly.

28

He promptly undertook to convince me that a human being actually could squeeze himself into this sandwich of a space. He slipped through the hole, extended his legs under the deck in one direction and his head and shoulders in the other and lay still, leaving me to contemplate his stomach, the only part of him still visible. With the hatch on, as it would be in stormy weather, the place would be as dark as a pocket, and airless.

Wide-Margin emerged grinning, expecting my approval. I nodded. After all, what quarters could one expect on a fishing junk? If the weather were not too cold or wet, we could sleep on deck.

"When the sea is rough, does it wash over the deck?" I asked.

The captain laughed and nodded vigorously.

Oh well, we would see what we would see. Travel problems, if you don't worry about them, often have a way of solving themselves.

But there was one other thing. I looked about, hoping my eye would light on it, then I wouldn't have to ask about it. The captain followed my gaze.

"Ah, you wish to see the engine."

Well, that wasn't it. But we went aft to see the engine. The captain lifted a hatch and there it was—a clean, well-kept little oil burner.

I looked around again. "What's down there?"

"We sleep there," and Yasuhiro lifted a hatch to reveal a cell as snug as our own.

"Yes, but . . . *where's the benjo?*"

"Ah, the benjo, the benjo. Very sorry, no benjo." He looked over the side.

"The lady . . ." I objected.

"Ah, *so desu*. The lady." Then he brightened. "But we will make a benjo, oh yes. Right back here, over the water." He took me back and indicated a point in space, just beyond the stern. "A little room. Will that be good?"

"That will be fine."

In general the boat was just what we wanted, picturesque and piratical, with the glamor of a sailing ship backed up by the efficiency of a motor, a craft small enough to fit the budget, but large enough to brave the dangerous tidal rips and whirlpools of the Inland Sea.

We took off in the dinghy for the mole where my wife had now been joined by several hundred citizens of Kanonji. The sea was more choppy than ever. Half way to shore Wide-Margin-of-Safety lost control of the treacherous little craft, a wave filled it, the boat turned turtle, and we were in for a swim.

The overturned boat, tossed about by the waves, struck me a blow that nearly bereft me of my senses. I thought confusedly that I must not drown because in that case I would lose my camera just as I had, in a similar upset, lost a three-hundred-dollar Contax in the waters of the Nile. I struck something else—it was the rudder of an anchored junk. Clinging to it, I took the camera from my pocket, reached up, and placed it safely on the deck. Then I climbed up and joined it. After a short wait another dinghy, a larger and more seaworthy one this time, put out from the mole, picked up the captain and myself and took us to shore.

The captain was all apologies. He assumed that our deal was off.

A kindly fishwife insisted that we come into her house, remove our wet clothes and don *yukatas*, summer kimonos. She washed the salt out of my clothes and ironed them—and refused to take a penny for her pains. I was touched by her kindness to a stranger and an American, the more so when I learned that her son, an aviator in the war, had been killed by our troops in New Guinea.

In an upper room looking out on the fishing fleet, we sat on the matted floor by a low table and sipped hot tea. The captain was crestfallen. I assured him that all was not lost. In English, I told him, we had a proverb: "A bad beginning makes a good ending." Calling for paper and pencil, we drafted a contract for a six-week voyage with Wide-Margin-of-Safety.

His demands were reasonable enough. For the boat and the services of three men we were to pay 2,500 yen a day ($7) with an additional charge for fuel, depending upon the amount used. The men would buy their own food, and we would buy ours.

For us this was eminently satisfactory—and for the crew as well, since it meant that they would earn more for six weeks of pleasurable cruising than for a year of toilsome fishing.

We returned to Osaka in high spirits. It would take four days for the men to construct the awning, build the convenience overhanging the stern, and put a floor in the fishbin bedroom. Then the boat would be brought to Osaka and our voyage would begin from there.

In the meantime we bought necessary equipment—heavy *futon* or comfortables for sleeping on deck, pots and pans, a few dishes, a little cutlery—and a Shinto shrine!

31

Fishermen, because they always face the unpredictable, are usually superstitious. The captain had, half in jest, remarked that my dunking in the sea on the first day was a bad omen. The shrine seemed to be the answer. We would place it on deck and dedicate it to Kompira, the Japanese sea god who is supposed to protect sailors. His sanctuary at Kotohira overlooking the Inland Sea attracts thousands of pilgrims, especially seafarers. We would go further—we would honor Kompira by naming our boat after him. Surely he would then feel bound to give it special protection.

But we were not going to trust fully a god we had just met. If he should prove irresponsible, and seas should sweep over the deck or the good ship *Kompira* should capsize, our valuables must be saved. The color camera had been wellnigh ruined by a few minutes' immersion in sea water. Camera experts in Osaka worked unremittingly for twenty-four hours before they could pronounce it out of danger. "If you had brought it in a day later," they said, "we couldn't have done a thing with it." Equally susceptible were Kodachromes, in which we had invested rather heavily, chiefly because of an assignment from National Geographic for an article and illustrations. The cameras, the Kodachromes, our whole project in fact, could be crippled by one brief ducking.

So, having purchased the shrine in one corner of the Daimaru Department Store basement, we turned to another corner of the same basement for tin boxes and plastic bags in which to store cameras and films. Two rolls of black adhesive tape and four of scotch were obtained to make

32

watertight the lids of the boxes. Then, guiltily hoping that the right hand knew not the sin of the left, we emerged from Daimaru's with our disaster-averting safeguards, natural and supernatural, under our arms.

4

SAILING WITH THE SEA GOD

ON A LOVELY MORNING in September the *Kompira* arrived at Osaka, took on her passengers and their duffel, was duly photographed by pressmen, some of whom had come all the way from Tokyo for the event, and sailed away to the west with all flags flying. We placed the shrine of Kompira at the foot of the foremast. It delighted the crew who made regular offerings of fish and rice before it throughout the voyage.

Now we met for the first time the two uncles of Wide-Margin-of-Safety. Their names were equally picturesque. One was Good-Fortune-in-Autumn. Would this name prove as inauspicious as the captain's? The other was Literature-Pursuing-Sixth-Son. It was true that he was the sixth son of his parents, but as for literature, he pursued it at a respectable distance. He had yet to read a book. Both uncles wore towels tied around their heads brigand-fashion. With brown faces twisted out of shape by a lifetime of squinting over a sunlit sea, and their great mouths studded with teeth like those of the killer whale, they looked as if they could rob a galleon or slit a throat with equal ease. We were to learn that they were both as gentle as lambs.

34

The wind was fair and we sped toward Kobe without benefit of engine. The two big lugsails towered above us, the larger reaching to a height of thirty feet. Each sail was equipped not only with a boom and gaff, but with four bamboo poles that extended across the entire width of the sail and were securely lashed to it. These poles, serving as battens, kept the sail stretched to the wind. The battens, in turn, were held to the mast by bamboo slats.

Such had been the characteristic sails of Asiatic junks for more than a millennium. Looking up at the antique combination of fabric, poles and slats, one could imagine himself Marco Polo seeing for the first time this curiosity of the Orient and wondering if he would ever be believed if he should tell about it upon his return to Venice.

Pegged with wooden dowels, built without nails, bolts or screws, weatherbeaten until its flanks were as grey as the whiskers of Confucius, the entire ship breathed of the long-gone past.

Well, not the *entire* ship. There was one thing that was brashly, painfully new. It was a large box built of fresh unpainted wood contrasting sharply with the old grey stern on the edge of which it perched. It projected backwards into space over the water. It looked like a piece of cargo that had been thrown aboard just as the ship was leaving and had only just made it.

I went aft to examine it. What could it contain? Observing a small door in the front of the box, I opened it, stooped down, and peered inside. The box was empty. I stood up to find the captain beside me, grinning his satisfaction.

"*Suki desu ka?* It pleases you?"

35

Then the light broke. This was the benjo. I stooped again to look in. Through a large opening in the floor I gazed down into the blue waters of the Inland Sea. The floor aperture was similar in size and shape to that to be found in any Japanese toilet. But being men of the world, the captain and his uncles knew that foreigners are not content with a hole in the floor—they require a seat. So one had been constructed above the large opening. But the opening in the seat was so small that it might have been designed for a two-year-old.

The master builder had now been joined by his two fellow craftsmen. Their pleasure and pride were touching.

"Enter, please enter."

I crawled into the box and tried it for size. Seated, I was curved like Cupid's bow, my head forced down to my chest by the low roof.

"Ah, we fix." The captain seized an iron spike and pried off the middle board of the roof. My head emerged through the hole. It did not seem to occur to my companions that this would affect the privacy of the contrivance in any way.

Being taller than the rest of the ship's company, I was fortunately the only one to be thus embarrassed. But even the shortest could not stand up in the business without emerging chest-high. This proved to be a convenience since the latch had been so cunningly devised that it sometimes locked the occupant in and it was necessary to reach down on the outside to open the door. If this did not work, one could always call for help.

Sometimes the temperamental latch relaxed too easily due to the violent vibration of the box when the engine

36

was in use. On such occasions a roll of the ship would swing the door wide open to a point where it could not be reached from the inside, and only another roll could close it.

When the rains descended the seat was soaked, and the occupant too, unless an umbrella were held over the hole in the roof—then the umbrella handle was very much in the way. This difficulty was solved one day by a stiff gale that carried away the umbrella.

It would all have been more simple without the seat. We would have had it removed, but the men were so pleased with themselves for having thought of it and exhibited it with such pride to all visitors that we hadn't the heart.

The cleanly Japanese never fail to wash on emerging from retirement. This nicety of polite society was not forgotten even on a pirate junk and the captain was always waiting with a dipper of fresh water to pour over our hands.

But though the situation had its ludicrous aspects, the enduring impression we brought away from these experiences was of the everlasting solicitude for our comfort, the unfailing tact, frankness and genuine delicacy of our shipmates.

To get back to our first day afloat. The breeze was soft, the temperature was perfect, the waves were blue jewels. We had the delicious feeling that we were shaking off the world.

But it wasn't quite true. It would be a day or so before we could pass yonder great island, Awaji, and enter the remote and sometimes mysterious inner reaches of the Inland Sea. Just now we were actually on Japan's main street. A half mile away on the starboard bow was the industrial and commercial heart of Japan.

Cities stretched continuously along the shore from Osaka, second largest metropolis in the nation with two million people, to the great port of Kobe, twenty miles away, with 850,000. And we knew that beyond those hills only twenty-six miles away was million-big Kyoto, third largest of Japanese cities, and for a thousand years the capital of Japan.

What a triumvirate are these three cities!—Osaka building industrial machines, Kyoto fashioning exquisite art objects, and Kobe shipping them to all parts of the world. Osaka and Kobe were flattened by war; Kyoto was spared because of its temples and art. Now it would be hard to find in any of them the scars of conflict—except in the minds of men.

The chimneys of three great shipbuilding yards belched a smoky welcome as we entered Kobe harbor and tied up at the American Pier. We were surprised and pleased to find waiting for us a cohort of officials who proceeded to limousine us around town, took us to the beautiful Kobe Mansion, (formerly a wealthy private home, now a remarkable hotel) for tea, and to the Hotel Seigaso for an elaborate sukiyaki dinner.

From such glories we returned to the American Pier and went to bed in the fishbin. Exploring the recesses of the place with a flashlight, I killed a spider and one of those bugs that frequent wet dark places. However we counted ourselves fortunate to find no rats or mice keeping us company.

When your head was on the pillow your nose was just six inches from the deck above. If you happened to get under a beam there was only three inches leeway. We tried to disregard the inevitable feeling of claustrophobia and went to sleep. I dreamed that I was crawling through places that became smaller and smaller until I was finally trapped. I came to with a start, and raised my head only to encounter the unyielding deck above. Mary woke.

"It's hot as Tophet here," I complained. "Let's get out of this."

The captain had said it would be too cold on deck—the Japanese habitually sleep between smotheringly thick futons in a tightly closed room. Accustomed as most westerners are to open windows, we found the sea breeze that blew across the deck more to our liking. The air was sweet and cool and Kobe harbor, so busy by day, was completely quiet. We slept blissfully until awakened by a sound like that of a truck stripping all its gears. But it was only Good-Fortune-in-Autumn and Literature indulging in that stentorian gargling with which Japanese males are wont to greet the dawn.

We sailed at sunrise. Kobe's provision stores were not yet open, so we would buy something for breakfast at our first landing, the fishing village of Iwaya on Awaji Island. We had brought along some canned goods for emergencies but we intended for the most part to live on the country.

But where was Iwaya? A heavy blanket of fog covered the sea. No land was visible except the hills of Kobe behind us.

The captain and Good-Fortune were having an argument. They pointed in quite different directions. Presently a fishing boat hove in sight and we altered our course to come alongside. The captain asked the way and the fisherman pointed.

We proceeded, but having failed to bring the pointing finger along with us we were soon in doubt again as to our bearings. The captain began looking for another fishing boat.

Were we going to thumb our way the length of the Inland Sea?

I had assumed that these hardy seafarers would know their way by a sort of sixth sense. But, after all, they were fishermen, not voyagers. Perhaps Captain Harada of the Kansai Steamship Company had been right when he had persuaded me to take along charts—not merely one or two, but no less than 21 of them, each covering a small area of the Inland Sea. Such detail was necessary, he said, because of the infinite number of obstructions.

We were already out of the marked and swept channel and had no way of knowing what lay under our bow in the way of reef or shoal. The ship carried no map or compass. And this on a sea that is popularly, or unpopularly, called Graveyard of Ships. I had to admire the nerve of a captain who would embark so nonchalantly on a hazardous voyage, but I had more doubt than ever of the suitability of his name, Wide-Margin-of-Safety.

I dipped into the hold and brought up a mighty roll of charts. Each was some three feet by four feet and there were enough of them to carpet the deck. I found the chart for this immediate area and called the captain. He made a brave effort to understand it but gave up and looked for another fishing boat.

Down in the baggage hold I rooted out of a suitcase a pocket compass that I had chucked in at the last minute, never dreaming that we would actually have use for it. Fortified by this inadequate instrument and the charts, I took over as navigator. The navigation was far from what could have been desired, but at least we did not beat a zigzag from boat to boat to ask the way. Destinations never appeared just where they should be, and islands bobbed up without the approval of the compass or the chart. Thus the five innocents abroad blundered their way through the Inland Sea, while Kompira chuckled in his shrine at the foot of the foremast but benevolently diverted our stem whenever we might have struck something too solid.

The morning mist had burned away before we reached Iwaya village. The sea was dotted with small boats in which the tentacles of octopuses waved. This is a famous octopus fishing ground. The method of catching the eight-armed fright is curious. An earthenware pot is let down at the end of a cord, the other end being made fast to a small buoy.

The octopus loves nothing so much as a dark hole and crawls into the pot. If the pot is drawn up gently, the tenant does not realize what is happening until it is too late.

Along the beach of Iwaya, octopuses, stretched out by bamboo sticks until they looked like kites, dangled from poles and dried in the sun. We passed them by and inquired for food. We were referred right back to the octopuses, for they were the only breakfast the village could offer us.

Mary boiled sun-dried octopus over the *shichirin*, char-

41

coal brazier, on the deck of the *Kompira*. The tentacles were not bad, once you forgot their similarity to snakes. The suction cups were as crunchy as nuts. The body, however, was as tough as rubber.

The eyes are supposed to be a great delicacy. They look very much like human eyes and after you have swallowed them you have the guilty feeling that they are continuing to look at you reproachfully from the inside.

We sailed over a sea of blue glass along the mountainous shore of Awaji Island to the sizable town of Sumoto. Here welcoming officials took us to see their most notable citizen, an eye-ear-nose-and-throat physician who pursues the fine arts in his spare time. One would scarcely expect a hard-to-reach island to be the home of one of the most famous of Japan's arts. Dr. Tatsuzo Matsutani is the father of Japanese puppetry. Out of bamboo and brocade, plaster and paper, he contrives puppets two thirds life size which are made so mobile by multiple controls that they do almost everything but talk. The remarkable Bunraku puppet shows in Osaka and other great cities have their inspiration in this island port.

So many things move in a Matsutani puppet that one operator is not enough. It takes three or four men to work a complicated puppet. They are before you in full view on the stage but their black clothing, covering every inch of face and body, is supposed to give them invisibility. From the point of view of the Japanese spectator, they just aren't there.

Dr. Matsutani insisted that we stay to dinner, lodged us for the night in a room in his hospital, and sent us on our

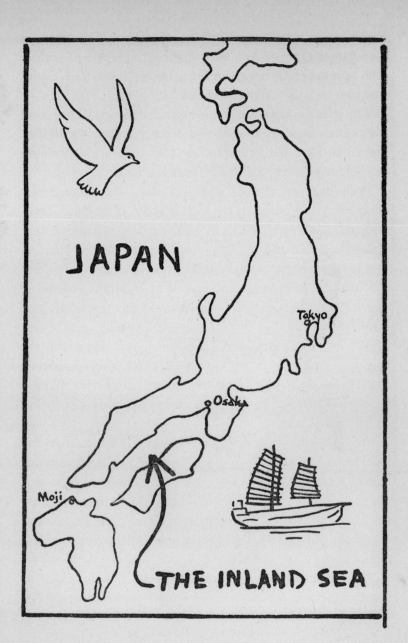

JAPAN

Tokyo

o Osaka

Moji

THE INLAND SEA

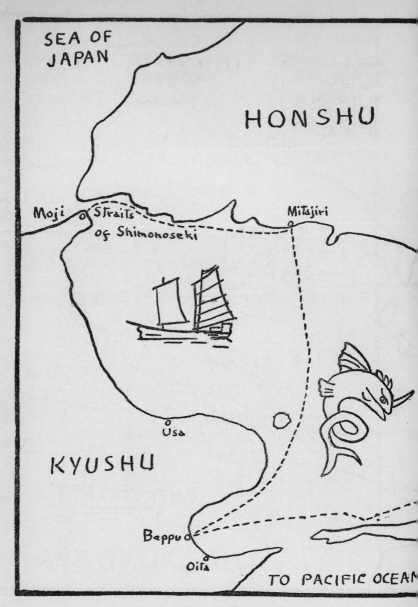

THE INLAND SEA

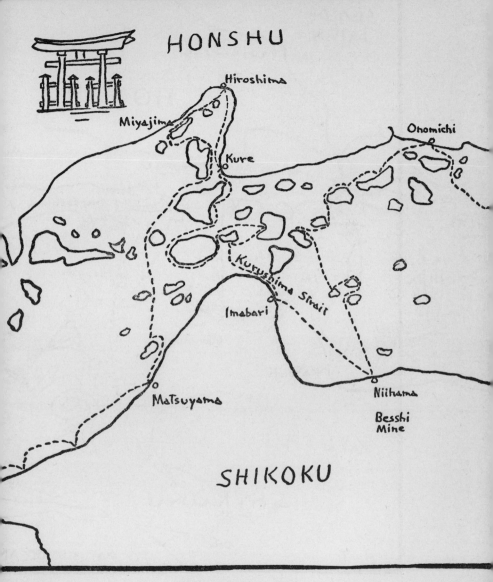

HONSHU

Hiroshima

Miyajima

Onomichi

Kure

Kurushima Strait

Imabari

Matsuyama

Niihama

Besshi
Mine

SHIKOKU

THE INLAND SEA

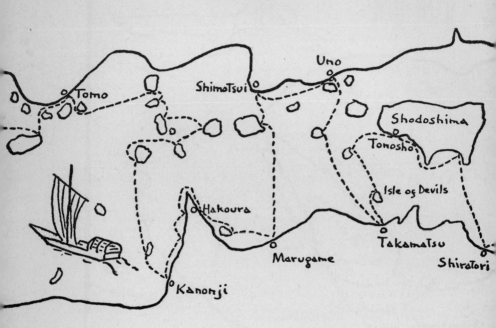

HONSHU

Tomo

Shimotsui

Uno

Shodoshima

Tonosho

Isle of Devils

Hakoura

Marugame

Takamatsu

Shiratori

Kanonji

SHIKOKU

THE INLAND SEA

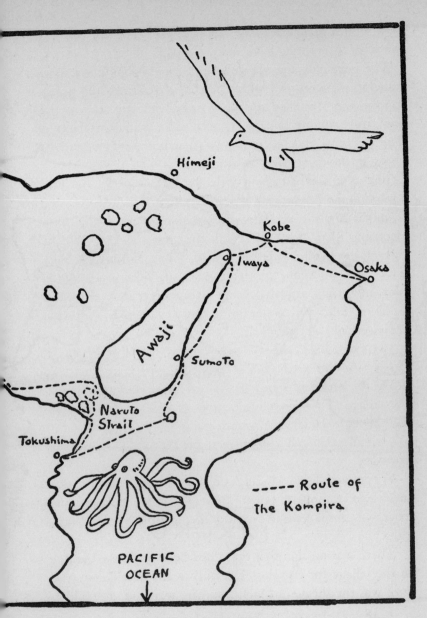

THE INLAND SEA

way with a good breakfast, all because, "We are grateful for what Americans have done for us."

The next morning we sailed out into a rolling sea. The cameras were stored below in the water-tight tin boxes. Canvas was stretched on the weather side to prevent the seas from coming aboard. It was only partially effective. The ship rose and fell in a way to strike a note of melancholy in the most cheerful stomach.

Just as it was getting a little hard to bear we slid into a smooth and lovely atoll that might have been transplanted from the South Seas. This placid lagoon was rimmed with charming islets that held at bay the angry waters. On one side of the lagoon was the quaint fishing village of Yura which we proceeded to investigate. Life here was a thatch roof and straw sandal type of existence that had little in common with the industrial activity of the Kobe-Osaka area we had left behind us.

We sailed on to the still more primitive isle of Nushima. Passing into the small harbor rimmed with fishing boats, we heard the sound of a bell. It seemed to be moving through the village. Then we caught sight of an old woman passing through the lanes ringing a gong.

"A funeral," said a fisherman on the dock, noting our curiosity.

We remembered reading of the ancient custom, now unknown in modern Japan. Upon the death of a citizen a crier was employed to ring out the people for the burial rites.

There was no sign that there had been any new building in the village for decades. The only really well-kept structure was the shrine of Hachiman, the war god, an ominous reminder that not all Japanese have forgotten war as an instrument of national policy.

Since the people of the village depend upon fishing for their livelihood, respect was divided between the god of war and the god of the sea. Fortunately the latter did not require a temple because nature had provided an erect rock projecting fantastically out of the sea and this was worshipped under the name of *Kami Gami*, Upstanding Deity. Because of its vaguely phallic appearance it was also an object of worship to women who desired the blessing of fertility.

All this and more the villagers patiently explained to us, for we had not been at the dock two minutes before all the village was there too. The islanders were much interested in our craft, never having seen the like, for there is more difference between the customs of various parts of the Inland Sea than between those of the coasts of Florida and California.

For their part, they had something curious to show us— a ship with an open bottom!

It was quite normal forward and aft. But amidships the keel had been replaced by a wooden grill through which the sea entered and filled the hold to a depth of about five feet. The slats of the grill were about an inch apart and tiny fish swam in and out at will. Fish that had been caught by line or net were dumped into this hold and, while the worthless midgets could escape between the slats, all fish of any size and value remained captive and could be kept alive and fresh until brought to port.

Looking down into the sea-going aquarium we saw large bonito and sea bream, big prawns, several eels, and an octopus. I expressed a desire to photograph the last-named. One of the young fishermen lowered himself into the hold, the water rising chest high, and dangled his bare foot invitingly before the octopus, hoping that it would fasten its vacuum-cupped tentacles upon his foot. Then it could be drawn out. The octopus was small and timid, probably a juvenile, and refused to cooperate. Finally it was scooped up in a small net at the end of a pole and I photographed it, squirming in the fisherman's hands.

Leaving Nushima, we sailed straight across an arm of the incoming Pacific with nothing between us and America —except some five thousand miles of salt water. Sleek black porpoises played around the ship. Far out we saw the spout of a whale. But the most astonishing spectacle was the sea serpent.

What it could actually have been I have no idea and I have a fair acquaintance with the denizens of the deep. It swam with its head well out of water and its tail licking the surface some ten feet behind. Its head was irregular and crested like that of a mythical dragon or giant iguana. It was not the streamlined head of a sea snake or moray eel or conger eel. It never went down during the twenty minutes we watched it. Evidently it was a land creature, quite without gills, yet it was many miles from shore and headed straight out to sea. It did not swim with the speed of a fish, but slowly and with effort as if propelled by the wriggling of the body rather than by fins. It showed no fear of the ship, even when we sailed within a few yards of it, and when we turned aside to make port it calmly continued on its course towards San Francisco.

It left us with the sobering reflection that there are more

50

things in the sea, as well as in heaven and earth, than are dreamt of in our philosophy.

Docking in the harbor of the city of Tokushima on Shikoku Island we were somewhat relieved to find no officials waiting to greet us. The fact is that, having misunderstood our itinerary, they were waiting for us at the port of Komatsujima some miles away. But we had not lain by the dock more than half an hour before the grapevine telegraph brought three newspaper reporters, one of them a young woman.

Newspaperwomen are rare in Japan and the kimono this one wore made her seem still more out of place. She shyly looked on as the men conducted their interview and, when urged to come forward, retreated so abruptly that she stumbled over an anchor and sat down hard on the deck.

Now she was all blushing confusion. She would have run away in utter disgrace and mortification. Mary gently detained her until she had got over her fit of tears and giggling, then gave her an exclusive story "from the woman's angle" that she could take back in pride to her city editor.

And so to bed on the deck, but not to sleep. A phonograph in a seamen's bar split the welkin with a badly scratched American record of "Silent Night"! Steam whistles blew and stevedores shouted as steamers docked or put to sea. Back and forth along the mole above our ship paraded the policeman who had been delegated to guard us. Not content with patrol duty, he came aboard periodically to wake us and tell us what good care he was taking of us.

5

NEAR DISASTER

I WOKE FROM the troubled sleep of our not too silent night to find daylight streaming in through the cracks between the strips of canvas that enclosed our sleeping quarters and to hear two strange voices.

Dressing, I went out on the afterdeck. Our captain was entertaining the captain of the *Taisei Maru* which had docked behind us during the night and whose enormous prow now overhung us like a cat about to pounce upon a mouse. The other visitor was a slender, frail-looking young man, Matsumoto by name, who represented the Japan Travel Bureau, government agency.

"Don't do it," the *Taisei* captain was saying. "You'll only get wrecked if you try it."

"But you take your ship through it," Wide-Margin-of-Safety objected.

"That's quite another matter. What's safe for a two-thousand-ton ship can be suicide for seven tons. But even big ships . . . Remember? . . ."

And he retold the story of the liner that had sunk in Naruto Strait with the loss of seventeen hundred lives.

Matsumoto chimed in. "Small boats never go through Naruto."

"Never?" said Wide-Margin incredulously.

"Never."

Wide-Margin smiled and looked away. I could see that he shared my constitutional distrust of that glib word "never."

I kept strictly out of the argument. While naturally interested in Naruto, and desirous of taking pictures of its turbulent waters at close range, I had no intention of persuading the captain to undertake an adventure that might mean the loss of his ship. Besides, I could see that he needed no urging. By the glint in his eye it was plain that pirate blood was stirring in his veins. However, he was willing to listen to experienced counsel—he knew nothing about Naruto at first hand, having brought his ship to Osaka by way of Akashi Strait on the other side of the Inland Sea.

The *Taisei* captain returned to his ship. But Mr. Matsumoto, evidently determined to keep an eye on us, decided to accompany us to Naruto town at the mouth of the strait.

He soon had reason to regret his decision. The sea was rough and he was thoroughly sick. He lay on his back on the deck until a wave washed over him. Then he stood up and disconsolately clung to the foremast, stumbling to the side occasionally to be rid of more of his breakfast. He doubtless thought bitterly that there must be easier ways to make a living than by assuming responsibility for a fool pirate and two more foolish foreigners.

Arriving at the docks of Naruto town, we were advised

53

by local boatmen to circle Naruto Strait by the Ko Naruto (Child Naruto or Little Naruto), a safe inland canal.

But what a pity it would be to miss one of the most dramatic phenomena of the Inland Sea!

But, we were told, we did not need to miss it—we could have a look at it from the steamer which daily takes Japanese tourists to view the spectacle. In fact the steamer would be leaving within half an hour.

This would be better than nothing. We boarded the steamer—only to be informed by her captain that he could not go near the whirlpools that day, the sea being too rough.

Nevertheless we decided to go and, to our surprise, Mr. Matsumoto volunteered to go with us. While we felt his constant attendance upon us to be less than necessary, we began to have respect for his fighting spirit. It requires courage to take a weak stomach out on a bad sea. The ship rolled violently and our companion spent the trip lying on the deck of the salon with his head over a box. We took turns holding his forehead.

The waves dashed over the prow and streamed down the decks. There seemed no chance of inspecting the whirlpools in such weather. But when we reached the strait the waves miraculously disappeared, the captain changed both his mind and his course, and we steamed into the channel.

Naruto is a mile-wide passage with rocky bottom between rocky headlands and obstructed by rocky islands. Through this bottleneck the tide from the Pacific Ocean rushes into the Inland Sea with the velocity of a mountain torrent. The incoming tide meets the ebb of the previous tide and the conflicting waters make giant whirlpools.

54

It was an eerie sight. For a time the surface about us would be as smooth as glass. Then in a perfectly quiet spot a peculiar boiling would begin. The water would rear itself up into a dome as if a hippopotamus were thrusting its back up out of the sea. Then the dome would begin to whirl.

Faster and faster it would spin, a deep pit forming in the center. Now it appeared that the up-draft of a moment ago had been replaced by a strong down-draft. It was easy to imagine the fate of a small boat caught in that centripetal whirl. Some of the whirlpools were fifty feet across, some much larger. Where the outer edge of a whirlpool encountered still water, waves were thrown up, and we were told that these are sometimes as much as thirty feet high. We later found this estimate more than corroborated in the Year Book of the newspaper *Mainichi* which reported Naruto waves fifteen meters (forty-nine feet) in height.

These waves are not straight and parallel as well-mannered waves usually are. They circle the whirpool, walling it in, and converting the interior into a horrifying pit.

We could see these whirling monsters only at a distance for the captain wisely refused to take his ship into the worst of the welter. When a whirlpool would begin to form dead ahead, our steamer would promptly change course to keep out of it. The edges of the whirling discs caught our bow and at such moments the ship would not answer to her helm, but staggered to one side or the other at the mercy of the merry-go-rounds. The ship did not attempt to sail through the strait, but only skirted it, then returned to Naruto town.

A debate was staged on the dock. Could the *Kompira* sail

the strait? Captain Wide-Margin-of-Safety was inclined to accept a wide margin of risk. The old tars of the waterfront were unanimous in warning him not to fool with the deadly Naruto. It wasn't just a matter of whirlpools, they said—there were devils under that channel. One of the most persistent of Japanese superstitions is the belief in *kappa*, a species of evil mermen or water goblins who delight in drawing humans down to a watery grave.

The prophets of doom won the day. It was decided that next morning we would sail the *Kompira* through the safe inland passage. Much disappointed, we put up at the Heiwa Inn for the night. Mr. Matsumoto, evidently feeling that his work had been accomplished, returned home.

Takehisa-san, a salvage engineer and owner of the hotel, came to converse with us in excellent English.

"So you have seen our maelstrom?" he said. "We are quite proud of it."

I was struck by his use of the word maelstrom. "You have been reading Edgar Allan Poe," I said.

"Oh, I have read *Descent into the Maelstrom* many times. I was interested in it because the Maelstrom and Naruto are so similar."

"Then you think Poe's description was fairly accurate?"

"Well, of course he was writing fiction and used a fiction writer's license. But the essentials were accurate. I've never been to Norway but I have the *Sailing Directions* for those coasts. Let me show you what they have to say about the Maelstrom."

He went out and returned quickly with a dogeared copy of *Sailing Directions for Northwest and North Coasts of*

56

Norway published by the U.S. Navy Hydrographic Office. He turned up the right page and I read as follows:

"Though rumor has greatly exaggerated the importance of the Malström, or more properly Moskenstraumen, which runs between Mosken and Lofotodden, it is still the most dangerous tideway in Lofoten, its violence being due, in great measure, to the irregularity of the ground . . . As the strength of the tide increases the sea becomes heavier and the current more irregular, forming extensive eddies or whirlpools (Malström). During such periods no vessel should enter the Moskenstraumen.

"These whirlpools are cavities in the form of an inverted bell, wide and rounded at the mouth and narrower toward the bottom; they are largest when first formed and are carried along with the current, diminishing gradually until they disappear; before the extinction of one, two or three more will appear, following each other like so many pits in the sea . . . Fishermen affirm that if they are aware of their approach to a whirlpool and have time to throw an oar or any other bulky body into it they will get over it safely; the reason is that when the continuity is broken and the whirling motion of the sea interrupted by something thrown into it the water must rush suddenly in on all sides and fill up the cavity. For the same reason, in strong breezes, when the waves break, though there may be a whirling round, there can be no cavity. In the Saltström [another tideway] boats and men have been drawn down by these vortices, and much loss of life has resulted."

"That," said the civil engineer, "is a pretty fair description of Naruto."

57

"We wanted to go through it," I said. "But they tell us we will have to take the canal."

The salvager of sunken ships gazed at us reflectively. "Do you really want to go through Naruto?" he said finally.

"Of course," I answered, but with sudden uncertainty. Were we climbing out too far on this limb?

"Then you shall go. I myself will pilot you."

I looked with new interest at the man who made his living from wrecks. "It's very kind of you to offer," I said. "But the captain is the one to decide whether he wants to risk his ship."

"Then I'll speak to him." And before morning he did. Wide-Margin-of-Safety at once fell in with the plan and, after breakfast, we all proceeded to the ship in a happy, though tremulous, state of mind.

Even with an able pilot the passage of Naruto was a dizzy experience. The tide tears through the defile at from eight to ten knots, a speed greater than that of many river rapids. This velocity is diminished during the slack, and our friend selected a time when the outcoming tide should have nearly spent itself. Even so, as we entered the strait, we seemed to be looking up a staircase. The pilot explained that the level of the water is often five feet higher at one end of the strait than at the other.

Powered by the engine only, we began to weave our way among the whirlpools. We were surrounded by holes and hills. We carefully avoided the pits but allowed the hills to crash against the prow and drench us with spray. The surface rose before us in different levels like great

58

steps. Some plateaus of water would be higher than our deck.

The little ship staggered like a drunken thing as she was caught by the whirling currents, now on one bow, now on the other. Cross currents rushed in from most unexpected angles. The boat would heel so far to port that everything on deck would begin to slide, and I, taking pictures, would have to embrace a mast—then the boat would as suddenly lurch as far over to starboard.

With all this frenzied movement going on it was odd to hear the pilot say, "We're not moving." Sure enough, taking a sight across trees on shore, it was evident that we were making no progress. The top speed of the engine was six miles an hour. Evidently a six-mile-an-hour current was holding us stationary.

Uncle Good-Fortune ran up a sail. This was nearly our undoing. A whirl of water swung the ship broadside. With the current pressing one way against the hull, and the wind the opposite way against the sail, our lee rail sank deep under water. A few inches more, and the shallow-draught, keelless ship would certainly capsize.

Uncle hastily pulled down the sail. This brought us upright. But we still lay broadside to the channel, and amid the confusion of raising and lowering the sail we had become caught in a circular current that now swept us around and around in spite of everything that engine and rudder could do to prevent it.

It took me a little time to realize that we were actually in a whirlpool and that the whirlpool was remorselessly carrying us nearer and nearer to its central pit. The din of the rushing water was terrific. I could see the pilot's lips move as he shouted instructions to Wide-Margin who was trying to coax a last burst of power from the engine. The two uncles were draped over the tiller and their faces were whiter than I had ever seen them before. Having spent most of their lives on the Inland Sea, they knew when to be afraid of it. As for the passengers, they completely forgot to take more pictures and clung like limpets to whatever was within reach. This was an instinctive reaction and quite needless since the boat was as steady as if it rested on a lily pond. No longer were there any waves to toss us about, no longer any conflicting currents. The water was all hellbent in one direction, as smooth and purposeful as a racing car. Round and round it went, spiraling down gradually toward a black pit in the center.

That pit looked as if it had no bottom. Now I could understand the Norwegian superstition, mentioned by Poe, to the effect that the abyss at the center of the Maelstrom penetrates the globe and issues in some remote part, perhaps the Gulf of Bothnia. Of course such a notion was entirely unreasonable, yet I could not help wondering where all this swiftly funneling water might go except into an underground passage. The floor of the Inland Sea is of volcanic origin, and in such formations tunnels of considerable size called "lava tubes" are not uncommon.

Another crazy fancy flashed through my mind. Our pilot earned his living by salvaging sunken ships. Had he diabolically plotted to sink the *Kompira* so that he could raise her?

Now we were half way down the slope of the whirlpool and shooting around at a speed that made one's head reel. The inside of the bowl was like translucent blue-green glass and one could not help being struck by the beauty of it, as well as the terror. Except for the whirling sensation, we suffered no discomfort. The ship showed no tendency to roll over into the pit. It rode at a crazy tilt, its decks lying parallel to the tilted surface of the water. Still we felt no tendency to slide, the centrifugal force of the revolution perhaps holding us in place. But that did not help us much psychologically and we continued to hang on to ringbolts and spars as if our lives depended upon it.

All this, which takes so long to tell, happened within a few seconds. We had not yet begun to think. Thinking came hard, not only because of the sickening whirl, but because of the thunder above us where the rim of the whirlpool ground against the nonrevolving waters, and the peculiar sucking scream that came from the pit below. That scream, our sailors solemnly testified later, came from the kappa that were waiting to receive us.

I tried to calculate our chances. We could hang on and go down with the ship. The buoyancy of her timbers would probably bring her up again at some distant point.

But the point might be too distant—we might be drowned in the meantime, as well as thoroughly macerated by the jagged rocks that were known to line the bottom.

Then I thought of what we had read the night before— something about satisfying a whirlpool by feeding it with an oar. I picked up an oar, one that belonged to our dinghy, and threw it so that it fell across the pit. It spun madly about a dozen times or more, then upended and plunged straight down out of sight. The funnel was now clogged with disturbed water, due to the interruption, but the effect was not great enough to alter the fate awaiting us.

However, it gave the pilot an idea. He cut the lashings of a large metal oil drum and toppled it overboard. It was half full of oil, precious fuel oil that I had paid for, yet I saw it go without regret. He had not been able to toss it into the center, but the weight of the oil and of the metal caused it to slide the rest of the way, and the air confined in the drum prevented it from sinking prematurely. It spun around, but with an awkward, sluggish, pitching movement that raised choppy waves and rapidly demoralized the perfect whirl of the vortex. The kappa made determined efforts to draw it down but always it bobbed up again. Gradually the pit filled with water, the slope of the pool became less abrupt and the whirl lost its power. Outside currents began to worm their way in, raising waves.

Presently there was no sign that there had been a whirlpool in this spot. The thrifty captain brought his ship alongside the floating drum and it was hauled back on board.

The steps rising ahead were lower now and the treads wider. Engine began to win over current. Still we did not breathe freely until, after another hour, we left the last of the rapids behind and drew into a sheltered cove. There waited a car that would take Takehisa-san back to Naruto town while we would proceed on our course. The pilot stepped ashore.

He wanted to know how we had liked the trip. We told him it had been a great experience and we wouldn't have missed it.

"Any time you want to do it again," he said cheerfully, "let me know."

"Thank you," I said. "Once is enough."

62

6

GRAVEYARD OF SHIPS

SPREADING OUR HUGE bat sails, we set our course due west. The magnitude of the Inland Sea here was amazing. To the north and west, no land was visible. We might have been on the ocean itself. The reputed thousands of islands were nowhere to be seen. From the north a heavy sea rolled down upon us across forty miles of open water.

On our left was Shikoku, one of the three great mainlands of Japan. It seemed good to have it near until one reflected that since it offered only a lee shore it was a danger rather than a comfort. The first safe port would be at the village of Shiratori.

After a considerable beating, we took refuge late in the afternoon in the quiet slip that served Shiratori as a harbor. The slip was only a hundred feet wide and bordered by thatch huts and rice fields. This was the smallest and most primitive place we had struck yet—or so it seemed until we went ashore in the dinghy, walked to the business center, and found that Shiratori is actually a busy town with a dozen factories turning out cloth gloves to be shipped to America.

That is a characteristic of Japanese communities—they

are bigger than they seem. Sumoto, already visited, had looked as if it might accommodate three thousand persons; it had a population of thirty-five thousand. Big Awaji Island, ridged with mountains from end to end, had looked uninhabited and uninhabitable—but tucked away unseen in its mountain valleys were 223,000 people, making it one of the most densely settled parts of Japan. Tokyo's tallest skyscrapers are one-third the height of Detroit's—but Tokyo has three times Detroit's population.

The Japanese live compactly—they must in a land smaller than California with eight and a half times California's population.

Americans ride two in an automobile big enough to hold seven. Seventy Japanese will crowd into a bus big enough for twenty.

I have seen a Japanese father take out his family of four for a ride on his bicycle. The only surprising thing about it is that his family was so small.

A western bedroom provides for two persons. A Japanese bed, consisting simply of the matted floor, is as large as the room itself and will accommodate two or twenty with equal ease. Japanese school children on tour frequently sleep one hundred in one large room of a Japanese inn.

The western bath tub is not expected to cleanse more than one person at a time. The Japanese tub will bathe simultaneously as many people of both sexes as can wedge themselves into it.

A western house is designed for the immediate family. A Japanese house, though perhaps half as large, is apt to be occupied by the "extended family"—that is, not only a

64

man, his wife, and their children, but also parents, grandparents, brothers and sisters, brothers-in-law and sisters-in-law, and a sprinkling of cousins. And houses, instead of being spaced in wide lawns, are packed side by side, each contriving however to maintain a tiny ornamental garden containing as many trees and plants, though in miniature, as a western landscape architect would plant in an acre.

Do we find in such crowding the secret of Japanese courtesy? The Japanese can be ruthless in war, as we know. Their savagery abroad is in part a reaction to the over-politeness they are forced to practice at home. In peace and among themselves no people can excel them in thoughtfulness and kindness. Living so close together, people are compelled to learn how to avoid stepping on each other's toes.

The practice of mutual consideration which sometimes makes the Japanese seem more Christian than Christians, is not due to religion at all, certainly not to the teachings of Buddhism or Shinto, nor does it mean that the Japanese are more angelic by nature than other humans.

It is due to grim necessity. It begins in the crowded home where children can scarcely move without bumping into someone and learn very early to respect the rights of others. Privacy is unknown in Japan and anyone who seeks it is considered peculiar and anti-social.

So we were doubtless thought anti-social and peculiar when, upon our return to the ship, we sought to avoid the scrutiny of several hundred onlookers lined up on either side of the slip by walling ourselves in with sailcloth. Literature-Pursuing-Sixth-Son started a fire in the shichirin, filled it with charcoal, and set it inside our canvas cabin.

The shichirin is the kitchen stove of the Japanese. It is an earthenware pot about a foot high with a small door in the side for draft and an open top on which may be set a pan or kettle. Another type of charcoal brazier in common use is the *hibachi*, which is finer in appearance and is used not for cooking but for heating the room.

We cooked our dinner and dined well on onions, eggplant, and two enormous four-dollar beefsteaks we had bought in town for twenty-five cents each. But our hope of privacy was short-lived. A smiling face came poking in under the canvas, then another, and another. Small boats plied back and forth between shore and ship and presently we had several score guests aboard. They let themselves in under the canvas until there was no more room and the rest stood outside on the deck and peered in through the cracks. They had a hundred polite but intimate questions to ask about our way of eating, sleeping, dressing and undressing. "We want to wait and see you go to bed," said one. An old man apologetically explained that we were the first foreign visitors the town had seen in twenty years, it being quite off the path of tourism.

All this was in marked contrast to our experience in Japan just before the war when the propaganda of the Japanese militarists against Americans and all other outlanders was so intense that a Japanese dared not visit the home of a foreigner. It was even dangerous for a Japanese to be seen speaking to a foreigner on the street. He would at once be haled to the police station and closely questioned. "Why did you speak to that foreigner?" "What did you say to him?" "What did he say to you?" And so on endlessly. Foreigners became completely isolated. There were no smiles for them. They met only blank looks or averted faces. Former friends passed them without a sign of recognition. The only persons who still took an interest in them were the police. Every day an officer would call and ask questions—your grandfather's first name?—what do you think of our policy in China?—why don't you go home?

Now all was changed. Temporarily at least. There were distinct signs of a return of nationalism and antiforeignism, but for the present the postwar submissiveness was still evident. The Japanese have enormous respect for anybody who can beat them. They are eager to adopt the ways of those who have shown themselves superior.

This eagerness is cyclical—it dies away in time and is replaced by bitterness and chauvinism. This cycle has been repeated over and over again in the history of Japan's contact with the outer world.

We enjoyed our guests and appreciated their interest but began to wonder where it would end. They had quite evidently settled down to wait for us to disrobe and go to bed. A sudden rainstorm saved the situation and sent them scurrying to their homes.

We laid our futons on the deck and retired. But the rain continued and rivulets from the open deck up forward came down the slanting surface into our cabin and soaked the edges of the futons.

We picked them up and retreated with them into the eighteen-inch hole. We left the hatch off. The coaming of the hatch diverted the rivulets so that they did not spill into our bedchamber. It was pleasant—hearing the driving rain and being perfectly sheltered from it.

But the roof of the cabin was, after all, just an old well-battered sail and the worn spots began to admit thin trickles of water that fell, some upon the deck, some through the open hatch.

So we pulled on the hatch lid and prepared to get along without air for the rest of the night. At least we would keep dry.

Or would we?

"It seems to be raining on my feet," Mary complained. This was impossible but when in order to tell her so I opened my mouth a stream of water poured into it. The seams in the old junk's deck were not waterproof.

Rather than be wet *and* suffocated we chose to be wet only and returned to the deck. It was not a highly successful night. We awoke at daylight, wet and cold, Mary expecting pneumonia while I chose lumbago. But the cheerful morning sun quickly dried us and there were no ill effects.

Emerging from the slip we found a spanking offshore breeze blowing. By sail power alone we sped across the Graveyard of Ships. Still to the northeast no land was visible, but northwest loomed the great island of Shodoshima.

This is a sea notorious for fog and storm. "Here's where the big ship to Beppu was sunk," Captain Yasuhiro said. "One hundred and twenty lives lost." The chart showed the location of a dozen other wrecks.

Shodoshima is the second largest island in the Inland Sea, twelve miles long, the home of eighty thousand people. It rose mountainously before us, a jagged blue wall three thousand feet high. We slid into the harbor of picturesque Sakate, a slanting village crowded in between abrupt mountains and the sea.

The long arm of our Kansai Steamship friend reached

even here and the local Kansai man was on hand to greet us. Throughout our entire trip, in fact, the arm never failed. Upon our departure from any port the Kansai official would telephone the Kansai office at our next port of call. At Sakate the Kansai man had enlisted the mayor and several other town worthies to walk us about and explain the importance of Sakate in the scheme of the universe.

When we made ready to leave we found three uninvited guests ensconced on the deck of the *Kompira* prepared to sail with us to the next port. One was a Japan Travel Bureau representative and the other two were Tokyo and Osaka newspapermen who were curious to see just what we did aboard ship. I'm afraid they didn't get much of a story but it was good to see how these wan, white escapees from the under-a-rock existence of great cities enjoyed the sunshine and sea air and the fragrant breeze that drifted down to us from the lovely hills of Shodoshima.

Mary made tea on the shichirin and served it with cookies and figs and *nashi*. Nashi are pears that look like apples and taste better than either.

7

THIS GIRL WILL WASH YOUR BACK

SKIRTING THE SOUTH SHORE of Shodoshima we came in late afternoon to breathlessly beautiful Tonosho. The town of eight thousand nestles among the hills on the shore of a still lagoon circled by high islets. The islets are connected by yellow beaches so that they look like a necklace of emeralds strung on a golden thread. At high tide these connecting links disappear.

It was at Tonosho that the officials set a valuable precedent. Ignoring our protestations that the deck of the *Kompira* made a comfortable bed, they insisted that we spend the night at the town's expense in a lovely seashore inn.

Thereafter it was standard practice for our captain, upon arrival at a new port, to take the officials aside and fill their ears with the story of the wonderful treatment we had been accorded in the last port. The eyes of the officials would grow round and one could see the determination forming in their minds that they were not going to be outdone. The mayor's car would be requisitioned to take us about, and often the mayor along with it, and we would be lodged at the best inn, entertained at an official dinner lasting as long as three hours from the initial saké to the

70

final soup, and tucked between thick futons for the night.

The captain's motives in instigating these plots were not altogether altruistic. He always managed to get himself invited as well. We are inclined to think of the Japanese as an undemocratic people. And yet there is a camaraderie between classes that would seem strange in America. This young fisherman's best shirt was chronically soiled and he was usually coatless and always tieless—yet he was readily included in the dinner parties, expressed himself freely to high officials and was treated as an equal by them.

On many an automobile trip, when it came time for lunch, the officials had the chauffeur and our fishermen eat with us. That just *might* happen in America. More likely the quality would not sit at the same table with the chauffeur and the chauffeur would not dine with the fisherman.

This instinctive feeling of the Japanese that a man is a man no matter what his station is a sound basis upon which to build a thoroughgoing social democracy.

But a distinction must be made between a social democracy and a political democracy. Socially, man to man, the Japanese are democratic. Politically, man to government, they are still the slaves of a theory of government two millenniums old—to wit, that the people should be ruled by a shogunate of powerful men using a symbolic emperor as a front.

The Japanese are a democratic people but it will be a long time before Japan becomes a democracy.

It is not surprising to find excellent inns in the large cities, of which there are many along both shores of the Inland Sea. But in nearly every small town as well, even on many a remote island, there was a lovely Japanese inn.

71

We would remove our shoes in the vestibule, put on soft slippers, and be led through shining corridors to an artistic room carpeted with *tatami*. The word tatami defies translation. It is usually mistranslated as "straw mats." This conveys the impression that the boards of the Japanese floor are covered with loose, thin mats. On the contrary, the tatami are heavy slabs or mattresses no less than three inches thick. They are uniformly three feet wide and six feet long and fit together perfectly so that they cover the floor completely from wall to wall without a crack. They are resilient. When you step in upon them with stockinged feet, having left your slippers just outside the door, you seem to be walking on something only a little more substantial than air. They are spotlessly clean, for a shod foot never touches them.

The chief feature of the room is the *tokonoma* or sacred alcove occupied by a beautifully designed hanging scroll and a flower arrangement. Sometimes there are chairs—usually one sits on the floor. This is no hardship, except at one of those three-hour dinners. Meals are served in the room at an ankle-high table. There is no public dining room in a Japanese inn.

But before dinner you must bathe, whether you want to or not. To come to dinner without having bathed would be as serious a breach of etiquette as to place one's feet on the table in the Waldorf Astoria.

However, bathing is no burden in Japan. It is the crowning joy of the day. The water is three feet deep and the tub is sometimes as big as a swimming pool. The Japanese bath is the most nearly perfect bathing device on this planet since the baths of Caracalla in ancient Rome.

72

Curiously enough, you don't go into the bath to get clean. You soap and scrub and rinse outside of the bath, using small buckets of hot water which, after having done its work, trickles away between the floorboards. When you are perfectly clean, and only then, you step into the tub. You crouch in it up to your chin for the thorough heating and relaxation it affords.

Usually the innkeeper, aware of the peculiar notions of his foreign guests, will see that they have the bath to themselves. However the proprietor does not consider that he will offend you if he sends in a man or a girl to wash your back.

The first time this happened to me I peevishly ordered the girl out, informing her that I would wash my own back. In a few minutes the proprietor came with another girl.

"You like her better?" he inquired. "*She* will wash your back."

I tried to explain my point of view but it sounded prudish even to me and was quite incomprehensible to the proprietor and the girl. He was visibly distressed and she began to weep.

"Oh well," I relented. "Come on. Wash my back."

Occasionally another guest, not forewarned, would stray in. Once a lovely young woman who found me alone propositioned me.

"I'll scrub your back if you'll scrub mine."

Being constitutionally a knight errant I could not refuse a lady in distress. I soaped, pummeled and rinsed her back. Then she went to work on me. In the midst of the process, my wife entered.

73

"Pardon *me!*" she exclaimed. "I guess I'm not wanted here!" and she started to back out.

But my scrubber was after her immediately. "Come. I will wash your back too." And she did.

We thought we had acquired a friend but when we encountered the same girl on the street she passed us without a sign of recognition. That is part of the etiquette of the Japanese bath. Acquaintanceships made in the bathroom are without sanction outside of it. And a lady who would reveal herself completely in the bath without thought of impropriety would, when dressed, be mortified if her kimono should part far enough to show her knee.

After the bath you don your *yukata* (summer weight kimono supplied by the house) and return to your room. A wonderful sense of well-being suffuses you as you seat yourself on a cushion placed on the floor before the low table. The maid brings in your meal on trays and stays to see that you eat it. Whenever your rice bowl becomes empty she refills it from a large wooden tub. If you do not eat four bowls of rice you are a weakling and the management worries about your health.

The rice is the background for the more flavorful foods. Between chopsticks you pick up thin iced slices of *sashimi*, raw fish, and dip them in soy sauce. You remind yourself that this is no worse than eating living oysters, and the fish, because it is absolutely fresh and uncooked, is rich in vitamins. There may also be several varieties of baked fish, shrimps and prawns. You may be served *oyako dombri*, mother-and-son dish, so called because it contains both chicken and egg. You may count yourself lucky if you get *chawan mushi*, teacup steam, a delicious steamed custard

74

of egg, mitsuba, mushrooms and chicken. Equally good is *kamo namban,* duck south barbarian, a soup of macaroni and duck. It gets its name from the fact that it was introduced by the barbarians who came from the south, that is, the Spaniards. There may also be codfish eggs, sea worms, eels, and cuttlefish. There will be a clear soup, quite refreshing, and any number of cups of tea, uncreamed and unsugared. The meal may end with persimmons, juicy nashi, huge grapes, delicate tangerines, or bananas from Formosa.

There is rarely any sweet dessert, such as a pudding. Sugar is little used in Japanese cooking except in *sukiyaki* which is a dish more relished by foreigners than by Japanese. Thanks to a moderate use of sugar and carbohydrates, Japanese food generates little acid and is acceptable to weak stomachs. It even becomes acceptable to the taste although after a few unremitting weeks of it one longs for a hearty beefsteak or a plate of ham and eggs by way of change.

Japanese food is to be preferred to Japanese versions of western food. You may have beefsteak if you ask for it but it is apt to be overcooked and smothered in a flavor-destroying sauce. Fried eggs are burned and crimped on the bottom until they look like browned crepe paper and taste like rubber. Bread, if you must have it, comes in slices as thick as books. The butter appears to have had a long hard trip—and so it has, all the way from Australia, in tins.

Of course I am speaking now of food as served in Japanese inns. In the large western-style tourist hotels or on Japanese cruise ships western dishes are competently prepared. It is only natural that a small inn that doesn't have more than one or two foreign guests a year should be no more proficient in cooking western style than would be the commercial hotel in Oshkosh if it should attempt to serve Japanese guests with the dishes of their own country.

On this particular night in Tonosho Japanese food was not considered good enough for us. A foreign-style dinner was served consisting of fried prawn, broiled chicken, potato salad and soup all served at once. This might have been all right if we could have begun to eat at once, but six town officials dined with us, and it is customary at such parties to spend the first hour sipping saké and beer while the food grows cold.

There was more than ordinary delay on this occasion because knives and forks lay on the table in place of chopsticks and none of our hosts wished to be the first to wield these barbaric tools. This cutlery happened to be unusually large, platter-sized rather than plate-sized, and as manipulated by the small Japanese the big metal weapons looked peculiarly awkward in comparison with slender and nimble chopsticks. The latter have much to commend them. How can we account for the West's total disregard of these clever implements, used with such success by half the human race?

Dessert consisted of a huge slab of bread and butter, a dainty for which foreigners are supposed to have a passion.

At midnight our guests, or hosts, departed and the maid came in to convert our livingroom-diningroom into a bedroom. She drew heavily padded quilts from a closet and spread them on the matted floor. The resultant couch was a good ten feet wide.

Two cylindrical sacks of oats were the pillows. These

76

might seem hard and granular but they were quite effete in comparison with the oldfashioned Japanese pillow—a block of wood placed under the neck so that the coiffure might hang in space and come through the night without being disarranged.

A paper-walled lamp (*andon*) was placed at the head of the bed with the switch within reach. Near it was put a carafe of water with a glass, and a tobacco box. The tobacco box contained a small hibachi from which you might light your cigarette, and a miniature bamboo spittoon!

If we had been dressed the maid might then have politely inquired, "Shall I undress you or do you prefer to undress yourselves?" But we were already in sleeping attire and had been since the bath hour. The yukata, a light, cotton kimono usually figured in blue and white, serves not only as bathrobe but is entirely proper as dinner gown, evening gown and nightgown. Being loose and free, it is the ideal costume for floor dwelling. It is even acceptable for street strolling on a warm evening when a suit would be tight and sticky.

The maid shut the *amado*, sliding wooden doors, facing the garden. It would be of no use to tell her that we wished to breathe the night air. She would be horrified. Night air is thought to be dangerous, full of miasmas and unnamable diseases. So we waited until she had left the room, then opened the amado.

This made it a simple matter for a burglar to step into the room. But a Japanese room is always open to thieves, day or night. You are never given a key to your room, for there is no lock to put it in. A New York hotel room without a lock would be inconceivable—no guest would accept it. He would not dream of going out for the day and leaving his unlocked baggage in an unlocked room. Yet you do that as a matter of course in Japan. I don't mean to draw an invidious comparison between the honesty of New Yorkers and the honesty of Japanese. Perhaps it is just a difference of habit. It may relate to the factor already mentioned, the respect for each other's persons and belongings made necessary by overcrowding. Whatever the reason, you may leave jewelry, watches, cameras or other valuables lying about the room during your absence without fear that they will be touched. Visiting several hundred inns during our years in Japan before the war and five months after it, we missed only one item—a comb. Since the maid had admired it we half suspected that she had taken it. A month later we found it where it had slipped behind the lining of the bag.

The night air rolled in, sweet and cool. We crawled in between the futons and turned out the light in the andon. Twenty feet away across the garden the ripples of the Inland Sea whispered on the beach.

It was quite idyllic—until the futon above you, as thick as a mattress, began to feel too warm. You laid it aside, and you were too cool. Later as the night grew colder you put it on again. But it was too short; your feet stuck out. And it was too bulky to tuck in around the neck. The sack of oats grew hard and you substituted a doubled-up *zabuton*, floor cushion. The bed beneath you was as firm as an orthopedic mattress and you tried to keep in mind that this was good for you.

But you knew from experience that there were various ways of circumventing these difficulties. The next time you would ask for an extra futon beneath, and two light futons on top instead of a single heavy one. You would also get an auxiliary quilt to lay over the feet. With these modifications you would sleep perfectly, but you would still prefer the deck of the *Kompira* on a rainless night.

For breakfast, instead of the usual *misoshiro* soup and pickles we were served eggs and fish steamed in an earthenware casserole. The bottom of the casserole was bedded with salt covered with seaweed. The combined flavor of seaweed, salt, fish and eggs made the dish unique and delicious.

Our official friends came early. They were to take us to visit the island's most famous scholar. They had increased from six to twelve, and since no automobile would accommodate all of us a bus had been chartered.

As we rumbled through the town the schoolmaster told us the story of the man we were to visit, Kan Yashiroda, an agronomist trained in Britain and America. Returning to his home country, he had developed a unique experimental garden just outside the town of Tonosho.

"But don't be surprised at anything," said the schoolmaster. "He's a little peculiar."

We dismounted from the bus and, fourteen strong, marched up the lane to a greenhouse. Outside it a workman was puttering about. He was a surly fellow in undershirt and shorts—evidently an employee and very ill-bred. He gazed with distaste and dismay at our advancing army and when the mayor greeted him pleasantly he replied in angry tones. Abruptly he struck off and our party followed.

"Who is he?" I asked.

The schoolmaster: "The owner of this garden, Kan Yashiroda."

Completely ignoring us, the agronomist tore past plants and trees of all sorts. They looked interesting but he did not pause to explain them. Evidently he was giving us the bum's rush.

"Why weren't we introduced to him?" I asked.

"I will introduce you," said the schoolmaster. But he couldn't catch him.

Finally with a burst of speed I came up with the unsocial pedant and said:

"I understand you speak English—you have spent much time in London."

"No," gruffly, "I do not speak English."

"You were in Kew Gardens in London, were you not?"

"Just for a few months."

"And in the Brooklyn Botanical Garden?"

He sourly admitted it. We noticed some plants familiar to us in California and called them by name. He mellowed a bit. There were specimens of parkinsonia, mesquite, Washingtonia filifera, date palm, Florida palm, barrel cactus, portulaca and several varieties of orchid.

"California," he grumbled. "Do you know Armstrong's Nursery?"

"Very well. We get our plants there."

"They used to send me their catalogue but the war stopped that. They won't send it any more."

Mary said she would have them send him the catalogue.

The garden was most remarkable. To walk over it was to make a world tour in an hour. The scholar, his interest in his work conquering his justifiable dislike of our wholesale invasion of his solitude, showed us the things he had gathered from all over the world. Here was cotton from Peru, coffee from Brazil, oil palm from Malaya, vanilla from Borneo, teak from India, pomelo from Siam, oranges from Spain, avocados from California, passion fruit from Australia, pineapple from Hawaii, date palm from the Canary Islands. We recognized many old friends and the agronomist's enthusiasm mounted by the minute.

Many of these plants had been introduced here for the first time in Japan and their adaptability to the Japanese climate had been proved. If adopted and cultivated by Japanese farmers, they would add richly to the range of foods of the Japanese.

We made some comment about the contribution Yashiroda-san was making to his country but he shrugged it off.

"I do it just for fun."

As we went away the schoolmaster remarked:

"He is very singular. He has nothing to do with other people. He has a stone slab for a table in his hut—stays there two days at a time without food, working on his notes. Almost crazy in his work."

8

THE CAVE OF DEVILS

IF WE HAD BEGUN to doubt the existence of the three thousand isles we were now reassured. Leaving Tonosho, we sailed into a sea of islands—islands like hats, islands like crowns, islands like cream puffs, islands like bouquets, islands like ships, islands like castles. Wooded islands, farmed islands, desert islands, islands terraced like birthday cakes, great smoothly rounded islands like humped-up bears, sharp jagged islands like broken pillars, islands that you could see through like triumphal arches, undercut islands that overhung the sea.

They were all different, yet in certain ways they were all alike. Every one was beautiful in its own fashion. And all were volcanic and mountainous. We did not see one flat island in our six-week voyage.

Some towered to a height of several thousand feet. Everywhere our hosts were determined to take us to the highest peak in the vicinity. We did more climbing in six weeks in the Inland Sea than in six years in California.

Because there is not one level plain on all the islands of the Inland Sea, rice growing is impossible. But sweet potatoes will cling to any slope. We think of rice as the staff of life of the Japanese. So it is on the mainland. On the islands the staff of life is sweet potato. Sweet potato and fish make island existence possible.

But many an island is too abrupt and rugged to do anything with except perhaps crown it with a temple. Many are just great, gaunt, towering rocks. Others are framed with patchwork fields from shore to summit. Some are beehives of activity, for half a million people live on the islands of the Inland Sea.

And yet, the lover of solitude can find it here in good measure. Scores of charming islets not suited to permanent residence are quite uninhabited, enchanted spots with black beaches or white beaches and aged pines, ideal places to step ashore, broil some fish over a campfire, have a picnic, and spend a night.

The stretch we were now entering had been designated by the government as the Inland Sea National Park. It may be the only one of its kind. I do not know of another park of islands on this planet but if there is one some reader of this book will doubtless write me about it. That is one good thing about writing books—the author learns so much from his readers.

The Inland Sea National Park cries aloud for visitors. Dedicated to the public, it is ignored by the public. Most of its islands do not see a foreign tourist from one year's end to another, and it is even off the beaten path of the indefatigable Japanese tripper. And yet it would be hard to find an island group to compare with it in loveliness. The islands of the Aegean Sea are brilliant, but glaring and harsh. The Thousand Islands of the St. Lawrence are agreeable, but one is like another. The islands of the Windward group of the West Indies are delightful but so far apart that you can enjoy only one island at a time. The same is true of the Hawaiian Islands. Climb a peak in the Inland Sea and you may enjoy as many as a hundred islands at once.

We were always amazed by the blueness of this enchanted world. The sky was a porcelain blue, the sea was an exquisite blue-green so clear that one could look down into it to great depths, and the boat seemed at times to be floating on air. The islands, especially in the morning, were wrapped in a soft mantle of blue haze.

But I did not set out to write a travel folder. To tell the truth, I have no desire that the Inland Sea be inundated with visitors. It is just as well that one lovely spot on earth should be allowed to retain its unspoiled charm.

We pulled in at a camel-backed island popularly known as Onigashima, Isle of Devils. We had been particularly eager to visit this island since it is the setting for one of the most famous legends of Japan.

The headman of the village was waiting for us on the small wooden pier and at once proceeded to show us the island's chief wonder, the great cave in the mountaintop. He led us through the quaint village and then up a steep path skirting terraces walled with stone. The path led finally to a black hole piercing the side of the mountain near the top.

We sat in the shade near the entrance to the cave and the headman retold the story of Momotaro.

"A long, long time ago there lived an honest old woodcutter and his wife. For many years they had prayed that they might have a child but their prayer had never been granted.

84

"One day the old man went to the hills to gather faggots while his wife went to the river to wash clothes. While doing this she noticed an object floating down the stream. With a stick she managed to draw it to her and was surprised to find that it was a large peach.

"She took it home and when her husband returned placed it before him. She had no sooner done this than the fruit split apart and a baby boy stepped out. The old couple, rejoicing, named the babe Momotaro, Peach Boy, and they kept him and brought him up as their own child.

"The boy grew up strong and brave, yet tender of heart. He wished to reward his foster parents for their kindness and was distressed that they were so poor and had to work so hard.

"Now the Isle of Devils—this island—was well known but honest folk dared not come near it for it was inhabited by ogres who had dug a great cave—the cave you see before you—as a place in which to store their stolen riches.

"One day Momotaro said to his foster parents, 'I am going to the Isle of Devils to carry off their riches; so please make me some millet dumplings for my journey.'

"This was done and he went on his way carrying the dumplings. But he was a generous boy and he gave one away to a hungry dog, one to a monkey, and one to a pheasant. These three, learning his purpose, volunteered to go with him.

"Arriving at the Isle of Devils, they found it girdled by a great castle wall. The pheasant flew over the wall and by signals reported the movements of the ogres. The dog ran around to the far side and by barking attracted the ogres in that direction. The monkey climbed over the wall and tore off the gate chain. Momotaro forced the gate and went in to battle with the ogres.

"He slew a hundred and took their chief, Akandoji, hostage. As the price of his release, he demanded treasure. The ogres went into their cave and brought out great stores of precious things and laid some before Momotaro. He went home laden with riches and maintained his foster parents in peace and plenty for the remainder of their lives."

The headman stopped speaking and the only sound was of the surf making ogre noises among the hollowed rocks far below. Wide-Margin-of-Safety lay in the grass, his head propped in his hands, gazing with big eyes at the headman. He was as fascinated as a boy although he must have heard this story a hundred times.

"Legends usually have a basis in fact," I said. "Why does the person or persons who invented this story connect it with this island? Was there a reason?"

"Yes, indeed, and a very good reason," said the headman. "In fact the real story of this island is even more dramatic than the legend." He turned to Wide-Margin-of-Safety. "You come from Kanonji, do you not?"

"Yes. How did you know that?"

"By your boat. It's the old pirate type. You know, of course, that the founders of your city were pirates who came from the far south more than a thousand years ago. You know too that they were the terror of the Inland Sea, raiding ships and capturing their cargo. But did you know that they stored their treasures in this cave?"

"That I never knew."

"It is true. They kept an army of guards on the island at

86

all times and they allowed no strangers to step ashore. Fishermen who came too near the island were angrily ordered away by savage-looking black men—for they were Indonesians—and it was easy for popular imagination to spread the rumor that they were devils. Also some word of the treasure that was hoarded here leaked out. So you see it was quite natural that some storyteller should invent a tale about a valiant warrior conquering the devils and taking away the treasure."

We went into the cave, the headman carrying an oil lantern. As it swung it brought bright crystalline flashes from the walls which were of black volcanic rock. The walking was easy and there were no stalactites or stalagmites to get in one's way.

"They were lucky," I said, "to find a place like this for their loot."

The headman stopped. "Oh, you don't understand. They didn't find the cave. They made it. Come, look at the wall."

He held the lantern up to the black surface. The mark of the tools was plainly visible. Volcanic rock comes in many degrees of hardness depending upon the minerals contained in the fluid lava, the intensity of the heat, the rapidity of cooling, and other factors. This was a fairly soft lavatic rock—nevertheless it was rock and the labor of carving out even one small room must have been prodigious.

"How big is this cave?" I asked.

"The part we know measures two square kilometers," the headman said. "But there are other parts that have not been explored. It is the largest man-made cave in Japan."

We went on through a succession of great rooms. "This was their council chamber. This is where they held their banquets. This room with the low door was the women's quarters. This room was the shrine, for the pirates were good Buddhists." A large Buddha was carved in the stone of an alcove. "And here is one of the secret chambers where the loot was stored. That great slab of rock was tilted in to conceal the opening."

"Is there anything in there now?" asked Wide-Margin-of-Safety.

The headman laughed. "I think not. The last of it was discovered and removed only a few years ago."

"But you say not all the cave has been explored. There might be other secret chambers, full of treasure?"

"Who can tell? It could be so."

Returning to the boat, Wide-Margin-of-Safety walked as if in a trance. The headman saw us aboard and left us. Wide-Margin came and sat on the deck beside me.

"Will you go with me?" he said casually.

"Where?"

"To the cave. Tonight."

"You don't mean that you have the itch to go treasure-hunting?"

"Why not?"

"People have been poking around in that cave for a thousand years, hunting for loot. What chance do you think we would have of finding anything?"

"But some was found only a few years ago."

I couldn't answer that one. "Anyhow why don't you wait until morning?"

"Because we'd be seen. You know—they might have

88

funny notions, that the stuff belonged to the village, or to the *ken*, or something. But I guess if it was put there by my ancestors," he went on defensively, "I have as much right to it as anybody, haven't I?"

The upshot was that when dinner was done and the village lights had winked out, Yasuhiro and I once more climbed the hill. There was no moon but the stars blazed and it was not hard to follow the path without turning on our flashlights. Once inside the cave, we clicked on the lights.

The cave was no better or worse than it had been in the daytime, but just the knowledge that it was now night and the fact that there were only two of us made the place seem infinitely more dark and mysterious. When a bit of stone fell beside me I jumped as if a cobra had struck at me. In a notebook I sketched our distances and turns so that we might be able to find our way out. Bats circled around our heads with a great throbbing of wings.

Wide-Margin investigated every crack. He would wedge himself into it and then reach as much farther back as he could. Suddenly he cried, "I've got something!"—and pulled out an empty lemon soda bottle.

In the shrine room he explored the Buddha for secret chambers, as it doubtless had been explored a thousand times before. In the room of the women he turned up some broken pieces of pottery and an ancient comb that might interest an archeologist, but not a treasure-hunter.

We went on back to chambers that we had not visited in the morning. I left the treasure-hunting to Wide-Margin and gave strict attention to my figures and sketches, fearful lest in more than a square mile of cavern we should be lost

89

and only our bones should be left as a poor reward for some treasure-hunter a thousand years hence. On and on we went, Yasuhiro tireless because of his excitement, I dragging my feet and thinking longingly of a comfortable futon on the deck of the *Kompira*.

Of course we found no treasure. When Wide-Margin was satisfied to call it a night, we turned about and put my notebook scratchings to the test. Eighteen paces straight ahead. A twenty-degree turn to the right. Then twelve paces. Forty degrees left. Fifteen paces. And so on. The system was proving highly successful—but suddenly it failed. Where a thirty-degree turn right was called for we faced a stone wall. There were four passages here to choose from and whether I had written "right" when I meant "left" or whether the tangent had been miscalculated, there was no way of telling.

We stood irresolute, peering into the four tunnels. I looked at my watch. It was a little before midnight. The echo of our footsteps having died away, there was no sound.

Suddenly this silence was broken by a distant laugh. It was so far away that one could not be sure it was a laugh.

"Did you hear that?" I asked.

Wide-Margin nodded. *"Tengu,"* he said.

Tengu are goblins or gnomes that haunt out-of-the-way places. Belief in them has persisted from pre-Buddhist times and there are several fine temples in their honor. They are supernatural beings in semi-human form but with enormous noses and dangerous beaks and claws.

I started down the passage along which the sound had come. "Not that way," implored Yasuhiro.

"It's no tengu," I assured him, although I was half ready to believe it myself. "Probably someone who has come to look for us."

We crept along as quietly as possible. When we came to a choice of passages we stopped and listened. There it was again, not a laugh this time, but a deep rumble so contorted by the cave walls that it might be the sound of human voices or only the rolling of rocks.

"It's the surf," I whispered.

"The surf doesn't laugh," Wide-Margin pointed out.

We crept on in the direction of the sound. Now we could hear it more plainly, a confused murmur broken now and then by an exclamation.

"Better put out your light," I suggested, turning out mine. The darkness did not add to our peace of mind. We linked arms and stepped softly toward the sound, our free hands extended forward so that we would not collide with a wall.

Presently we could make out a faint glow of light ahead. The sound was stronger now and it was no rolling of rocks or splash of surf, and it sounded too human to come from any tengu. It was not cheerfully human, but vaguely sinister and we went on more cautiously than ever.

We came to a sharp corner and peered around it. Before us opened up a great room that we recognized at once as the council chamber. About twenty men were milling around by the light of oil lanterns which they held in their hands and a brighter gasoline lantern that hung from the ceiling. More treasure hunters? No, they were not looking for anything, but merely arguing with each other.

Presently they seated themselves on the rock floor and

one stood on the stone platform to address them. He was too far away and my ear for formal Japanese was too poor to catch all he had to say, but I got words and phrases. They were expressions that I had often heard in militaristic Japan before the war but that had supposedly been wiped out by Japan's defeat and her regeneration as a peace-loving nation.

"Japan can only be saved," cried the speaker, "by *fukko*." Fukko means return to old ways. He called for the revival of *bushido*, the spirit of the samurai warrior. He declared that Japan must rid herself of foreign tyranny. He had much to say about *yamato damashii*, the soul of old Japan. Japan must turn her back on western ways, which were enfeebling the nation. Democracy was not for Japan. Japan had fallen by the sword, it could be redeemed only by the sword. Japan must not forget her dream of a Co-Prosperity Sphere embracing all Asia.

But what really sent a chill down my back was the speaker's summons to his listeners to engrave upon their hearts the imperial rescript of Japan's first emperor, Jimmu Tenno: "We shall build our capital all over the world and make the whole world our dominion."

I retreated into the shadows and drew Yasuhiro back with me. It was the same old, bitter story, the story that we hoped had been ended by the surrender and the occupation. There had been reports in the newspapers of these secret gatherings of dyed-in-the-wool militarists who itched to regain power and lead Japan into new and bloodier adventures. And it was in the Japanese tradition to use a cave for such plottings, if a cave were handy. During the Satsuma Rebellion in 1877 the great cave beneath the island of Enoshima was the rendezvous of northern conspirators in league with the southern rebels. As for the Cave of Devils, it was easily reached by boat from the cities of the mainland a few miles away. A landing could be made on the side of the island opposite from the village so that no villager need be aware of it.

The only way out, so far as I knew, was through the council chamber. Should we reveal ourselves to the plotters and try to explain that we were not spying upon them but were merely looking for hidden treasure? Who would believe that?

It would be just as well to keep out of the way of these hyper-patriots, especially since some of them seemed to have had a bit too much saké. Probably among their number were men who had been purged by the Allied Occupation for their part in Japan's military adventure, and this public disgrace would make them less than friendly toward foreigners. One speaker followed another, whipping the malcontents up to a higher and higher pitch of excitement.

There was nothing to do but wait for the end of it. Giving up all thought of our good bed, we stretched out on the rocky floor. The men were shouting, cheering and chanting now and our uneasiness lest they might take a notion to explore our passage made sleep impossible.

The night seemed endless and the floor, which was smooth enough at first, developed points, humps, ridges and razor blades.

When at last the voices died away we stole out and found the council chamber empty. Not far beyond it a patch of daylight indicated the exit. We came out on the mountain side. To see the sky above us and breathe the fragrant morning air was like emerging from a bad dream.

Trampled weeds showed where the men had descended the steep slope to their boat. We followed the path down the opposite slope to the *Kompira*.

Yasuhiro kept muttering, *"Dame desu! Dame desu!"* It is hard to translate, but it expresses deep dissatisfaction.

"Never mind," I said. "You can come back some other time and look for treasure."

"Oh, I wasn't thinking about that—but about those men and what they want to do—take us into more wars. I was only fifteen when I was drafted. They sent me to New Guinea. It was bad. I have a little boy—sixteen months old now. I hate to think he'll ever have to go through anything like that."

9

ORIENTAL RIP VAN WINKLE

THE WATER GYPSIES, considerably rumpled by their night in a cave and on deck, were hardly prepared for the reception they got at Takamatsu. A hundred people waited on the pier. The mayor presented Mary with a bouquet half as large as herself. During the long wait for us it had already begun to wilt, so she told Uncle Literature to put it in a bucket of water on deck. He misunderstood and dumped it into the hold.

The Women's Club extended greetings. Boy Scouts wanted autographs. Seven news photographers took pictures. One of them asked that Mary pose holding the mayor's bouquet.

There was a frantic search for the bouquet. Literature, always slow to react, finally realized what was wanted and dug up the flowers. They had been dropped in a compartment occupied by some sea eels and cuttlefish, results of the morning's fishing, and some of these indecorative creatures had to be shaken out of the bouquet before Mary was willing to clasp it to her bosom and pose for a picture.

The crowd escorted us off the dock and into the offices of the Kansai Steamship Company where ceremonial tea was served while "the press" interviewed us. "And now," said the mayor, "you must see the sights of Takamatsu. First we will go to a toilet paper mill."

The reason for this choice became evident when we learned that the mayor owned the mill. He was justifiably proud of it. We saw the entire process from trees to tissue. Great pine logs were reduced to chips, the chips were crushed to pulp, the pulp rolled into paper. The paper is unusually fine and soft. It is not merchandised in rolls, but in sheets a foot square. When we had completed our circuit of the great mill we were honored with a going-away present, a bale of toilet paper a foot square and two feet high.

Thence in the mayor's Dodge car to a lacquer factory to see the execution of one of the superb arts of Japan. We were not allowed to come too near the trays, vases and other articles to which the lacquer was being applied. If you chance to be allergic to lacquer and touch a freshly lacquered piece you will break out all over and suffer agony for weeks.

Then by car to the base of Yashima and by cablecar to its summit, nine hundred feet high. Here is a lovely pine forest through which the weak-legged can be toted in a *kago,* a basket on poles like a palanquin, carried by two men and dating back to the days when there was no wheeled vehicle in Japan. At an inn overlooking the Inland Sea we enjoyed a noble lunch and an unforgettable panorama of blue sea bounded by many-hued mountains and sprinkled with scores of islands from sorely remembered Isle of Devils to great Shodoshima.

But if our day's sight-seeing had begun with the strictly

96

Unlike the giant octopus of the mid-Pacific, its small cousin in Japanese waters may be handled with impunity. Its tentacles, boiled and sliced, are a common food and octopus eye is a choice delicacy.

The *Kompira* was a 7-ton, 45-foot fishing junk with two primitive batwing sails and auxiliary motor. The eye painted on the prow is believed to help the ship to find its way.

Cooking was done on the *shichirin* (charcoal brazier) seen in the right foreground beside the teakettle. Behind is a tub of fresh water, a bucket, and drum of fuel oil. On the left are the open hatches of the sleeping hold and baggage hold. Aft, left to right, Literature-Pursuing-Sixth-Son, Good-Fortune-in-Autumn, and Captain Wide-Margin-of-Safety.

Every Japanese ship customarily carries a small Shinto shrine as a sort of marine insurance. Offerings of fish and rice are placed within. Our shrine was dedicated to the sea god, Kompira, after whom the vessel was named. Note the millennium-old method of battening the sail to the mast.

The sleeping arrangements were primitive, yet highly satisfactory. The Japanese *futon* were warm, the sea air like a tonic. But on stormy nights it was necessary to descend into the 18-inch-deep hold. In many villages the officials insisted upon lodging the water gypsies in the best local inn.

A world of boats. Inland Sea towns, especially those on the islands, have little use for trains, trams, and automobiles. The most common busses are the "sea busses," small steamers that ply regular routes among the islands.

Upon the assurance of the priest that the *Kompira* could pass under the torii, Captain Wide-Margin-of-Safety tried it. The foremast struck the lower beam, the stout wood split, the wire forestay snapped and flailed the crew, the rigging was damaged, vermilion splinters of the sacred torii showered the desk. The symbolic water gate belongs to the Miyajima Shrine built in 811 A.D.

The tide boiled through Naruto Strait with the velocity of a mountain torrent. The conflict between ebb and flow creates gigantic whirlpools reminiscent of the Norwegian Maelstrom described by Poe.

The famous long-tailed cocks of Kochi must perch high to exhibit
their plumage. The longest tail on record measured 24 feet.

Kneeling on the resilient *tatami*, using a floor mirror, our captain's wife critically studies the kimono. She put it on at our request, but was so unfamiliar with its workings that her husband had to help her. She prefers western dress.

The old Japan is not gone. A kimonoed supplicant worships at the shrine of fertility. Each woman whose prayer is answered with the birth of a child writes the sex and the date of birth on a stone and contributes it to the shrine.

The mayor of Miyaura tries on for size a part of the 500-year-old leather armor of the daimyo of Matsuyama, preserved with 1500 other national treasures in an island temple remote from the paths of bombers.

In the half misty light of early morning one of the many imitators of Fuji rises from the Inland Sea. The island is called Aki Fuji.

Ten medieval castles, or their ruins, crown high points of the Inland Sea region. Maintained in almost perfect condition is the 600-year-old castle of Himeji.

Most of the 3,000 islands and islets of the Inland Sea are inhabited, and cultivated to the peaks. They are of every shape, but all volcanic and picturesquely mountainous. In six weeks we did not see one flat island.

The only place in Japan where nets bring up tropical fish. The hot springs of Beppu extend under the bay and raise the temperature of the water thirty degrees, making it congenial to fish brought from the South Seas by the Black Current. Elsewhere they die in the chill northern waters; here they multiply.

A room in a fine Japanese inn is without furniture or ornament, except for the scroll and flower arrangement in the sacred alcove. The floor of the room is covered with *tatami*, 3-inch-thick straw mats. No shoe ever desecrates them.

Hiroshima, city of the first atomic bomb, has been entirely rebuilt, except for the Industrial Hall which is preserved in its ruined state as a memorial of August 6, 1945.

utilitarian it ended with the thoroughly artistic, the charming Ritsurin Park. Perhaps our hosts had simply been saving the best for the last. At any rate what we saw reassured us as to the essential tact and delicacy of these Japanese. Ritsurin is a public park big enough for a hundred thousand people but so intimate wherever you may happen to stand that it seems to have been made for you alone.

There is seldom a sweeping vista in a Japanese garden, rarely a broad lawn or other large open space. The Japanese garden is a place of unexpected nooks and corners, irregular outlines, rocks, stone lanterns, arched bridges.

The aim of the landscape architect is to achieve an effect of what might be called cultivated wildness, or careful naturalness. A woodland glade may be so naturally covered with moss that one never dreams that every bit of it was planted by hand. The hillocks look natural, though in most cases they are man-made. There is never a straight path in a Japanese garden. The designer, taking his cue from Mother Nature, abhors straight lines.

There are usually no beds of flowers in a Japanese garden. In fact flowers are seldom seen, except where they grow in seeming naturalness here and there in the woods. One reason that the Japanese garden makes little effort to be colorful is because the costumes of the visitors are supposed to supply the color.

Ritsurin's lovely lake spanned by curving bridges is typical. One seldom finds a Japanese garden without water. It may be a large lake; it may be a small pool; it may be only a waterfall or brook; but water there should be to satisfy the Japanese love of beauty.

About the water there are always rocks. Japanese gar-

97

den designers believe in rocks. Many of the rocks in the ancient gardens were donated by the *daimyos*, the feudal lords, and bear the inscription of the givers. It does not matter if a rock weighs a ton or two; if it is beautiful it will be pounced upon by some landscape architect and transported many hundreds of miles to grace a new garden.

To close the day we attended the inauguration of a new dance hall, modernistic to the last degree, where beauties in western evening dress danced soulfully to the music of *Sentimental Journey*.

And so, as the guests of the town, to the Kinsei Inn which our hosts had assured us was *ichiban ii* (number one good). It was just that. We deposited our bulky present in the place of honor, the sacred alcove, dismissed our friends and gave ourselves up to slumber that was all the sweeter for the stony sleeplessness of the previous night.

Morning saw us leaving our good friends of the highly recommendable city of Takamatsu and setting forth into a world of legend and romance. Over a windless surface so unwrinkled that we could study the beauties of the sea bottom, we directed our course toward a perfect volcanic cone of an island called Ozuchi. It was an uninhabited island, small, rising steeply to a point, and clothed with camellias and wisteria.

It is also called the Isle of the Serpent because it is here that a great snake is supposed to guard the Buddhist scriptures that Prince Shotoku buried in the sixth century to insure that he would have a good life after death. Persons who dare step ashore report that there are indeed many snakes on the island, presumably the descendants of the great serpent.

But the place is chiefly renowned, not for the island itself, but for the waters beside it. For here dwells the god of the sea in person. There lies his palace before your eyes—but hardly within your reach, for the highest of its towers are five fathoms below the surface of the Inland Sea.

We looked down upon it from the gunwale of the *Kompira*. Perhaps the unimaginative would say that it was only a huge white rock, as big as a large house, and those were only brightly colored fish, not princes and courtiers, that passed in and out of its openings. But any Japanese who had heard from childhood the wondrous tale of Urashima would know that it was a palace and nothing less.

As we gazed down upon its gleaming battlements, Uncle Good-Fortune-in-Autumn retold the story.

Now it happened in the long ago that a fisherlad of a small village of the Inland Sea went out to fish. The boy's name was Urashima. Hours passed and he caught nothing. He was about to go home utterly discouraged when he hooked a tortoise. The tortoise is a sacred thing in Japan and the boy, with many apologies, removed the hook and let it go.

The tortoise offered to reward the boy for his kindness. "If you will mount my back I will take you on a wonderful journey." The boy consented and was carried swiftly to Ryugu, the Dragon Palace beneath the sea.

Out came the vassals of the sea king to welcome him. Urashima was led into an inner chamber of the palace where the king's daughter, the beautiful Princess Otohime, sat among her maidens. The walls of the palace were of alabaster and ivory. Coral pillars were reflected faintly on floors paved with pearls. The tapestries were embroidered with all the wonders of the sea. The maidens regaled Urashima with songs and dances and he was served with rare delicacies.

He married the princess and for three dreamlike years lived with her in the sea palace. But at last he began to long for his home, his village, his people. In vain the princess tried to console him.

"I wish to go back," he said. "But only for a little while. Then I will come again."

"If you must go," said the sorrowing princess, "take this jewel case as a keepsake in remembrance of our love. So long as it is closed we remain united. Do not open it—if you do we shall be lost to each other for ever."

On the back of a tortoise Urashima sped homeward. But when he emerged from the sea and waded ashore he stood bewildered. His cottage was gone, all the houses were different, he recognized none of the people. Forlorn and lonely he wandered through the unfamiliar streets. He stopped passersby and sought in vain for news of his family and his friends. He returned to the shore and gazed out longingly to the spot where, beneath the waves, lay the home of his beloved. Her box was under his arm—there might be something in it that would speak of her. Forgetting her warning, he opened it.

A cloud of purple smoke came from the box and rolled away toward the hills. Suddenly realizing that he had done wrong, he tried to seize the smoke and return it to the box but it could not be done.

A terrible weariness came over him, his black hair turned white, his sturdy, beautiful limbs withered, he crumbled into dust and fell dead upon the shore.

For three years in the Dragon Palace were equal to three hundred years on land!

As we gazed down through the wavering water to the white domes and minarets, the balconies and open palace doors, a vague figure undulating with the movement of the sea came out of the palace and seemed to be pensively gazing toward the shore. It may have been the princess or it may have been a dimly lit sea bream or flounder.

Any notion that the Japanese, with their talent for copying the West, derived their story from Irving's Rip Van Winkle is corrected when we learn that the legend of Urashima was told in the *Nihongi*, "Chronicles of Japan," written in the eighth century.

Being already in our bathing suits, we tried to swim down and have a look inside the sea king's palace. But we lacked the power to descend to that depth. The problem was solved by embracing an anchor and going down with it. The luminous caves extended far within and from them burst out a school of startled *tai*. The tai or sea bream is a delicious food fish. We promptly forgot the palace and the princess and ascended to get out the lines and fish for lunch.

The Inland Sea is narrowest at this point and by early afternoon we were approaching the north shore. Here we saw how the land area of Japan is being extended at the expense of the sea. A mile-long dike is being built to turn Kojima Bay into rice fields. All the way to Shimonoseki the same process is going on—bays are being diked off, filled in, and converted into farms.

In fact a proposal has been made that the entire Inland Sea be drained to add to Japan's cultivable area. This does not appeal to the islanders. To them, fishing is of top importance. Perhaps it is equally important to Japan as a whole. Eighty-five percent of Japan's animal proteins come from fish. Japan markets more fish than any other nation on earth. One and a half million persons are engaged in the industry, and 450,000 vessels. The motorized fishing boat is the rule, and yet the age of sail has not vanished. Standing on a height overlooking the Inland Sea one may count half a hundred sails within view at one time.

Fishermen have been benefited by the Occupation-inspired Fisheries Law. Formerly many seas were closed to the average fisherman because the fishing rights in those waters were held by monopolists. It was most confusing and distressing. The sea between these two islands belonged to one landlord, while the area between the next two belonged to another. Each great bay might have a different proprietor. The new law is intended, by a gradual process, to abolish all such exclusive rights. Just how rapid the process will be depends upon the struggle between the forces of reform and reaction. A system of cooperatives has been established to improve the fisherman's lot.

We pull in at Uno and the Kansai man whisks us to the office of the mayor who lodges us in a hotel and later comes with six of his officials to dine with us.

First an hour is spent in sipping saké and beer. Then come raw fish, broiled fish, vinegared fish and fish paste. It is impolite to be ravenous, therefore these dishes are merely toyed with. Then appear fried lobster and potatoes. They are allowed to pass unnoticed and are succeeded by *tempura*, breaded prawns served with seaweed and mushrooms. The dish is removed without having suffered much damage and large beefsteaks are placed before us. They are hot and look good. But we must not touch them until our host, the mayor, leads off. The beefsteaks wait for an hour, slowly taking on a sad and wintry complexion, while a geisha sings some plaintive ditties accompanying herself on a *samisen*.

It is now within an hour of midnight. The dinner suddenly picks up speed. Everyone leaps to the attack and cold steak, cold rice, cold soup, cold tea, pickles, and fruit all disappear at once.

The next morning we saw the wonders of Uno, for this is the home of the greatest shipbuilding industry of Japan. We walked through the busy yards of the Mitsui Shipbuilding Company where big vessels of thirteen thousand tons or more were perched in drydock getting their final fitting before being dispatched to Danish, Norwegian, Philippine and other foreign purchasers.

For Japan is not only building ships for herself but for customers all over the world. This is a really stupendous fact when one considers that eighty percent of Japan's merchant fleet, once the world's third largest, was sunk during the war. Japan was left with only one passenger liner, five ocean-going merchantmen and a few hundred small coastal vessels.

And under the surrender terms she was forbidden to build any ships for herself larger than five thousand tons or faster than eleven knots.

But SCAP lived and learned and in 1949 this policy was reversed. The reason for the change of heart was that it was costing the United States too much to ship goods to Japan in U.S. bottoms. About twenty-five cents out of every rehabilitation dollar that America was spending on Japan went to defray shipping costs. In December 1949 restrictions were removed and Japanese shipbuilders were given the green light.

They went at their job with typically Japanese energy. Starting almost from zero they have already reached three-fourths of their prewar capacity. Japanese ships are swiftly reappearing on the seven seas. Twenty-three sailings a month are advertised to southeast Asia, the United States and Africa. On the New York run alone Japan now has forty-seven new, seventeen-knot freighters. Prewar production figures, enormous because Japan was preparing for war, are expected to be exceeded in 1956. The shipyards are not only keeping up with Japan's demands for new ships but are building for foreign customers since Japanese shipbuilding costs are substantially below even the very moderate costs in the shipyards of Great Britain or Scandinavia.

Uno abounded in factories of all sorts but it was not all industry. It had a place for sentiment too. Our visit happened to coincide with Old Folks' Day appointed by the mayor in honor of the aged. A special feature, free to citizens over seventy years of age, was a theater party. It drew 830 old-timers to the city's finest theater where a stock company played an old-fashioned samurai melodrama. Upon filing out, each guest received a gift from the hands of the mayor.

I did not remember that an Old Folks' Day had been celebrated in Japan before the war and said as much to the mayor.

"We didn't need it then," he said. "Everybody respected

the aged as a matter of course. There has been a great change since the war. Our young people have gone too far in adopting western ideas of individualism. They have rebelled against the discipline of their elders. They think democracy means they can order their own lives without any advice from older people. I believe it is just a part of the general postwar excitement and they are gradually coming back to their senses. Occasions like this help to remind them of the debt they owe to parents and grandparents."

We sailed through a maze of islands to Shimotsui. Much as we appreciated the kindness of welcoming committees, we were relieved to find no one waiting on the pier to receive us. We would have this night to ourselves.

But we had not climbed half way up Mt. Washiu before a little man came panting up behind us to say that he was from the *yakuba*, town hall, and we were to be lodged at the Shurokuen where a feast would be held in our honor.

If our peace of mind was demolished by this news it was restored when we reached the top of Mt. Washiu and gazed upon a scene the like of which mortal eyes rarely enjoy this side of paradise. No artist could reproduce it, no poet could describe it. I shall not try even in prose, which is more supple than poetry. But I can at least give the ingredients of the panorama: a good hundred islands surrounding us on the east, west and south; a low sun shining out from clouds of blood and gold across a porcelain-blue sea; two score white sails of fishing boats returning to port for the night; pines a century old hanging over the water as if to bless it; all against the background of the towering mountains of Shikoku on the other side of the Inland Sea.

How tremendous must have been the earth's inner strength to throw up those mountains and these isles, all of them volcanic. A number of them were perfect volcanic cones, and we recalled the comment of a geologist that this place is notable because it is the only spot on earth where one can stand and see seven volcanic peaks. Second best, he said, is a spot in Mexico where three can be seen at once.

Nature confers a blessing upon those who worship her, and we went down to our three-hour dinner with mellowed hearts and tolerant spirits.

The morning sea was rough and the *Kompira* bucked both wind and tide as we crossed to Marugame, sighting by a castle on a hill above the town.

A must of Marugame is a visit to the castle. Incidentally I have failed to mention that picturesque medieval castles are a prominent feature of the landscape about the Inland Sea. Castles dating from feudal times that fortunately came through the war unscathed look down from the hills of Osaka, Himeji, Sumoto, Marugame and Matsuyama while in many other places half ruined keeps and walls tell of past glories.

The Kansai man insisted upon telephoning for a car to take us to the castle. After he had been on the phone for half an hour without results, we set out on foot. But we had gone only a block when someone had the bright idea of putting two chairs into the open truck of a motor tricycle. At the peril of being flung out every time we made a turn we traveled in this state to the foot of castle hill. Then we proceeded to climb to the castle, now utilized as

106

a water reservoir—doubtless the most useful purpose it has ever served.

By this time the city hall man had caught up with us. He produced a car out of his sleeve and landed us at the sumptuous Hinode (Sunrise) Hotel for dinner, bed and breakfast. Autograph hunters came. Each carried a brush and a strip of cardboard two inches wide and a foot long and you were expected to furnish a fine specimen of calligraphy. Their compliments on our work were polite but not wholehearted.

This is a city of fans and salt. We spent the next day visiting fan factories and inspecting the salt industry.

Most of the salt with which the Nipponese season their food comes from the Inland Sea. Sanded fields adjoining the shore are inundated with sea water which impregnates the sand with salt. The salted sand is raked up and placed in concrete bins where water is poured over it to wash out the salt. The saturated water goes to the factory, passes through four huge evaporators which dissipate the water, and there is the salt ready for shipment—great snowy piles of it to be put up in straw sacks each weighing forty kilograms.

We were presented with two ten-pound sacks of salt as souvenirs of our visit. The captain took them to the boat and they joined our bale of toilet paper in the hold.

Not far inland was the shrine of our guardian angel, Kompira, the sea god. It would be impious indeed to pass it by without doing obeisance—so we took train to Kotohira and climbed the eight hundred steps to the mountaintop shrine.

Tens of thousands of pilgrims, mostly grateful seamen,

107

come every year and one of the buildings of the temple is filled with models of ships supposed to have been saved from disaster by the friendly intervention of this god. Hundreds of miniature shrines used on shipboard have been deposited here. Wide-Margin-of-Safety volunteered that after our voyage was finished he would make a special pilgrimage to Kotohira to place here for benediction and safekeeping the little shrine that stood at the foot of our foremast.

We went down through an aisle of magnificent cryptomerias to one of the loveliest hotels in Japan, the Kotohira Kadan. It clings to a hillside overlooking a romantic river crossed by an ancient covered bridge. The hotel is rather a collection of thatch-roof cottages perched here and there on the mountainside among great pines around a pool and cascade. You have a house to yourselves with your own bath and your own servants.

A slightly odd custom of this delectable inn is that of taking all your clothes, after you have removed them for the night, and placing them in the safe in the main house. The reason is given that robbers sometimes come down the heavily forested mountainside and break into the cottages. The cynically-minded might suppose that the true purpose was to prevent guests from decamping without paying their bill—but such an interpretation would be quite wrong.

By way of no less than 104 tunnels our train bored through the mountain massif that constitutes most of the great island of Shikoku and came out in the castle-crowned city of Kochi on the shores of the Pacific.

A unique art of Kochi is the raising of *onagadori,* or long-tailed fowls. I call it an art rather than industry because a bird with a tail twenty feet long is not of great utilitarian value, nor is it meant to be. The breeders of such birds pursue their vocation as other men paint pictures—because they are artists. They keep their birds as pets and are not anxious to give them up, even at a price. If they do so the fee will depend upon the length of the tail, at the rate of about two dollars a foot.

In olden times the onagadori were raised for the feathers which were used to adorn the tops of samurai lances in the processions of the daimyo.

Only the cocks have long tails; the hens are quite inconspicuous. The average growth of the tail is two and a half feet a year. The longest tail on record measured twenty-four feet. Each bird is kept in a tall narrow box, its tail draped over a hanger. Once in three days it is taken out for a ten-minute walk. Someone must walk behind it, carrying the tail.

After our experience in the Cave of Devils, we should have had enough of that kind of diversion. But when the city fathers of Kochi proposed a visit to the Ryuga Caves we weakly yielded. "It's only a mile," they said.

But a mile can seem like ten when it is through the gloom of an underground labyrinth, following a guide going ahead with an acetylene lantern which throws the black shadows of his legs back upon the spot where you must make your next step, over slippery boulders, crouching double under dripping stalactites, squeezing through holes, climbing up over rocky buttresses, up stone steps, up precarious Jacob's ladders.

There is a steady sprinkling as of rain from the stalactited roof. Thousands of bats cling to the roof or swoop within inches of our heads. Hundreds of thousands of roachlike creatures that thrive on bat dung swarm over the walls. A stream contests the passage with us and sometimes we must walk ankle deep. Cataracts tumble in from mysterious tunnels. There is a waterfall thirty-five feet high and another eighteen feet.

Wet, bruised, exhausted, we come out on the mountainside where we must make a long and slippery descent through pouring rain to an inn. There we have a comforting hot dinner—and insist upon eating it while it is hot.

Recrossing the island, we pause to shoot the rapids of the brawling and beautiful Yoshino River—then continue to the Inland Sea coast and rejoin our ship. The breeze is fair, the sunshine is salty and sweet, and it is with great satisfaction that we put the land behind us.

Through an islanded paradise we sail to Hakoura (Box Bay) and come again upon the trail of the Japanese Rip Van Winkle. For it was in the quaint village on this perfect crescent of beach that Urashima is supposed to have lived. And just off yonder picturesque Hakosaki (Box Point) he did his fishing and met the tortoise that carried him to the sea king's palace. The bay and point are, of course, named after the box which he brought back to the village as a gift from the princess of the sea and indiscreetly opened. On the shore we talk with a whiskered patriarch so old and shriveled that he might be Urashima himself just before he crumbled into dust. He shows us the place where Urashima opened the box. The spot is marked by a stone memorial. Near it stands a tablet to the king of the sea. To the folk of this village, the story of Urashima is not legend but fact.

And if we are not convinced of its truth by the presence

of the tablets, the old man has another proof to offer. He points to the round purple mountain that rears its bulk just behind the village. That, he says, is the congealed smoke that rose from the box. And the name of the mountain is Purple-Smoke-Came-Out Mountain.

Faced with this mountain of evidence, who could doubt the tale of Urashima? We nod silently and retire to the *Kompira*, for there is no city hall and no inn at Hakoura. The whole bay is our bedroom and the moon rises over Purple-Smoke-Came-Out Mountain. We sleep on deck and the air is fresh and cold and good.

10

THE "NEW" JAPANESE WOMAN

THE TAIL OF A TYPHOON swept us around great Point Mi Saki into the broad stretch of the Inland Sea known as the Bingo Nada or Bingo Sea. The main swirl of the typhoon was far out in the Pacific but we got enough of it to be glad to put in at Kanonji.

This was the home port of our captain and crew. As we neared the harbor we were met by a great fleet of one hundred and fifty ships all putting out to sea for the night's fishing, regardless of stormy weather. Every ship was like our own, rakish and piratical, a true descendant of the pirate fleet that had sailed up from the South Seas a millennium ago bearing the founders of Kanonji.

The men on their decks looked as free and fearless as our own Wide-Margin-of-Safety. One could imagine that they were sailing forth to attack a flotilla of Spanish galleons and would return at dawn with their holds full of golden loot. But Wide-Margin deflated this dream by explaining that they were after lobsters.

However, we were to learn later from other authorities that there is just enough left of the piratical tradition to

112

make it prudent for other craft, particularly the yachts of the idle rich, to give the Kanonji fleet a wide berth.

The city hall was out in force to meet us, and motored us to the excellent Iketoku Inn. We were ushered into a lovely room and impressively informed that Prince Akihito, the next emperor of Japan, had slept there. The officials stayed for dinner.

"I burn the boat tomorrow," was Yasuhiro's startling announcement. Marine insects bore into the hull and once a month it is necessary to burn them out. All the next day the *Kompira* perched in drydock while flames crackled beneath it. At the same time minor repairs were made and the seams that had admitted water to our sleeping quarters were calked up.

Yasuhiro timidly inquired whether we would prefer to spend the second night at the hotel or in his home. We chose the latter much to his delight and confusion—and to the confusion but probably not delight of his pretty little wife, Asako, who reminded us that a fisherman's house could not make us as comfortable as the hotel that had harbored the Crown Prince.

We entered the house through an unfloored storeroom filled with coils of cables, fishing tackle, canvas, nets, tubs, and machine parts. Adjoining it and raised above its level were two tatami-floored rooms and up a steep stair was another. These three small rooms were home for eight people—Yasuhiro, his wife and son, and Yasuhiro's father and mother and grandmother and sister and brother. Since the house already accommodated eight persons it was not too difficult to find room for two more.

The uncles lived apart but they and their families came

over to spend the day. Curious neighbors dropped in—visitors from overseas are as rare as elephants in Kanonji. Our upstairs room overlooked a street on one side and a *kamaboko* (fish paste) shop on the other. People congregated in the street and courtyard, lifting their gaze to the upstairs windows, two boys climbed on a roof to see better, children slipped into the house, crept up the dark stairs and peered into the room, schoolboys came with card, brush and inkstone for samples of our calligraphy.

A young druggist, a friend of Yasuhiro's, came to show us his stamp collection. Another friend of the family, a young lady named Atsuko which might be liberally translated Hot Baby, asked questions about the profession of writing for she aspired to be a journalist. She had been through primary, lower secondary and higher secondary and planned to go to the College of Foreign Studies in Tokyo.

But when it comes time to eat, all ladies, except my wife, disappear as if by magic. They may have heard of the new day for women but they still do not presume to eat with the men. Even enlightened and ambitious Hot Baby cannot be persuaded. Asako, the captain's wife, brings up the ingredients for sukiyaki, a dish which must be cooked on the table before the guests. But since tradition does not allow her to remain at the table she blushingly declines to do the cooking, and the captain and Mary, armed with chopsticks, manipulate the meat, cabbage, onions, beancurd and slabs of fish paste in the bubbling shoyu, water and sugar in the iron pan over a charcoal fire. What is left after

114

we are through is taken downstairs to be consumed by the women.

We don't take kindly to this sex discrimination but we would be most impolite to make an issue of it. It is not our business to dictate manners in our host's menage. We can only hope that the presence of the American woman at the feast with the men will awaken some new ideas.

Asako is a lovely girl, but shy, and much afraid of doing the wrong thing. Poor girl, she is the minority party in this house. Japanese custom requires that the bride move in with her husband's family. Asako must take instructions not only from her husband but from her mother-in-law, her grandmother-in-law and her sister-in-law. And she must be circumspect in her dealings with little Hideki, her sixteen-month-old male child. She cannot order him about as she would a daughter and she is expected to obey his every wish unless to obey would do him positive harm. He is already showing signs of awareness that he belongs to the master sex.

"But," some reader protests, "I thought all this was changed by the Occupation."

Our present visit to Japan was to cover five months, six weeks of which would be spent on the Inland Sea. Perhaps it would be just as well at this point to look ahead and summarize what we learned during those five months concerning the status of women in post-Occupation Japan.

The Allied Occupation of Japan must rank in history as one of the most generous projects ever undertaken by a victor in aid of a defeated enemy. Its roots lay in the spirit of America and the British Commonwealth. That spirit was admirably interpreted by General MacArthur, and his idealism was transmitted to his assistants all down the line. No missionary of the Gospel ever labored with more devotion than that displayed by the average SCAP[1] official in his zeal to spread the MacArthur gospel of rehabilitation and reform.

Of course it was not all pure altruism. The American ego derived quite a bit of satisfaction from the role of teacher and mentor. And the receptive attitude of the Japanese gave the instructors a warm sense of achievement. It is always pleasant to be in a position to tell others how to behave; and still more pleasant to have them obey with alacrity, at least while one is watching, no matter what they may do later behind one's back.

Most of the SCAP personnel were young Americans without the experience of the British and French in dealing with alien peoples. The majority of them had never before been away from home. They did not speak the language, and had a vague idea that Japanese civilization began in the year of 1945. Their chief himself knew little about the Japanese at first hand and kept them at arm's length during his tenure in Japan. He rode from the Embassy to the office and from the office to the Embassy, refused to receive Japanese at either home or office, did not attend Japanese functions or conferences, and got his information as to what was going on from his subordinates. This well screened information gave him an over-optimistic impression of what was being accomplished. Hence his naive and sweeping generalizations as to the overnight democratization of Japan.

[1] SCAP—the Occupation. The initials stand for Supreme Commander for the Allied Powers.

"Never in history," he said concerning the new status of women, "has there been a more far-reaching and dramatic transformation."

At least it might honestly be said that never in history had men worked so hard for women. The Allied armed forces, predominantly male, went all out to improve the lot of the Japanese female. Whatever the program lacked in understanding of the real needs of the Japanese woman, it was sincere and wholehearted, a magnificent demonstration of the American faith that this is a wonderful world and can be made even better.

The right to vote is the greatest gift of the Occupation to Japanese women. It is moreover likely to be permanent, for when did women ever give up anything they had once gained? Woman suffrage was not completely new, having been exercised in some local elections, but never on a national scale.

The women promptly took advantage of their new privilege. In the first postwar general election, April, 1946, women won thirty-nine seats in the Diet (Japan's parliament or congress). This gave women eight percent of the total number of seats.

The enthusiasm that had prompted a heavy vote by women ebbed somewhat in later elections and at present women hold twenty-four seats in the Diet.

In regional elections women are elected to prefectural assemblies, city councils, and town assemblies. A few have been made village headmen. According to a 1950 United Nations Secretariat report Japan's various legislative assemblies contained 3.4 percent women—double the American figure of 1.7 percent.

Women are now members of such important Diet committees as labor, welfare, education, justice and foreign affairs. A woman lawyer became vice-minister of justice; a woman leader in the labor movement became vice-minister of welfare; a woman became vice-minister of foreign affairs; a woman became chairman of the repatriation committee; a woman was appointed chief of the newly established women's and minors' bureau. Women head the home demonstration section which carries an extension program to rural women, the child care section of the children's bureau, and the nursing section of the medical bureau.

Women have been appointed conciliation commissioners in the 276 family courts established under the new Civil Code.

Most women do not have the education necessary to fill such posts. The schools and colleges for women have always been inferior to those for men. The curricula for girls' schools have been based upon the feudal ideals expressed in *The Greater Learning for Women* written in the seventeenth century. This work was keyed to the thesis that a woman must "look to her husband as her lord and must serve him with all reverence and worship." The purpose of education for women was to prepare them to be "good wives and wise mothers." They were trained to stay home. The old Japanese expression *hakoiri musume* (box-enclosed maiden) was significant.

Now schools are coeducational and boys and girls use the same textbooks. All tax-supported universities have been made coeducational. In addition to these public institutions, twenty-six new private women's colleges have been founded.

Marriage has been made safer for women. The new Civil Code outlawed the idea of the husband's superiority over his wife. Henceforth man and woman were to be equal. Young people might choose their own mates. In case of the husband's death, inheritance would not go solely to the eldest son as previously but would be shared by the widow. The privilege of divorce was not to be the monopoly of the male. Women could bring divorce proceedings against their husbands.

In the early days of the Occupation democracy was a popular word. In Kagoshima a contest was held to select the most democratic husband. There were sixty-five candidates. Each was given a questionnaire including such questions as "Do you encourage your wife to improve her talent?" "Are you interested in discussing current topics with your wife?" "Do you come home straight from your work, or do you prefer to go to a party by yourself?"

First prize went to a sixty-eight-year-old doctor who was judged to have been most considerate and cooperative. When his wife came home late from women's meetings he went to the station to meet her. He helped her with the housework, ate at the same table with her, and walked beside her on the street. Second prize went to a railroad official who was not only good to his wife but had removed discriminations against women workers and established equal pay for equal work. Upon receiving the prize he stated that now that he was publicly recognized as a democratic husband he could carry a bundle for his wife without feeling embarrassed. The contest was given much space in the newspapers and doubtless had a good effect in many homes.

Women in industry are protected by new labor laws. Overtime for women is limited, night work restricted, generous leave prescribed in cases of illness or maternity, equal pay required for equal work.

Women may be found in almost every sort of business or profession. There are today even women police—two thousand of them—something never known before in an oriental country.

In Tokyo girls may be seen walking hand in hand with their boy friends on a summer evening, sitting with them under the trees at the edge of the imperial moat, going with them to dances and shows. They dress in *yofuku*, western clothes, which they wear with much more distinction than before the war. The kimono is, alas, on the way out. Even around the Inland Sea it is gradually disappearing. Knowing that Asako would look lovely in a kimono, I asked her to put one on for a picture. She did, but with great difficulty. "I've forgotten how the *obi* goes on," she complained. She dislikes the kimono and never wears it except at New Year's and festivals. "I can't move in it," she says, "and it's too expensive." It took her a good hour to dress, and that only with her husband's help.

Recently a Japanese garment expert came out with a "five-minute kimono" that can be slipped on as easily as an overcoat. It had a brief vogue, but the trend toward yofuku continues.

When all the postwar changes are listed they seem to add up to a real revolution in the lot of the Japanese woman. Certainly there has been improvement—but scarcely a revolution. Rather we must call it evolution, and slow evolution at that.

The kimono, for example, has been on the way out since 1868. On my first visit to Japan in 1915 I wrote about its "disappearance." It is still disappearing and will probably keep on disappearing for another century or more. It is one of the loveliest costumes in the world, transforms a kitchen wench into a queen, perfectly conceals Japanese bow legs, and though inconvenient for school wear or business is still prized by Japanese women for use at all dress-up functions.

As for the new freedom, it must be kept in mind that Japanese women have always enjoyed more freedom than their Asiatic sisters. They have never suffered foot-binding as in China or harem seclusion as in India. They have usually handled the family finances and have always done the shopping. Those of them who became mothers-in-law, and most of them did, exercised an authority unknown in Europe and America.

Nor is their participation in industry a new thing. Japan has been a great industrial nation for half a century. Women flocked into factories and business offices when their men went to war against Russia in 1904. They did it again in the First World War and many of them stayed after the war was over. The great textile industry has depended almost entirely upon women. Women have been employed in factories of all descriptions, making everything from fans to artillery. For decades girls have been leaving the country to go on their own in the cities where they took jobs in shops or offices, attended dances, saw motion pictures, kept unchaperoned "dates" and chose their husbands or lovers. Those who were determined to complete their education might do so since, although the imperial universities were closed to them, there were a good number of private colleges for women.

Many of the new laws are still only paper laws. The new "equality" was violated even in the offices of the Occupation itself. Women were placed in inferior positions and received lower pay than men. In most cases parents still insisted upon choosing mates for their children, in spite of the fact that Article 24 of the new constitution stipulates that marriage shall be by mutual consent of both sexes.

A typical case was that of Haruko, a nineteen-year-old Tokyo girl, who was kept a prisoner in her room because she would not marry the man her parents had selected for her. She preferred a Japanese-American boy she had met in Occupation circles. One night she escaped to a friend's house but the police tracked her down and returned her to her parents. They locked her up again and only began to realize they were on the wrong track when she attempted suicide. Then they used reason instead of force, impressed upon her the traditional duties of a Japanese woman, and finally persuaded her to give up her sweetheart and marry a man she had never seen.

This was in Tokyo where the foreign ferment was most active. The same thing would not be likely to happen in the country—there the girl would submit without question.

To get a true idea of what effect the new laws had had in the country, the Natural Resources Section of SCAP made an intensive study of thirteen typical villages. This is what they had to report concerning the status of women:

"Real social equality with men is not publicly accorded women in any of the thirteen villages. Joint participation

122

of men and women in non-familial social functions is un-heard of. Generally men and women have social gatherings separately or the women prepare and serve food to the men and then eat by themselves in the kitchen.

"The increasing participation of women in community political activities is not necessarily accompanied by a cor-responding improvement in social status. At Yoshida, where the female voting percentage was consistently higher than in any of the other twelve villages, where more women appeared to have knowledge of their legal rights under the Constitution and the Civil Code, and where there was even a woman in the village assembly, the social status of women seems to be the lowest of any of the villages.

"Except in Honami, where more than one hundred farm women are members of the village agricultural coopera-tive, women took little part in economic organizations. Because membership in cooperatives is nearly always by households, women do not attend meetings unless their husbands are ill or otherwise unable to go. No women hold office in any of the agricultural cooperatives. . . .

"Although Article 762 of the revised Civil Code permits ownership of property by wives, independent of their hus-bands, women still seem to follow the traditional practise of having their property registered in their husbands' names. Again, although the revised Civil Code stipulates that a widow is entitled to inherit some portion of the family property upon the death of her husband, no cases have been reported of women having yet inherited under this provision.

"Because family property generally is inherited intact—in the Japanese saying, 'even unto the rat's dung in the closet'—by a single heir, it is difficult for a widow, under existing traditions, to share in the inheritance. The majority of women interviewed were doubtful about the practicality of the inheritance provisions of the revised Civil Code and favored the continuation of the old custom. They held the general view that the land holdings were too small to justify division among individual family members and that such action would be economically harmful. Widows felt that it was 'only right' that the son who takes care of them after their husband's death should receive the entire inheritance."

The position of our little friend, Asako, in her husband's household is still customary in post-Occupation Japan. Says the report concerning the women of the thirteen villages:

"In most places the slightest arrogance on the part of the daughter-in-law is sufficient cause for her being sent home to her parents and divorced. Furthermore, in some villages the mother-in-law still measures the rice to be cooked at each meal and the daughter-in-law cannot even approach the rice bin. She can only assume the responsibility for running the household on the retirement of her mother-in-law, when she is presented with the rice paddle as the symbol of her new status. Reportedly in most villages women rarely become the mistresses of their own households before the age of forty."

While there is no question that in some respects Japanese women have advanced since the war, in other ways they have suffered a grave setback.

The care of home and family is a greater task than it was. Bombing destroyed all modern household facilities and

124

these have as yet been only partially restored. Before the war gas and electricity had begun to be used for cooking. Now most households have gone back to firewood and charcoal. Everything in the home is done the hard way. Tremendous inflation has cut the purchasing power of the husband's wages and the family cannot afford labor-saving devices, even if they were available.

More serious has been the moral setback. The new ideas from the West have tended to disrupt the family. Formerly no member of the family would make any important move without the approval of the family council. The new doctrine of individualism permits each member to go his own way. Formerly upon the death of the father the eldest son was the head of the family. Now no one is responsible, each member seeking his own advantage.

"Moral conditions are very bad now," a wise Tokyo mother told us. "In the United States you have had a long time to get used to certain freedoms. Here we were suddenly thrown into them and don't know how to use them. Freedom isn't something you can put on like a coat. It must grow from the inside. Freedom must come from the spirit."

Japanese mothers have never been more distressed and bewildered. Said one, "I feel like a hen that has hatched a brood of ducklings and sees them heading for the pond."

The trouble is that many of the newly-hatched only think they are ducklings but when they reach the pond discover too late that they can't swim.

This new license in the name of liberty, causing young people to revolt against the discipline of their elders, has brought about an alarming increase in crime and delinquency. "Everything old is bad," is the philosophy of many of the younger generation. The SCAP investigation of the thirteen villages revealed a post-1945 condition of moral laxness. "Lack of obedience and 'talking back' to parents, precocious smoking, arrogance, and thievery were reported on the increase by worried parents. They tend to attribute these conditions to a confusion of the new democratic ideas with license, the relaxation of the former rigid discipline of the schools, and the elimination of the former *shushin* (morals) course from the school curriculum."

The worship of American power was perhaps gratifying to some Occupation officials but was not good for the Japanese. It was illogical to adopt Western ways simply because the West had defeated Japan. This placed adulation of force above consideration of what was good for the people. It transferred obedience from the old Japanese military hierarchy to the new Allied military hierarchy. At first there was blind respect. But as the shortcomings of the new bosses became apparent, disillusionment set in and young people felt lost, without anchor and without star.

Add to this spiritual confusion the mental damage done by the war. A country that has not suffered wholesale attack from the air cannot know what this means. All Japan's great cities except Kyoto were partially or wholly destroyed by bombs and fire. Many of the smaller cities were wiped from the map. The atomic bombing of Hiroshima and Nagasaki was more dramatic but no more unnerving to the individual woman in her home than the arrival of an ordinary bomb in the middle of the kitchen was to another woman in any one of the hundreds of devastated towns.

The result is millions of minds that are permanently shocked, warped, distorted. A SCAP officer appointed to study this problem collected a large file of typical cases. One will suffice here:

"K— is seven years old, the daughter of an educated middle-class woman and a university student. . . . Twice during the war the house in which she was living was burned in raids, once when she was evacuated from Tokyo to Kofu for several months. She experienced the fire raids of 9 March and 25 May, 1945. She seems completely normal until she hears a siren or fire alarm, which she connects with the fire raids. When this happens, even at a distance which makes the sound very faint, she stops her most boisterous play, begins to moan, and whimper, starts to tremble uncontrollably, becomes increasingly hysterical until she is screaming and twitching. The attacks sometimes last more than an hour."

The file abounds in the tragic stories of persons of both sexes and all ages left mentally unhinged by the experiences of the war years. This widespread derangement should be taken into account when we judge the current behavior of the Japanese.

Nor is much comfort derived from religion. Today the Japanese live in a religious vacuum. The most earnestly propagated faith before the war was State Shinto. A militaristic government used it to buttress their plans to conquer the world and make the divine emperor king of all. The collapse of the military and the complete discrediting of State Shinto turned many people against religion of any sort.

Buddhism never was an inspiring religion in Japan. It

was a religion not of life but of death—funerals were conducted by the Buddhist priests, and ancestors were honored in Buddhist festivals. Even professing Christians often turned to Buddhist temples for burial rites.

Christianity had a decided vogue immediately after the war. It was the religion of the conqueror, therefore it must be good. Evangelists swept thousands into the Christian churches. But by 1950 this wave of enthusiasm had largely spent itself.

Today there are fewer Christians in Japan than there were three hundred years ago. In the seventeenth century Japan had five hundred thousand Christians in a population of thirty million. Now she has 370,000 Christians in a population of eighty-six million. Then nearly two percent of the Japanese were Christians. Now less than one-half of one percent are Christians. Despite the self-sacrificing work of an army of missionaries, it can hardly be said that Japan shows promise of becoming a Christian nation.

Apparently she is destined to go her way without reliance upon supernatural consolations. But for the time being at least, the loss of faith in the Sun Goddess and in the divine origin and destiny of Nippon has left a people open to any counsel of cynicism or despair. The collapse of old values has been felt most keenly by the women, since they have always been more devoted than the men to religious observances.

II

THE GI AND THE GEISHA

SEX HAS PLAYED a large part in the postwar troubles of the Japanese woman. As a GI bluntly put it, "It's their own fault for being so damn attractive."

It is not surprising that the delightful little "moose" of Japan should have turned the head of the woman-hungry soldier. The word moose, by the way, was the Yank soldier's invention derived from the Japanese *musume*, girl.

No invading army was ever more well-behaved than the Allied soldiers upon their entry into Japan. The Japanese were astounded. The men had expected massacre, the women had anticipated rape. Women and children had been sent in great numbers to the comparative safety of the country. But the invaders came in with smiles and bows, gave cigarettes to the men, candy bars to the children, and politely ignored the womenfolk.

Perhaps the ladies were slightly piqued by such lack of attention. At any rate there was soon a change in their attitude. Instead of keeping themselves out of the way, they set about putting themselves in the way of the conquering barbarians.

Most had no evil intent—they merely responded to

kindness and courtesy. Acquaintanceship budded into friendship, friendship in many cases ripened into adoration, for the Japanese female had never known such a considerate male. The age of chivalry which still cast a lingering glow over Europe and America had never touched Japan. Japan had its own rich virtues, but deference to woman was not one of them.

It was heady wine for the Japanese girl, walking beside her man instead of six paces behind, going first through doors, seeing him carry the bundles and bare his head upon meeting and parting. Besides he had both the means and the inclination to give her a good time while her Japanese men friends had neither.

Etiquette required the Japanese boy to keep aloof and wait for his elders to arrange a meeting with some personable girl. No such inhibitions restrained the American, Briton or Australian. And their freedom from such conventions was contagious; many Japanese girls met them on their own grounds with a frankness and intimacy that they would not have dared to show to men of their own nation.

Every man could have his moose. Thousands took advantage of the opportunity—and thousands still do, now that the Occupation has been replaced by the "Security Forces" which garrison a defenseless Japan until she is sufficiently strong to defy her traditional enemy, the U.S.S.R.

Many of the girls involved are of good family and the finest type of Japanese womanhood. They expect to be taken seriously. Many of the officers and men of the allied forces are just as fine and just as serious. This is indicated by the fact that up to March 19, 1952, eight thousand U.S. servicemen had married Japanese girls and had taken their brides to America. Thousands of others had wedded Japanese brides with the intention of staying in Japan with them or taking them home later.

But for every one of these men who were willing to face the problems of interracial marriage, there were perhaps a hundred who did not care to wade in so deep. They wanted a moose but not a noose. To meet their needs the "*aprés guerre* geisha" came into being. The after-the-war geisha was not necessarily a geisha at all but any girl willing to make herself agreeable through the long night hours without expecting any more lasting alliance. Some of them were actual geisha but they were apt to be expensive, usually costing ten dollars an hour. The highest type of geisha kept herself aloof from such traffic, jealously preserving her status as an entertainer and artist. But the fat wallets of servicemen caused many to slip.

A far greater number of the aprés guerre geisha are taxi dancers, barmaids, waitresses, prostitutes, and "pompom girls." Pompom is a play on the Japanese word *ponpon* meaning the stomach and pompom girls are those who go with foreign soldiers for the sake of food, cigarettes, dresses and other material advantages to be paid for with "love."

Just who is the victim in these transactions it is sometimes hard to say. The girls often give as good as they get. A Tokyo taxi dancer pulled the same trick on several dozen hapless servicemen. In the dance hall where she was employed she would dance with a likely-looking prospect, pretend to be overcome by his charms, show great interest in learning his name and address, and date him to meet her at a certain rendezvous the next day.

When the time came, he would be there but she would not. While he waited for her she ransacked his quarters and made off with everything of value. Then she moved to another dance hall and repeated the routine.

The police finally caught up with her but not before she had made forty soldiers very red in the face.

As any foreign correspondent who was in Japan during the Occupation will testify, great care was exercised by the authorities lest anything but the "truth" should go to the outside world. The "truth," according to these official mentors, was that the Occupation was "doing fine." Thus there were no ifs or buts in the highly encouraging report published throughout America and Europe January 24, 1946 to the effect that MacArthur had outlawed legal prostitution in Japan. The Japanese government had been ordered to annul all contracts binding women to bondage. General MacArthur acted, he said, under the Potsdam Declaration guaranteeing respect for fundamental rights.

An age-old scandal had been abolished. No longer would fathers be permitted to sell their daughters to the highest bidder. No longer would girls be bound by their debts to brothel keepers.

The proprietors of brothels customarily took half of a girl's earnings for food, lodging and overhead. She must then make payments against the cost of her purchase, and also she was expected to buy from the proprietor her cosmetics and other articles including kimonos at three times their real worth. The result was that she went steadily more deeply into debt. Now by one stroke of the powerful MacArthur pen her debts were cancelled and she was free to walk out and become a respectable citizen.

132

The intention was excellent as are all the intentions of this great humanitarian. But the public impression that the Yoshiwara had breathed its last was not well founded. There is more prostitution in Japan today than at any time in history. The presence of womanless foreign troops, and the general breakdown of morals following the war, are contributing causes.

Another cause is the greater attractiveness of the profession now that a woman may go in business for herself rather than work for a rapacious landlord. One girl when asked why she didn't quit the game now that she had the protection of the law said, "Why should I? It has almost doubled my earning power."

There was no exodus from Tokyo's Yoshiwara. Said one resident: "With the terrible housing shortage we'd rather stay here." Of the 310 sumptuous and elaborate houses in this district before the war only nine had survived attack by the B-29's, but new houses were rapidly thrown up to accommodate the rush of foreign customers. Girls were readily recruited into the service.

A typical case was that of a girl who had been working in a teahouse on the Ginza. Her customers were Japanese and she complained that they were noisy and rude. She considered her status much improved when she was able to move to a good house in the Yoshiwara where she could earn many times more money by giving pleasure to polite Americans.

Innkeepers may no longer hold women in bondage. They must accomplish their purpose in a more indirect way. Therefore they offer accommodation, food and clothing in return for sixty percent of the woman's takings.

No contract is signed and the woman is theoretically free to leave at any time.

At the close of the war a great Tokyo munitions plant closed its doors and its owners faced bankruptcy. But presently they had an idea that proved to be their salvation. They reopened the plant as the world's largest brothel under the name of the International Palace. They rightly gauged the hunger of the occupying armies and the plant did such a tremendous business that Americans dubbed it Willow Run—because it processed its product on such a huge scale. Each woman "processed" fifteen GIs a day at $3.30 each. Half of this went to the management. Thus the two hundred fifty women employed gave the International Palace a daily revenue of $6,002. The owners were satisfied. It was almost as good as making munitions.

A newspaper correspondent, Mark Gayn, visited the International Palace May 10, 1946, more than three months after legal prostitution had "ended" in Japan. The place had by that time been put off limits for Allied troops and those who visited it must do so on the sly. He found that practically all the girls were deeply in debt to the company for clothes and cosmetics. He asked them if they had heard of the MacArthur directive canceling all such debts. They had not.

The correspondent, who stood on good terms with the Occupation authorities, did not risk their displeasure by sending this item to his home paper. But he jotted it down in his journal and later included it in his book, *Japan Diary*.

The girl market in Japan is chiefly in control of one man, Hitoshi Narikawa, who manages fifty thousand operators. He looks like Santa Claus and is known as Papa-san.

134

When the MacArthur directive was promulgated he promptly obeyed it. He notified the women in his six thousand houses throughout Japan that they were liberated. They were free to leave—but if they did they must not expect to be taken back.

Only five hundred of the fifty thousand accepted their liberty. The others said they'd rather stay.

"It wasn't that they loved their work," Papa-san explained. "It was merely that they didn't want to be unemployed, homeless and hungry. And anyhow, they liked the chance to meet an occasional kind American soldier."

So the girls stayed, but on a new basis. Papa-san merely charges them rental for the rooms.

The girls are not forced to pay their debt but if they insist upon doing so, good. If they don't, it's all right. But they must not be surprised if they have an accident sometime at the hands of Papa-san's thugs.

The fact is that the sense of honor is so acute in Japan, even in the lowest strata, that many girls feel bound to work out their debts in spite of a law that permits them to abscond without payment.

Many girls have been emancipated by compassionate GIs. A soft-hearted officer who had just bought out a sixteen-year-old girl for five thousand yen ($280) was asked why he did it.

"Just because she's young and beautiful," he said. "And she speaks English."

His friend replied, "Speaks English! The only words she knows are Mama, Papa, and Nice Boy."

"Yeah," acknowledged the officer, "but man, how she times them!"

135

Japanese villages in the vicinity of U.S. army bases complain of the influx of women to serve the needs of soldiers. In Nishitama village three miles from Yokota Air Base seventy houses are occupied by one hundred and twenty girls whose patrons are exclusively American military personnel. Their activities make a deep impression upon the children and young people of the village. Recently when a teacher of the junior high school asked his 140 pupils to write themes on "Present-Day Social Conditions" nearly a score of them wrote on this subject.

"Some described in detail," reports the *Nippon Times*, "and with youthful candidness what they saw when they took a peek through paper-sliding doors. Some of the passages are quite unfit for print."

Parents and teachers in all such communities, silent and fearful during the Occupation, are now expressing their resentment in no uncertain terms. Many American soldiers agree with them whole-heartedly and one wrote the following letter to the paper.

To the Editor:

Much has been said and written about moral laxity in Japan. Yet we (the Security Forces) have been instrumental in bringing about this condition. Townsmen and villagers near the U.S. bases have tolerated us in silence mainly because we are the occupying force. I wonder what the reactions of our home towns would be if they were subjected to the same humiliation and shameful behavior by foreign soldiers. We are now planting the future outbreak of resentment against us. No nation will forget the moral humiliation it was subjected to. Unless army personnel is better controlled we will soon lose any semblance of respect.

An officer, U.S.A.F.

Parents of impressionable young people do not like it when professional prostitutes set up housekeeping next door; but how much more painful it is when their own daughters are involved. The great majority of girls used by soldiers are amateurs. Professional women know what to expect. It is the amateurs who really get hurt.

A girl was brought unconscious to a hospital in Hiroshima. She came to long enough to tell her story, then died. She had been raped by twenty Australian soldiers, then left lying in a wayside lot. The soldiers, when questioned, explained that they had just been out for a "bit of fun."

So many incidents of the sort occurred in Hiroshima that the Australian troops, assigned to occupy that city, came to be known as *yabanjin*, savages.

The methods of the Americans were less brutal and those of the British were almost refined. The latter depended upon blandishment and persuasion, and I came upon a group of British soldiers earnestly studying the chapter entitled "Phrases in Cupidland" in Sheba's valuable little handbook, *Japanese in Three Weeks*. They were learning to say, "I worship you," in Japanese: *"Anata wo suhai shimasu."* They pored over the Japanese equivalents for I live for you only, My love for you is all my life, I love you long and I love you true, When you are gone darkness comes into my soul, My heart goes pit-a-pat when you kiss me, Each parting is a grief unspeakable, You are sweet as a demure violet, Dear heart you are mine alone.

137

The use of such expressions is all in the day's fun for the soldier. He does not realize that they are nothing less than dynamite to the heart of a young girl who has never heard such terms of endearment from the lips of a Japanese. The girl wants to believe what she hears and serious misunderstandings are the result.

Little Tomiko, dragging a bashful GI after her, came into the office of a journalist, Miss Yoko Matsuoka, who had previously befriended her. The girl knew no English and the GI no Japanese, except a few love phrases. Tomiko announced jubilantly that her friend was going to marry her and take her to America.

Miss Matsuoka turned to the GI. "I understand you intend to marry Tomiko."

"No, I ain't promised anything like that. I'm going home in three months."

"What do you intend to do with her?"

He shrugged. His copybook Japanese had evidently won him what he wanted from the girl and he had no further interest in her. But he had some decency. And the journalist wrung a reluctant promise from him, then said to Tomiko:

"He has no intention of marrying you. He will support you until he leaves, but he will not take you to America. You misunderstood."

Two GIs, headed for the U.S., looked out of the window of the train about to pull out and bade a last farewell to two weeping Japanese girls. Evidently the girls knew no English, or not enough to understand the heartless wisecracks of their departing lovers. A sobbing question, "When you come back?" was answered with a laugh:

"Come back? When you damn Japs bomb Pearl Harbor again, baby, I'll be back!"

We stayed a few days in the home of Missionary I. L. Shaver in Oita. A pretty moshi-moshi girl (telephone operator) from the Oita Telephone Exchange came to consult the missionary. She wanted to find Jimmy Blank, a GI who had been like a husband to her but now didn't come to see her any more. He had promised to take her to America. He had given her an auto tab of his car, his name on a piece of paper, and a snapshot of his sister.

She was in a highly emotional state. She could not eat or sleep, she was so lovesick. She was crazy about her GI, she said. She was wild to go to America. She was afraid he had been sent to Korea. He might be killed.

"If he dies I want to die too."

She couldn't get any information about him. Whenever she called up the camp and asked for Jimmy, every man who answered the phone said, "I'm Jimmy."

Mr. Shaver undertook to telephone for her. When he did, he was told that Jimmy had leave until twelve that night. He wasn't using his leave to see her.

Whether the girl's hint of self-destruction was carried any further I do not know, but not a few of these international incidents have ended in suicide. In a number of cases it has been a double suicide when the soldier and his sweetheart could not see their way clear to wed and could not bear to part. An Air Force lieutenant, about to return to his fiancée in America, was poisoned in a geisha house by his Japanese friend who then took her own life. This is the only death on record of a soldier of the Occupation at the hands of a Japanese.

Usually the soldier is allowed to go and forget, and if there is any dying to be done, the girl does it. The suicide rate, always considerable in Japan, has risen sharply during the last few years.

The volcanoes are the favorite scenes for such acts of quiet desperation. Since the volcanoes are regarded as Shinto shrines it is an act of piety to give oneself a living sacrifice, a burnt offering, to the gods. The smoking craters of Asama, Mihara and Aso receive scores of the lovelorn every year.

Two GIs on the way down the slope of Mt. Aso met a weeping girl on the way up. When she sank to the ground they went to her assistance and somehow learned her story. She loved an American who had gone home. She had gowned herself in her best ceremonial kimono and had come by train all the way from Fukuoka to end her life here.

The GIs led her to a hotel at the base of the mountain, fortified her with a good meal, took her in their jeep to Kumamoto where they put her on the train for Fukuoka.

The number of GI babies is unknown, the Occupation having discouraged the taking of a census that might reveal the unpleasant truth. Any mention of the question in the press or on the radio was disapproved and the Japanese radio announcer who referred to the birth of the first GI baby as "the first Occupation present" was fired.

Now the subject is freely and bitterly discussed. The government, as a matter of international courtesy, still refrains from making a census. The lowest unofficial estimate places the number of Madame Butterfly's children at twenty thousand. The great Tokyo newspaper, *Yomiuri*,

140

declares that "international orphans with blue eyes or black faces who do not know their fathers or mothers now total two hundred thousand throughout Japan."

Perhaps a reasonable guess would be that Occupation troops have fathered one hundred thousand half-Japanese waifs.

Of course there are more to come. Another Tokyo paper calls attention to the fact that "the number of half-breeds will be on the increase in view of the stationing of U.S. forces in Japan for a relatively prolonged period."

Every day press and public become more acid, and more obloquy is heaped upon the mothers of mixed bloods. The half-castes are becoming outcasts. They are considered morally unacceptable. Other children make fun of their light hair, or ridicule the kinky hair and black faces of children fathered by the negro troops. Mothers dye fair hair black, but nothing much can be done with a black face.

Americans who suppose that their godlike attributes are the envy of the rest of the human race would be astonished at the Japanese antipathy for "faded hair, washed-out skins, beetling brows, big noses, and hairy chests." Particularly now that Japan has begun to swing away from her postwar adoration of western power, race prejudice is reasserting itself. The Japanese consider themselves racially purer than Americans—and with good reason. Japan is no melting pot. True, the race combines Mongolian and Polynesian strains, but the blending was completed more than a millennium ago. The Japanese are ethnically one of the most homogeneous peoples on the face of the earth.

This gives them no reason for pride, because a "pure" race is not necessarily better than a mixed race—in fact the odds are on the side of the mixed race. But people do not need good reason to be proud, and with the resurgence of nationalism in Japan anything alien is looked upon with increasing dislike and suspicion.

The *Yomiuri* suggests that all these unwanted half-breeds be sent to the United States. These children, says the paper, "are now coming of age to join public schools. How will they feel when looked at every day by other children in school?

"We understand Germans appealed to American women who responded and took such orphans in Germany to an organization in Washington, D.C.

"America is a melting pot of races, so these orphans would not be as forlorn over there as here in Japan."

There is also a move to send a few thousand GI babies to Brazil to be adopted by some of the three hundred thousand Japanese in that country. Brazil is even more of a melting pot than the U.S. and far more tolerant toward racial minorities.

But even if some of the children are successfully exported, the great majority must stay in Japan and make the best of it.

There is agitation on the part of Ku Klux Klanlike elements in Japan against allowing Eurasians and Negrasians to attend the public schools. It is said that the presence of these "children of crime" would contaminate respectable children. Segregation is demanded. The oldest of the children are now of age to enter school. A government spokesman insists that there will be no discrimination. "So far we have made no racial distinction and we don't intend to."

In the meantime private institutions have been caring for

GI babies. Egon Hessel, Kyoto missionary who has a hand in every sort of good work, took us through one of his kindergartens. Among the black-haired Japanese there was a single little brown-haired tot. Her GI father is with his family in America, but he sends forty dollars a month to support the child and its mother.

This is an exception. In most cases the fathers accept no responsibility for their Japan-born children. In many cases they do not even know that they exist.

A good-hearted Japanese woman, Miki Sawada, turned her father's farm in Oiso into a home for deserted Occupation babies. With contributions from Japanese and Americans she is caring for more than one hundred unwanted children whom she describes as "innocent victims of this age of war and violence." GIs connected with the Tokyo Army Hospital gave four thousand dollars. Joe Louis contributed the proceeds of a boxing exhibition. Persons in Richmond, Virginia, contribute three hundred dollars a month.

Our Lady of Lourdes Baby Home in Yokohama cares for 175 orphans. Sister Mary, chief nurse, needs funds to start a boys' school. "The poor things," she says. "The Japanese children will make them suffer if they go to public schools. Children can be very cruel, you know."

Other homes are being supported by American servicemen. "These are our responsibilities," was the slogan of the U.S. Naval Air Station at Atsugi in a drive that raised $2,200. A Battery in Yokohoma donates $250 a month.

This spirit of goodwill needs to be applied for prevention as well as for cure. But the chance of this is slight so long as the ratio of American servicemen to American women in Japan is about 100 to 1. The men moreover are for the most part young, just at the age when they begin to look most insistently for female companionship. Armies since the beginning of time have been baffled by this problem.

Many servicemen, obeying a natural impulse but unwilling to indulge it to the injury of others, are marrying Japanese women. This need not be considered a comedown for the American soldier. In a great many cases he marries above himself, into a family of means, culture and position. His bride may have the better of him in education and breeding. He deserves to be congratulated, not condemned for "going native."

Such marriages may help in the long run to solve the problem of half-caste children. With the increase in the number of legitimate Eurasians, the stigma attached to the illegitimate will fade. As Japan becomes racially more cosmopolitan, she should become less rabidly race conscious. That will make Japan a safer and better neighbor.

America too will be a safer and better neighbor if she chooses to receive cordially the Nipponese brides of returning servicemen. For them life in a strange country is a trying experience and may easily end in disaster for themselves, their husbands and their children. In some cases Japanese wives in America have organized "War Brides' Clubs" and travel long distances to get together once a month to discuss their problems of adjustment in this new land.

That is good, but it is still more important that these women, instead of isolating themselves, be drawn into community activities with their American neighbors and that their children should experience no discrimination in school or on the playground. The Japanese have rare qualities of culture and character to contribute to American life.

Whether on the whole the Japanese woman has been advanced or retarded by foreign intervention it would be hard to say. Perhaps her lot has been improved in spite of the Occupation, as well as because of it. The one really precious gift that has been conferred upon her is the suffrage. Probably she will keep it. So far as I am aware history records no instance of women being deprived of the suffrage once they have won it. With it the Japanese woman can, if she puts her mind to it, gradually free herself from a web of tyranny and humiliation twenty centuries old.

12

SKYSCRAPER UNDERGROUND

LEAVING THE PIRATE STRONGHOLD, we recross the Inland Sea through a fantastic world of storybook islands where any sort of supernatural being might live and any impossible thing happen. Some islands rise abruptly from the sea in rocky precipices topped by a cap of forest. Others slope more or less gradually, though a thoroughly reasonable slope for farming is rare. Most are scalloped along the edge into charming bays with yellow sand beaches. These bays are separated by bold rocky promontories stuck with pines at all angles. On the most picturesque hilltops are apt to be *torii* and shrines.

In the bays are quaint villages with thatch or tile roofs—never rusty sheet iron. Each village has erected an efficient stone breakwater to make a snug harbor for the fishing boats.

We stop to explore the islands of Mushima, Kitagishima, Kobishima, Hashirijima and arrive just before sundown in the dream harbor of Tomo on the northern shore of the Sea.

Soon we have been conducted up a hill and flights of polished stairs to a room on the third floor of the Tokiwa

146

Hotel where from our balcony overhanging the sea we look out upon a scene that would make an Italian turn his back on Lake Como.

We are perched on a peninsula and practically surrounded by the Inland Sea. Alternating belts of smooth and rippled water stretch away to infinity. Fishing boats with square sails wing their way to port, the fisherman helping the slight breeeze by working the sweep. The sea is checkered with the little white squares. The sunset glow dramatizes the green and gold of numberless islands, some of them so small that they look like round furry caps set down on the sea, others climbing high and crowned with pagodas. The blue-and-purple mountains of Honshu and Shikoku form the backdrop.

So much prized is the view that even the bathroom is enclosed in glass and a sign on the wall announces that this is the only place in Japan where you can see five *ken* while bathing. Within the reach of the naked eye lie the states of Tosa, Kagawa, Ehime, Okayama and Hiroshima.

Idyllic sailing weather carried us on the next morning toward Onomichi. Though we curved and twisted to get through the narrow passages between islands, the wind followed us like a faithful spaniel. A huge balloon jib rigged to the foremast fairly lifted us over the waves. As for the sea, it is here more like a river, the mountainous village-sprinkled shores lying so close together.

We had been going about an hour when a motorboat overtook us and a policeman clambered aboard. He explained gruffly that he had chased us all the way from Tomo. We searched our consciences. How had we transgressed the law? Still grumbling over the inconvenience we had caused him, he reached inside his uniform and drew out a foot-long card and a brush. He wanted a poem.

After a night "on the town" in a choice Onomichi inn, we entered a new Inland Sea. Here the islands were no longer dainty and quaint, but enormous, businesslike brutes swarming with towns and humming with factories. It does not seem fitting that a group of islands should be a manufacturing center—but this is. On the map a maze of red lines marks the routes of "sea busses," small steamers that serve the island towns. Between the islands wriggle narrow water lanes through which the tide rip races as if late for an appointment.

Yet even the factory-fringed islands are magnificent in their upper reaches of farm and forest rising to a final burst of jagged peaks. And sprinkled in among the big busy fellows are little odd-shaped and fortunately uninhabitable islets that have all the romantic flavor that an island should have.

If factory islands are a surprise, how much more surprising is the island of Ikuchi which has along with its chimneys and power lines a Nikko that out-Nikkos Nikko. The gorgeous aggregation of temples that is Nikko is visited by tens of thousands of tourists every year—and yet here is a far superior wonder that is probably not looked upon by any foreign visitor from one year's end to another.

A dozen superbly designed temples, bell towers and pagodas in red, blue, white, silver and gold, glorify the Shinshu sect of Buddhism. Surrounding the buildings is a great wall pierced by a mighty gate that is in itself one of the architectural treasures of the Orient. Grand staircases, balustrades and platforms of white marble are reminiscent of the Summer Palace near Peking. One of the temples is a treasure house of Japanese relics; another contains a sanctified version of the comic strip, a series of finely sculptured and painted scenes telling the stories of the Buddhist saints.

The name of this hidden marvel is Kozoji and ten years from now it may be in the guidebooks. It is not there now because it is well off the beaten track of tourist travel, and because it is new, little more than ten years old. So modern is its spirit that recently all of its six hundred monks formed a labor union and went on strike!

Somehow we escaped the attention of Ikuchi officialdom and went to sleep on the deck of our boat in the harbor. At four in the morning there was a deep boom that seemed to come out of some ancient past. A long silence, then another boom, but on a slightly higher note this time. Quite evidently the sound came from the bell towers of Kozoji. The two bells alternated with long peaceful pauses between. It was hard to reconcile the tranquil sound of them with the gay, almost giddy gorgeousness of the temples where brisk little monks go on strike.

Past frantically busy shipyards we sailed toward a plume of smoke emitted by a great black copper smelter that had one entire island to itself. Not a sprig of green was visible on the island. The smelter had formerly stood on the mainland but when its fumes ruined the vegetation for miles around it was banished to its present location. The company was worried lest the island should prove too small, but they have found a way to remedy that. The immense quantities of slag ejected by the smelter have already enlarged the property by fifty percent.

We now cross open sea, pausing to look down through the clear water to the barnacled decks of a ship sunk by a typhoon three years ago, and sail into the harbor of industrial Niihama, a city of sixty thousand individuals each with his own chimney. Such is the impression one gets of this city of smokestacks outlined against the wall of mountains two thirds of a mile high. Our little ship timidly pulled up to a pier under the frowning scrutiny of monstrous plants for the manufacture of nickel, zinc, aluminum, ammonium sulphate and penicillin. The thunder of machinery, the pall of smoke, and a heavy rain, all conspired to make our deck an unattractive bedroom and we raised no objection when the mayor, who had graciously come to have tea with us in the Kansai office, put us up in the Sumitomo Club for the night.

Niihama is occasionally visited by foreign businessmen since it is on the mainland, accessible by railroad, and industrially important. But there is no foreign hotel. Visitors must stay at the club maintained by the Sumitomo mining interests. Apparently some previous visitors had been unacquainted with Japanese ways, for it had been necessary to post this notice on the wall:

"No shoes are allowed in a Japanese inn. When slippers are placed at the entrance for use by guests, wear them only when walking on the corridors, and not in the matted rooms.

"The guest is expected to use his room as sitting room, bedroom and dining room combined unless otherwise provided.

"It is the custom to take the Japanese bath after the body has been cleaned and the soap rinsed off outside the bathtub and soap is not used inside the tub. The management requests bathers to conform to this custom."

The chief sight of Niihama is outside of it. Moreover, this remarkable sight is out of sight.

The Besshi, eight miles back of Niihama and buried a mile deep in a mountain, is one of the world's greatest copper mines.

I had had quite enough of caves. The mayor and his aides who dined with us insisted that I must go through the Besshi Mine. I declined—and the next day found myself in the lockerroom at the mine's maw, removing my clothes lest they be damaged by the drippings and donning miner's shirt and pants, canvas boots, and a black patent leather helmet equipped with a clasp to hold an open-flame acetylene lamp. The helmet was too small, the pants too short, and I had the general appearance of a slighty surprised visitor from Mars.

My wife would not accompany me, for three reasons: (1) She didn't want to, (2) The management didn't invite her, (3) The miners didn't want her, because: (a) They imagined a woman's presence in a mine causes accidents, (b) They go naked.

Captain Wide-Margin-of-Safety, who would rather miss a party than a tunnel, was going, also a Colonel Ryder from GHQ in Tokyo. Together with several mine executives as guides, we boarded a trolley which presently plunged into the tunnel.

As it did so, every man removed his cap in deference to the god of the mine. This is supposed to insure safe passage. The ceremony is repeated upon emerging into the blessed light of day.

Our train consisted of half a dozen cars equipped with seats but no walls or roof. The train roared through the tunnel of solid rock with such a din that if you wished to speak to your neighbor, mouth must be placed to ear and you must shout at the top of your lungs. The car rocked violently from side to side. The Colonel and I had reason to regret that we overtopped our Japanese companions by almost a foot. This brought our heads within eight inches of the trolley wire. The wire packed six hundred volts. When I removed my hat because of the increasing heat I was sharply advised by an executive to put it on again. He shouted in my ear something about electrocution. The rough roadbed continually bounced us up and down, uncomfortably close to sudden death.

Trains of ore on the way out passed us. The air was stifling and the noise deafening. The tunnel seemed endless. My fingers ached from clutching the rungs of the seat to hold myself down.

We stopped and the manager said we had come a mile. The same trunk tunnel, he said, ran on for another mile.

The air was oppressive with a damp heat that fogged the lens of my Rolleiflex and blurred my glasses so that I had to remove them. To the flicker of our acetylene lamps, we walked, choosing between stepping on the slippery ties or in the mud between them. One of the Japanese volunteered the information that this obstacle race sends many men to the company hospital with broken legs.

Presently we stepped into a cage and dropped a third of a mile.

We came out into a cave as big as a church occupied by the enormous power plant whose heartbeat sends electric life throughout the great mine. This plant was buried two miles inside the mountain. Each of the huge machines had been made out of units small enough to be brought in through the tunnels, then assembled. An enormous blower labored to lift the stagnant air out of the tunnels—but since there were two hundred and fifty miles of tunnels, this task was an almost impossible one.

Near the power room was the brain room, the main office of the mine, a place of desks and stools and walls hung with diagrams. Here in the heart of the mountain we were served tea! Everyone received it with much formality and polite sucking of breath, despite the fact that the attendant who served it was perfectly nude.

This however did not seem unreasonable in view of the heat. Our clothes were soaking wet with steam from without and sweat from within. Each of us had been furnished with a towel before entering the mine, and found full use for it. Our faces flowed, and water streamed out from under our helmets.

Near nakedness alternated with nakedness in the style show of the copper mine. Some workmen wore a G-string effectively, some ineffectively, most did not bother with it at all. When the manager summoned an engineer who had been working on the generators, the man came modestly holding his cap over his essentials.

Stark naked men repaired tracks, loaded ore cars, ran electric locomotives, operated the machines, dug into the walls with automatic drills, did carpentry, worked over books in the main office, bowed before a Shinto shrine a mile underground.

It is not quite correct to say that they were naked. Most

of them did wear helmets. Many also carried a towel which was usually draped around the neck.

They looked as if they had returned to the age of primitive man, and it was extraordinary to see these cavemen lift their hats to us and bow as courteously as if they were dressed in afternoon suits and high hats at an imperial garden party. Not only did they salute the visitors, but they were continually lifting their hats and bowing to each other. Responding to their courtesy, I nearly stepped into a shaft 160 meters deep.

The greatest shafts are the elevator shafts. The man who operates a cage covers a good deal of perpendicular territory in a day. From bottom to top his trip is two thirds of a mile.

The Besshi Mine is a skyscraper inside a mountain. There are forty floors in this skyscraper. But unlike the floors in other skyscrapers, these are numbered from the top.

The first floor is the highest level, although this is still far below the top of the mountain. The fortieth floor is the basement—but only temporarily, for work will proceed to still lower levels. The distance from the fortieth floor to the first is 3712 feet. That makes the Besshi skyscraper three times the height of the Empire State Building.

The 250 miles of corridors have taken 260 years to dig. Progress was slow when it was a job for chisel and hammer. Modern machinery has speeded up the burrowing, and the tunnels are now being extended at the rate of four miles a year.

Twelve hundred men are employed underground, six hundred above. There are fifteen hundred houses for the men and their families, six stores, four hospitals, one school.

The mine was founded by Sumitomo 260 years ago and remained in the control of that mighty family until after the war when a MacArthur directive broke up the great industrial combine and Besshi became an independent company.

Has this been a good thing or not? I put the question to a high executive after we had emerged from the mine, stripped off our sodden garments, resumed normal attire, and sat down to partake of the inevitable tea.

The executive shook his head. He could not speak English, but he could write it. He wrote in my notebook:

"Under Sumitomo we could work indeferently with profit or loss of this mine in a short time. Now we must operate fearfully in the care of share of stock."

In other words, it would be a matter of indifference if the mine should operate at a loss for a short time provided it were backed by powerful financial interests such as Sumitomo. As an independent company, however, it must rely "fearfully" on its own resources.

The mayor of Niihama when asked the same question explained that all the industries of Niihama had been Sumitomo before the war. Now they had been broken up into five companies. None of the five had enough capital.

At Uno we had explored the same question with officers of the Kamioka Mining Company. There the huge copper smelter and sulphuric acid plant were a study in still life, not a wheel turning. The plant had been in trouble ever since it had become an independent company. It had formerly been a part of Mitsui. I asked the manager what he thought of the breaking up of the zaibatsu.

"I think it wrong, because smaller units cannot function so efficiently."

A Kyoto industrialist gave a slightly different answer. His company had controlled such diverse interests as an electric railroad, the Takarazuka Girls Revue, and a baseball team! Now these, and a dozen other enterprises, had been sent each on its separate way.

"Was the break-up of the zaibatsu a good or a bad thing?" I asked him.

"Good!" he said emphatically. "But it won't last."

13

THE FOUR GOLIATHS

THERE WOULD HAVE BEEN no war with Japan but for the zaibatsu. Its fate may determine whether Japan will again embark upon a war for world conquest.

Zai means wealth and *batsu* means clique. The name is apt, for the zaibatsu is the wealth-clique that owns and operates Japan.

The zaibatsu is the group of powerful families dominating Japanese industry. The term is applied particularly to the four greatest of the great families: Mitsui, Mitsubishi, Sumitomo and Yasuda.

These four clans alone controlled before the war nearly three fourths of the capitalization of all Japanese business. Most of the other fourth was controlled by lesser families of the zaibatsu.

Each of the zaibatsu began in one industry such as coal mining or shipping. But during the past century they have steadily broadened their interests until now their tentacles extend into businesses of every description. A zaibatsu expert with GHQ described Mitsui thus:

"A comparable business organization in the U.S. might be achieved if, for example, U.S. Steel, General Motors,

Standard Oil of New York, Alcoa, Douglas Aircraft, E. I. Dupont de Nemours, Sun Shipbuilding, Westinghouse Electric, American Telephone and Telegraph, RCA, IBM, U.S. Rubber, Sea Island Sugar, Dole Pineapple, U.S. Lines, Grace Lines, National City Bank, Metropolitan Life, the Woolworth Stores, and the Statler Hotels were to be combined into a single enterprise."

Nor were the combines content with Japan's business. They took over its politics as well. The Seiyukai Party, the GOP of Japan, was in the pocket of Mitsui. Mitsubishi bought up the Minseito, counterpart of the Democratic Party in the United States. Yasuda exercised great political power through his support of the military and the secret societies.

Since the big families controlled the wealth of the nation, the munitions factories, the steel mills, the shipyards, all the means of making war, they alone could decide whether there should be war or peace. Speaking of the families General MacArthur said, "The integration of these few with government was complete and their influence upon government policies inordinate, and set the course which ultimately led to war and destruction. It was indeed so complete a monopoly as to be in effect a form of socialism in private hands." And ambassador for reparations Edwin W. Pauley reported, "Not only were the zaibatsu as responsible for Japan's militarism as the militarists themselves, but they profited immensely by it. Even now, in defeat, they have actually strengthened their monopoly position."

By the Deconcentration Law of December, 1947, eighty-three zaibatsu holding companies were dissolved and fifty-

158

six members of zaibatsu families were purged—that is, excluded from positions of responsibility in public or business life. Holding company securities were offered for sale to the public. Few Japanese however had the money to buy them.

The new law had been passed by order of SCAP (the Occupation) but it had no public support. The conservative Japanese government was against it, the Diet was against it, small businessmen whom it was intended to free from the bonds of monopoly did not care to be freed, and the people saw no reason for changing an economic system that had made Japan the greatest power in the Far East.

Curiously enough the Japanese had never resented the zaibatsu. Being a people who crave leadership, they rather liked being fathered by the big families. Competition is no virtue in Japanese eyes. The Japanese businessman has no wish to "go it alone." He welcomes the chance to merge his business in a great combine that will carry him over years of depression and assure him a small but steady income for the rest of his life. Bankruptcy is practically unknown in Japan. When a small company fails it usually "fails successfully." That is, it places itself under the protection of a larger concern and goes on with the same personnel almost as if nothing had happened.

Cooperation is the word in Japan, not competition. There is a feeling in Japan that competition involves a high degree of waste.

American business and diplomatic circles also worried lest the break-up of the zaibatsu should delay Japan's economic recovery.

Disapproval, both Japanese and American, discouraged

SCAP. The most severe measures against the zaibatsu were relaxed. Prime Minister Shigeru Yoshida who had strongly protested against the dissolution of the zaibatsu was inclined to overlook violations of the law. The leaders of the zaibatsu had been consulted when the law was drawn up and it had been framed in accordance with their advice —therefore they did not find much difficulty in circumventing it. In many cases the "purged" zaibatsu officials still kept control of their enterprises through dummies.

The Supreme Command Deconcentration Review Board examined 325 operating companies to determine whether they should be made independent of zaibatsu control. The Board divorced eleven companies and recommended changes in eight others. Thus ninety-four percent of the companies were not touched.

Sadly commented the *New York Times*: "The breaking up of the corporations was the chief objective. This has been amended and watered down to such an extent, it is likely not more than ten corporations will be materially affected."

And the *Christian Science Monitor* mourned: "Behind the scenes the same individuals and their network of control associations and interlocking monopoly agreements are exercising tremendous power."

Independent manufacturers still could get raw material allocations only by consent of the trusts. They were unable to obtain financing from banks because the banks were still under zaibatsu domination.

Even the occupying troops were balked by the monopolies. When Eighth Army Procurement ordered materials from the supposedly independent Daiwa Sangyo Company, the order was refused. When company officials were asked the reason for the refusal they frankly explained that they were under orders from Mitsui not to deliver the goods.

With the failure of SCAP to carry out what it had so gallantly begun, the system of exploitation of the many for the benefit of the few was speeded up. By 1950 eight banks controlled eighty percent of Japanese industry according to the British Commonwealth delegate on the Allied Council for Japan.

Since the passing of the Occupation there has been nothing to stop the returning tide of the zaibatsu—nothing but an unenforced law. Twelve offshoots of Mitsubishi have recombined. Three former Mitsui firms have reunited. Firms in every line of industry are throwing off the masks they assumed for the time being and are resuming zaibatsu names. The firm temporarily called Asahi Trust and Banking Company reverts to Mitsubishi Trust and Banking Company, East Japan Heavy Industries becomes Mitsubishi Nippon Heavy Industries. Nishin Chemical becomes Sumitomo Chemical. Seika Mining becomes Sumitomo Coal Mining. Tokyo Trust and Banking goes back to Mitsui Trust and Banking. Kawasaki Wharf feels more comfortable as Mitsui Wharf, and Nitto Soko Tatemono as Mitsui Bussan. Dozens of other cases might be cited.

At the same time zaibatsu shares which had been sold to the public are now being bought back by the trusts and the trend toward broader security ownership and the development of an independent middle class is being checked. Economically, Japan is stepping backward toward feudalism.

Political freedom is dependent upon economic freedom. So long as the Japanese are willing to accept the serfdom of a system of industrial monopoly, there can be little hope that they will accept the principles of democracy in their political life.

14

WHEN PIRATES MEET PIRATES

NIGHT IS AS LOVELY as day on the Inland Sea. It is a shade more exciting as well, since then it is impossible to look out for floating mines and rocks.

We left Niihama late in the afternoon and made most of the trip to Imabari after dark. The air was balmy and the sea was like a sheet of black glass. In it were reflected brightly the lights on the shore, and dimly the shadowy masses of islands and mainland mountains. Lighthouses winked. A dirty old lantern lashed to our foremast peered out myopically through a red eye on one side and a green eye on the other. The sailors sang and the engine chugged and we had not a care in the world.

This vagabond life ended abruptly when we stepped ashore at Imabari to be met by heavy officialdom, ushered to a hotel, and dinnered from ten to one A.M.

It seemed that we had hardly begun to sleep before there was a polite "*Ohaiyo de gozaimasu*" outside our door and the city fathers were ready to take us toweling—for is not Imabari the greatest towel city in Japan and the second greatest on earth?

We visited a goodly proportion of the sixty-three towel

factories of Imabari. In this city woman's place is not in the home—it is in the textile mill. In one vast room 530 looms stretched away into the dusty distance. In prewar times there were more—one mill had two thousand looms. But they are not doing too badly even now. A factory of average size turns out a million towels a year.

Beside each loom hang cards perforated as for a player piano. By some mysterious art the perforations in these cards determine the pattern in the towel. The cards, all connected, pass through a mechanical brain above the loom and the holes in the cards regulate threads in the weave, altering according to the design. A fabric with no design needs no cards. A very intricate design requires thirty-five hundred cards.

In towel production America is first, Japan second. But Japan's export trade is greater because her towels are cheaper. She exports to South Africa, Southeast Asia, Iran, Iraq, Pakistan, Afghanistan, Hong Kong and India. A bid is being made for the American market as well as the European.

One would expect that towels made by so artistic a people as the Japanese would carry a beautiful oriental design. But the designs were painfully commonplace. We learned the reason when we visited the Ehime Prefectural Textile Laboratory where the designs are created.

"We get most of our ideas," the manager said, "from the Sears and Montgomery Ward catalogues. We consult them to find out what Americans like."

When I suggested that these institutions, though admirable, are not necessarily the last word in art and that the laboratory would do better to rely upon Japanese art sources than upon mail-order catalogues, my suggestions fell on deaf ears.

It was a city too big for its size. We drove from one traffic jam to another. Yet we never heard the driver rail, no matter how needlessly or stupidly the car was blocked by bicycles, wagons, *fu* carts, or stubborn pedestrians. If someone had carelessly left his cart blocking the road, our driver would dismount, go into one shop after another until he found him, get him to move his cart, then beg his pardon for putting him to so much trouble. "*Sumimasen*," he would say, "I humbly apologize." The other would also apologize and there would be an exchange of bows before we could proceed.

It was all a part of the Japanese pattern. During five months in Japan I did not hear one harsh or impatient word spoken by anyone—except perhaps by me when I became impatient of the patience of our Japanese companions.

"Look out for mines," we were told as we left Imabari. Near the entrance to Kurushima Strait we looked down to the shattered hulk of a mine victim. The sowers of mines had paid special attention to Kurushima since it, like Naruto, is a bottleneck, the closing of which would seriously check traffic through the Inland Sea.

The tide poured through Kurushima with a rush of bursts and falls that make the narrow passage look like a mountain torrent. The whirlpools caught our little ship and set it spinning, quite heedless of the rudder. The engine seemed powerless and we had learned the danger of raising a sail in such an emergency.

On one side was a rocky island and on the other a high, rocky hill of the mainland. We were swirling closer to black rocks that lined the mainland shore. It occurred to me that this might be the end of our trip. At least the cameras and films were in watertight containers. Good-Fortune was at the tiller, Wide-Margin at the engine, and Literature and I were armed with oars to fend off the rocks.

There was a splintering crash as the stem struck something unyielding and the boat heeled over until water flooded in over the port rail. Those of us who had nothing to hang onto slid across the deck. The boat slowly righted itself. The crash had checked the whirling. With a reversed engine and some poling we got free of the rock. Now we were out of the whirlpools and in a rather mild eddy. Crawling along close to shore we pulled through the strait and into the open stretches of the Aki Nada, Autumn Sea.

Past fantastic high rocks we sailed to the village of Miyaura on the island of Omishima. The mayor was waiting on the pier and walked us through the town to the 2000-year-old Oyamazumi Shrine, mellow and moss-covered, breathing of a past so ancient as to make Americans and even Britons feel juvenile.

Here is enshrined the Rain God to whom a famous medieval priest indited the poem:

> *May thy Milky Way run down to the Earth,*
> *To become the merciful rainfall on our farms!*
> *O, our glorious descending god!*

For some reason this shrine has been chosen to house most of Japan's authorized national treasures in armor. We besought the priest, for the sake of a picture, to take from the glass case and put on the magnificent suit of armor that had been worn by the daimyo of Matsuyama five hun-

166

dred years ago. He declined, but not for the reason that we had expected. It was not because the treasure was inviolate, but because he was not strong enough to wear it. The armor, though made of leather, is very heavy. The helmet alone must weigh as much as the heaviest of western saddles.

The priest called in a wiry laborer who donned the armor and stepped outdoors for the picture. An attempt to place him in the sun was foiled by the priest who feared that even momentary exposure to direct sunlight might fade the blues and reds of the costume. Our model puffed and panted under his burden and the perspiration rolled down his face.

"Men are not what they were in those days," lamented the priest.

The gray-brown shrine two millenniums old contrasted strongly with the multi-colored wonder ten years old that we had seen on one of the great industrial islands of the Bingo Sea. The islands of the Autumn Sea were also large but as different as the difference between the names of the two seas. Here life was slow and meditative and steeped in memories. The modern world seemed very far away. Forests of aged trees covered the hills. Villages were few and as old-time as a painting by Hiroshige. One expected to see two-sworded samurai stalking through their lanes.

An ancient schooner with bamboo-slatted, bat-wing sails much like our own had seemed to be following us all afternoon. At dusk we sailed in between the picturesque islands of Osakishimo and Okamura and drew up before the fairly large village of Mitarai. I noticed that the schooner dropped anchor a few hundred yards away.

It was now quite dark and we were not expected in this village. We anticipated the pleasure of sleeping on board, but the village was noisy with the clacking of wooden *geta* and the shouting, clapping and singing of two or three drinking parties. We suggested to the captain that we sail on a few miles to some quiet cove.

He was willing but his shipmates were not. The uncles had been staying on board every night while the captain and we had been luxuriating in hotels. Literature and Good-Fortune had hoped to take this night off for a bath, a bit of talk with the fishermen on the piers, and a bed ashore.

We put them ashore and promised to come back for them in the morning. Then we set out to sail a few miles farther north. What was my surprise to see the schooner up anchor and follow us.

We came to in a tranquil bay where there was no sound but the fiddling of crickets—and the splash of the schooner's anchor an eighth of a mile away. The moon was almost full. The air was cool but not cold.

"A wonderful night for sleeping," I remarked.

Mary was eyeing the schooner. She said, "A wonderful night for a murder."

We were not too much worried. Thanks to the gentlemen of the press our craft and its strange errand had become fairly well known and we had frequently been approached by boatloads of the curious. Still we made one concession to caution and did not remove our clothes and change to

168

pajamas as we usually did before slipping in between the futons.

I intended to keep one eye open. They both closed at once and I knew nothing for many hours.

Then I woke with a slight start. It seemed to me that I had been awakened by a soft jar or bump. Possibly the dinghy alongside had bumped the ship's hull. It was hard to believe since there was scarcely enough breeze to raise a ripple. In fact it was impossible to believe, for I now remembered that the dinghy was on deck. The captain had been working on it during the day, carpentering a new thwart, and tacking a sheet of plywood across the forepeak to make a storage chamber. He had left his tools in the boat—perhaps one of them had fallen. But there wasn't enough motion to make anything fall.

I dismissed the question and lazily studied the shadow of the mast cast by the moon upon the side wall of our canvas cabin.

But here was another impossibility. To throw a shadow on the side wall the mast would have to be on our beam.

A chilling sensation crept through my ribs. The mast was not ours. Another ship lay alongside.

I flung off the futon. At the same instant there was a shuffling sound and the shadows of two men appeared on the side wall. The shadows stooped, the edge of the canvas was raised, and I looked into the indecipherable faces of our two visitors.

Came a voice, "*Gomen nasai*, I beg your pardon."

"*Doitashimashite*," I replied, "Don't mention it."

"You are the Americans?"

"Yes."

"Do you have a gun?"

"No."

"That is good because we do not wish to make any trouble. We think you have much baggage and good cameras."

"I am afraid you will find us very poor pickings."

Mary stirred. "Are you talking in your sleep?"

"No, Mary. A couple of friends have dropped in to see us."

Mary sat bolt upright.

"*Gomen nasai.*" Both men apologized at once. "*Sumimasen.*"

"What do they want?"

"Everything they can get, I'm afraid. But they won't make any trouble if we keep quiet." And to the men I said, "Let's go out on deck and talk this over." I had a vague idea that the captain and I might push them overboard.

To rouse the captain I thumped my shoes noisily on the planking as we came out on deck. Alongside us was the mysterious schooner of the afternoon. In the act of climbing over onto our deck were two more men. My hopes of resistance faded.

There was the clattering of a hatch aft and the captain emerged, still half asleep.

The four visitors bowed, the captain bowed, and civilities were exchanged. The spokesman for the pirates, and evidently their chief, explained their errand. "And we like your ship," he said, "we will take it too."

"You know you can't do that," Wide-Margin said in a voice that betrayed his struggle to keep it under control.

"The police will catch up with you long before you can get this ship out of the *Aki Nada*."

The chief laughed. "Before the war we would have been afraid of the police. Not now."

There was some truth in what he said. The police, stripped of its arbitrary and oppressive powers by the Occupation, was only gradually reasserting its former authority. The great cities might be effectively policed, but not the far reaches of the Inland Sea.

Our captain had another objection to offer. "These Americans are friends of Japan. You would not wish to harm them."

"Certainly not," said the chief. "We will not harm them in any way. In fact, if you have some saké we will drink to good relations between Japan and the United States."

"I humbly apologize," said Wide-Margin. "I have no saké. But you will harm the Americans if you rob them."

"Not at all. They are rich. All Americans are rich. As for your ship, you will not lose. They can buy you a new ship."

Nothing is ever accomplished in Japan, not even a robbery, without plenty of preliminary discussion. We talked for two hours. There was no fire in the shichirin so Mary could not make tea, but she brought out a bottle of grape juice and served it in plastic cups. As the east began to gray the pirates showed some eagerness to have done with conversation and be off.

"You have been most kind," said the chief. "But now we really must go." He ordered his men to launch our dinghy. It was put over the side. We were ushered into it. "Now

171

you are free to leave," said the chief. "Thank you and *sayonara*."

Wide-Margin began to ply the sweep. "You are only four men," he called back. "And it takes six to man those two ships. Had you thought of that?"

"Don't worry about that," laughed the chief. "We have friends out yonder who will lend us a hand. In the meantime we'll take your ship in tow." He and his men began rummaging into the hatches. "Where's your baggage?" he called.

"In the hold—that one—just forward of the mainmast."

"The keys. You'd better give me the keys for them."

"They're not locked."

"Well, stand by for a few minutes," roared the chief. "There may be some more questions we'll want to ask you."

We hove to and waited.

"What can we do?" said Mary. "Surely we can do something." When she got no answer she became a shade bitter. "You [she meant me], the dauntless explorer, and you [that was for the captain] with pirate blood in your veins— and all we can do is run away!"

The captain blushed and said nothing. Feeling frustrated, I savagely kicked aside the tools in the bottom of the boat to make room for my feet. Then I looked down at them. Could they be used as weapons? Hardly. There was a good hammer but it would not make much impression upon the thick skulls of four sailors. There was a screwdriver and a box of screws, a box of nails, a box of tacks—and a brace that Wide-Margin had used in boring the holes for the new thwart.

172

I picked up the brace. It had a big three-quarter inch bit in it.

A crazy scheme began to form in my mind. I called the captain's attention to the brace, holding it below the gunwale so that it could not be seen from the ship, for dawn was now well on its way.

The captain looked bewildered. Then comprehension came into his eyes. He began languidly operating the sweep as if to bring the boat back to the ship.

The men were still rummaging in the various compartments of the hold and the chief saw our return with satisfaction. He probably thought us very obliging.

But instead of drawing alongside the *Kompira*, Wide-Margin circled to come up under the bow of the schooner on the far side from the *Kompira*. Here we were quite out of sight. There was no one on the deck of the schooner.

The captain seized the brace and slid over the side. He was quite at home in the water, either on the surface or beneath it. He submerged, selected a spot in the second futtock well below the water line and began to bore. His feet did not reach bottom but the water pressure held him up against the hull and gave him leverage, and I aided by clutching his hair, worn long in the postwar style of Japanese young men.

His South Sea progenitors could have stayed down for three minutes and he was quite capable of half that—but it required less than a minute to bore a clean hole through the inch-thick strake.

Coming up for breath, he went down to bore another hole, and repeated the performance until four thirsty mouths were drinking in the Inland Sea.

Mary now had an inspiration of her own. She took up the box of tacks, opened it, and scattered the contents over the schooner's deck. Japanese sailors always go barefoot.

The captain boarded the boat and resumed his place at the sweep. We came out from under the shelter of the schooner's gunwale to see that the pirates had pulled a number of suitcases and duffel bags up out of the hold of the *Kompira* and were engrossed in going through their contents.

A sharp order from their chief, and they abandoned their search for treasure to man the schooner, fix a towline to the *Kompira*, and run up the schooner's sails. The tacks at once began to have a demoralizing effect upon their previously sweet natures. If the Japanese language contains no profanity it is at least well supplied with expletives and they were used now.

The morning breeze was light but enough to draw the line taut. Our brave little *Kompira* began to move out of our lives. If the breeze quickened before we could reach her, or if the captain had merely bored into a watertight compartment, the game was up. We had calculated that such an ancient vessel would not be compartmented, but we could be mistaken.

Wide-Margin put everything he had into the sweep, and I used an oar as a paddle. As we gained the side of the *Kompira* the chief shouted, "Stand off!" But our captain made fast the painter and we climbed aboard.

The pirates were now too fully occupied to give us further attention. They hopped and howled, got down on their knees to pick up the offending barbs. It was some moments before they discovered that their ship was down by the head. They tore off a forward hatch and looked in.

The chief called for buckets. The old craft was evidently not equipped with a pump. Nor could any ordinary pump have checked such an inrush of water.

I threw off the schooner's towline, Mary took the tiller, Yasuhiro started the engine.

On the other ship all the men were bailing. With no one at the tiller, the ship came up into the wind, the wooden battens across its canvas beating like flails. Now a man was going down into the hull with rope ends to try to plug the holes. The ship's nose was digging deeper every moment and her poop rising higher.

We chugged by within fifty yards. Wide-Margin raised his head through the engine hatch, cupped his hands around his mouth, and yelled, "*Gomen nasai!*"

There was no answering courtesy from the schooner.

Whether the raiders lost their ship or stopped the leaks we did not wait to see.

We reached Mitarai at sunrise. The two uncles were already on the pier, fishing. They were relieved to see us.

"We were worried," said Literature-Pursuing-Sixth-Son, "because the people of the village say there are some bad men about. We humbly trust that you had a quiet night."

15

MIRACLE IN HIROSHIMA

THE BLASTING of a twenty-ton cargo boat into small bits by a floating mine had brought the minesweepers and we saw them hard at work as we sailed on toward Kure.

Since Kure had been one of Japan's chief naval bases, Allied airmen had thickly sowed the waters with drifting terror. Most of the mines had long since been swept up, or had died a natural death. Enough remained to provide an occasional sensational explosion, but they actually did not cause as much loss of shipping as did the everlasting rocks and reefs.

Two vessels steaming abreast of each other a few hundred feet apart dragged a heavily weighted cable, each ship having an end of the cable aboard, and the sagging bight of the cable was expected to gather in the mines which were then carefully exploded. The work was slow, and could be exceedingly dangerous. Many sweepers with their crews had been lost.

We followed the example of other vessels and gave the sweepers a wide berth. A sweeper was identified by a black ball at the foremast head and another at the yardarm. Other

craft must under no circumstances pass between the sweepers nor approach nearer than five hundred yards on the
beam or a thousand yards astern. We more than doubled
these precautions, and passed on to Kure.

In the harbor a number of British warships lay at anchor,
their spick-and-spanness contrasting with the forlorn appearance of rusty red wrecks of Japanese ships now being
sold bit by bit as scrap iron.

City Hall took us on a lengthy automobile ride through
the long narrow city and past the great skeletons of the
bombed-out Japanese naval arsenal.

Facing Kure is the huge island of Etajima where had
been located the Japanese naval academy. We sailed along
its coast past many miles of caves dug into the seafront
hills. These had been used by the Japanese army to store
munitions. Now they were used for the same purpose by
the U.S. Army in connection with its operations in Korea.
Large signs warned shipping not to come within two
hundred yards of shore. When we edged in a little closer
in order to get a photograph, guards shouted reprimands
in a mixture of Japanese and English.

Far down at the end of the bay the city of Hiroshima
was emerging from the mist. It was with deep emotion that
we looked upon the scene of the world's first atomic bomb
attack.

On the pier we faced a rather formidable reception committee made up of an assistant to the mayor, a Japan Travel
Bureau representative, the Kansai agent and eight reporters
with notebooks and cameras. They took us at once to the
office of the mayor, Shinzo Hamai, an earnest, studious
young man who explained the project to turn this former

stronghold of militarism into a memorial for world peace.

Hiroshima is one of the seven largest cities of Japan. It is built on land that did not exist seven hundred years ago— the delta formed since that time by the many-mouthed Ota River. It is now being man-extended by fill-ins reaching out into the bay.

The mayor took us to the roof of the City Hall where we looked down upon the city as upon a map. Not far away was the Atomic Bomb Dome, the gutted Industrial Museum which is being preserved in its ruined form as a memento of the blast.

But we looked in vain for any other sign of disaster. The great city had been completely rebuilt. For two hours Hamai-san pointed out new developments and told his plans for the future. Great wide boulevards course through the new city which is punctuated by regular squares and sprinkled with parks and playgrounds.

The bolt from the blue at a quarter after eight in the morning of August 6, 1945 destroyed seventy thousand houses and wiped out sixty percent of the city at one stroke.

The Japanese government estimated the number of killed at seventy thousand and the injured at 130,000. Mayor Hamai takes exception to these figures, claiming that those killed numbered more than two hundred thousand if the fatalities resulting from the injuries and diseases caused by the atomic blast are also taken into account.

"One out of every two persons then in Hiroshima perished on that historic day or immediately after it."

An American newsreel cameraman who flew over Hiroshima following the surrender said, "The city was just a flat expanse of emptiness. You could play billiards on it."

But the ashes had hardly cooled before rebuilding began. The prewar population of four hundred thousand, reduced to ninety thousand by death and flight, is now back to the prewar total.

General MacArthur said in a message to Hiroshima on the occasion of the second anniversary of the atomic attack:

"The agonies of that fateful day serve as a warning to all men of all races that the harnessing of Nature's forces in furtherance of war's destructiveness will progress until the means are at hand to exterminate the human race and destroy the material structure of the modern world. This is the lesson of Hiroshima. God grant that it be not ignored."

Hiroshima, at least, is not ignoring it. The city's ambition is to become the pivot of the peace movement for the whole world. It has assumed the name of "Peace Commemoration City." The plan calls for the construction of a Peace Hall, Peace Park, Peace Boulevard, and Peace Commemoration Gardens.

The nucleus of the peace city will be the Peace Hall being erected at the heart of the atomic blast. It is to have a seating capacity of two thousand five hundred and will be used mainly for international conferences. Peace Plaza which lies before the Hall will accommodate twenty thousand people.

Magnificent Peace Boulevard, one hundred meters wide, runs to Peace Park which is being laid out with all the skill of which Japanese landscape architects are capable.

If the bombing of Hiroshima capped all the horrors of war since the beginning of history, it is some comfort to

179

know that the goodwill manifested by conquering peoples toward a defeated one has also been without parallel. No matter how naive and unaware of reality the Occupation may have been at times, its heart has always been in the right place. Through unofficial as well as official channels the sympathy of the American and British people is evident wherever you turn in Hiroshima.

Catholics of all the western world are helping to construct the colossal Memorial Cathedral for World Peace, promoted by the Reverend Hugo Lassalle who has served Hiroshima for twelve years.

Five orphanages care for 250 war orphans with the help of "moral foster parents" in America and Britain through the medium of Norman Cousins, editor of *The Saturday Review of Literature*.

An appeal to four hundred foreign universities brought generous contributions to Hiroshima Uuiversity and hundreds of tree seedlings for the campus. Hiroshima sadly lacks trees. A building may rise from the ashes in a month but the growth of a tree can hardly be rushed. Only seedlings, millions of them, and time, can give the city the pleasing mantle of green it had in the old days.

Twenty-three schools abroad have donated books to the International Peace Library in the university. Doctors and nurses in Hawaii contributed a thousand medical books to the Red Cross Hospital. Californian residents of Japanese birth have built a splendid children's library in Hiroshima.

Houses for war widows are another benefaction from the west. Also in the Eba section of the city a project known as "Houses for Hiroshima" was begun three years ago by

Dr. Floyd Schmoe, a Seattle Quaker. He collected funds from hundreds of friends in many parts of the world. The development is known as Eba Village and at its center is a community house financed by an American woman who had a taste of Japanese barbarity when interned in the Philippines during the war.

High on a hill in the eastern part of the city is the research institute of the Atomic Bomb Casualty Commission. Jointly staffed by American and Japanese doctors, the institute is studying the physical effects of the atomic bomb. Those effects may still be seen in the faces and figures of many of the people of Hiroshima. They are a constant reminder of the savagery of war and the dedication of the city to peace.

Never again, vow its citizens, will Hiroshima invite attack by becoming a war city. It was in this city that the Emperor Meiji established his headquarters as commander-in-chief of the imperial forces in the Sino-Japanese War. It was from this port that soldiers sailed for the war front at that time as well as during the Russo-Japanese War, the "incident" in China during the thirties, and the two World Wars. Some philosophic Hiroshimans consider that the city got what it deserved. They are determined that it shall not deserve it again.

We came close to one of the personal tragedies of Hiroshima when we entered our hotel that evening. An unexpected "Good evening" in English came from the family room behind the vestibule.

A woman with an abundance of blond hair surrounding a deeply-lined face introduced herself as Wanda Yamatoda.

"The proprietor of the hotel isn't used to receiving foreign guests," she said, "so he called me in to find out what you would like."

We explained that we were used to Japanese inns and would give no trouble. But we invited her into our room for a talk.

Wanda was an American who had married a Japanese and had come with him to Japan in 1941. Of course that was just the wrong time to come. In December of that year the war broke. Her husband went to war and came back to die of cancer. His widow, left without means of support, suffered great privations.

Worse than that, being an American, she was in constant danger of arrest and torture. Other foreigners of her acquaintance disappeared without a trace.

She was taken to police headquarters and questioned as to just what she thought of the Japanese and their policies. She had reached the point where she hardly cared what happened to her, so she told them exactly what she thought, good and bad. They were very angry, but one stood up for her. "She's right," he said.

There were more of these inquisitions, but her independence and frankness won respect and she was never subjected to actual torture.

When the atom bomb fell upon Hiroshima she was inside a building more than two miles from the center of the blast. Others were killed all about her but she was unhurt.

"Sometimes I think it would have been better if I had died then."

Now she was teaching English and was getting along well enough. She had never taken to Japanese ways and had given up trying. She had a careless almost gay manner and laughed frequently but there was an aching despair back of her laughs. She could not afford to return to America. There was no American community in Hiroshima. Still young, but lost-eyed and wrinkle-faced, she was a sorely displaced person, a victim of war unmercifully spared by the atom bomb.

Still more pitiful were Hiroshima's armless or legless or faceless mutilés, or those mentally deranged. The miracle of Hiroshima had restored the buildings of the city, the stores, temples, schools, but could never wipe out the physical and psychological legacy of those ten seconds on August 6, 1945.

16

THE RIDDLE OF EDUCATION

A SPARKLING DAY took us on from the city of the atom bomb toward the sacred island of Miyajima.

A Japan Travel Bureau man, Yamaguchi-san, chose to sail with us. He was a learned young man, having been professor of psychology and philosophy in Kyushu University.

"How did you come to leave a professorship to work in a travel bureau?"

"One reason was that I couldn't live on a professor's salary. Another reason was that students are no longer serious. They won't study. They won't obey. They have been infected with illusions of liberty, independence, democracy. They don't know the real meaning of these words. They rebel against discipline, want to run the class, run the professor, run the university."

"But don't you think they will settle down in time?"

"I think they will. But in the meantime I prefer some other field."

Professor Yamaguchi was not alone in his opinions. We had heard them expressed by teachers and principals in all the schools we had visited along the Inland Sea.

184

"Students since the war are no longer diligent," Morau-san, teacher of English in the Tonosho High School, had said, "except in baseball."

"It was very easy to control students before the war," said Professor Goto of Oita University. "Now they want to go their own way. However, there is gradual improvement."

A teacher complained that his students say to him, "We don't have to bow to you any more and you can't tell us what to do. Everybody is equal."

A class sitting for an examination found the questions hard and marched out of the room. One of them, when the teacher sought to detain him, explained, "We don't like the examination and we won't take it. And under the new constitution you can't force us."

The present rebellion of youth is a natural reaction to the excessive strictness of prewar days. Under a militaristic government the schools were run with army regimentation. Students did not dare think for themselves. They had no scope for initiative. They were not invited to express their opinions. They were expected to take in, not to give out. Teaching was by rote and individual inquiry was discouraged. The purpose of the educational system was not to educate, but to train recruits to carry out plans of military aggression. Nationalism was the keynote of education.

The task of the Occupation, or SCAP as it was usually called to telescope the unwieldy title of Supreme Commander for the Allied Powers, was to abolish military training, remove military-minded teachers, substitute new textbooks, and prohibit State Shinto which glorified a divine emperor and the right of a divine Japan to rule the

185

world. Of the 490,000 teachers before the war nearly half were discharged or resigned before they could be discharged.

The American 6-3-3-4 system was introduced—six years of elementary school, three of lower secondary, three of higher secondary, and four of college. Previously only six years' education had been compulsory and free. Under SCAP's directive the new law prescribed nine years of free and compulsory education.

Women's schools and colleges had always been inferior to those of men. Now they were placed on an equal footing. The system was made coeducational through the ninth year.

Parent-teacher associations were established and adult education programs started.

Formerly the Minister of Education had exercised the power of a czar over all the schools of the country. Thus they could be bent at will to any nationalistic purpose. This arbitrary power was broken and local school boards were given great freedom in choosing textbooks and courses of study.

Most of these changes have great merit, or would have if they could be made to stick. But they do not touch Japan's most desperate educational problem—the Japanese language. Written Japanese is probably the most difficult language in common use today. It is more difficult than Chinese from which it was derived because many new hurdles have been added to it since it was imported from China in the fourth century.

"Japan in its two millenniums of history has copied

many things from the cultures of many nations," says Robert King Hall, professor of comparative education at Teachers College, Columbia University. "It is quite possible that this was the most disastrous of all its importations. To the occidental student of western languages, all written in some variant of a phonetic system, it may be difficult to appreciate fully the monstrous handicap which the Japanese writing system has imposed upon that people."

Japanese is a system of ideographs, picture symbols, comparable to the hieroglyphs of ancient Egypt but far more complex. It is impossible to tell by looking at an ideograph how it is supposed to be pronounced. It is not even possible to be sure of the meaning since a single character may have a dozen different meanings depending upon the context.

The Japanese do have a simplified phonetic system called *kana* in which each syllable is represented by a mark. However this system is scorned as being too easy, and as failing to bring out all the nuances of Japanese thought.

More than forty percent of an elementary student's time is spent in learning to read and write. Even with this great expenditure of time, he learns very little. It has been found that the average graduate of the six-year elementary course has acquired about six hundred characters. Newspapers, even those which make a deliberate effort to limit the number of characters, use 3500. Approximately nine thousand characters must be understood if university reference books are to be read. A scholar needs from twenty thousand to thirty thousand.

Speaking of the inefficiency of Japanese education, Dr. Inazo Nitobe once said:

"The use of Chinese ideographs is the root of all evil in this respect. A large part of the school life is spent in mastering some four thousand ideograms, most of which are pronounced in three or four ways and written in at least three ways. The waste of energy thereby incurred is worthy of the most serious consideration and can be prevented only by the adoption of transliteration, that is, the use of the Roman alphabet instead of Chinese ideograms."

Japan has a higher proportion of children in school than the United States. The nation has claimed 99.6 percent literacy. However this was an error in translation, the word "literacy" being used when what was meant was "attendance." The official statistics show that during the years 1935-1939 the proportion of children under fourteen years of age attending school was 99.6 percent.

But true literacy, enough literacy to be able to read a newspaper, a magazine, or a book, is quite another matter.

Most of the directives of General MacArthur passed over the heads of the Japanese people because of their inability to read them. A study of four major SCAP directives showed that 31 percent of the characters used were beyond the comprehension of half the graduates of the compulsory educational system.

An elementary school teacher reported that in his large class of sixth grade pupils, only two were able to read the new constitution.

A study of workers in fourteen factories revealed that only 17 percent could read the history of the war years sponsored by SCAP and published in all Japanese newspapers in order to give the Japanese the truth about the operations of their militarists from the Mukden Incident to the signing of the Surrender on the *Missouri*.

A check in downtown Tokyo indicated that one adult in ten could read the names of war criminals who had been arrested and tried by the Allied Powers.

How can democratization of Japan be accomplished when most information is inaccessible to the people?

Language difficulty lowers the efficiency of business. A Japanese typewriter carries a total of 2,863 characters. Under such a handicap speed is impossible.

Linotype machines cannot be used in printing plants. All type must be set by hand. Instead of twenty-six letters, the Japanese compositor must wrestle with a minimum of 3500 characters.

A Japanese index is a sour joke. There is of course no alphabetical clue, and I have seen a Japanese student search twenty minutes for a word that would be turned up in ten seconds in an alphabetical dictionary.

Blind persons may be better educated than those who can see because they do not have to spend forty percent of their school time in learning ideographs. Japanese Braille is phonetic.

Pedantry blocks reform. Scholars take pride in their hard-earned knowledge and oppose a simplification of language that would place the common man on their level. Pundits frequently write material which they know cannot be understood by those to whom it is addressed. When SCAP proposed that the new teachers' manual be written in simple, understandable Japanese, a Japanese professor, former minister of education, objected on the grounds that if the Japanese teachers could read it without difficulty they would be "insulted."

To study Japan's educational needs SCAP brought to Japan an Education Mission made up of twenty-seven distinguished American educators. After detailed study in conjunction with Japanese educators, the Education Mission recommended "a drastic reform of the Japanese written language." The Mission advised that the use of Chinese ideographs should be abandoned in the popular written language and that a phonetic system should be adopted using the Roman alphabet.

Could so radical a change be made? Attention was called to the experience of Turkey. There the vigorous Mustafa Kemal abolished practically overnight the complicated Turkish writing system and replaced it with a twenty-eight letter Romanization. No such sudden change was recommended for Japan.

Many liberal Japanese educators supported the plan. Curiously enough, opposition to it developed mainly within SCAP itself. The Education Division of the Occupation was against it. The project died before it was born.

Perhaps it is just as well. The very modest success of other SCAP reforms gives little assurance that this one could have been carried through. It is hard for those who think of Japan as a vigorous modern nation, which it is, to realize how firmly it is bound by its traditions.

With the passing of the Occupation there is a gradual edging back to old ways. The Minister of Finance says Japan cannot afford to give nine years of free education. A good portion of the public disapproves of coeducation because of a number of painful incidents reported in the newspapers, the killing of girls by sex-bewildered boys. Shinto has crept back into the curriculum and a text made mandatory by the ministry of education in all schools is openly hostile to Christianity, declaring that this religion is incompatible with Japanese traditions. The education minister has announced his intention to restore courses in "morals" in the senior high schools. These courses had little to do with morals and much to do with the excitation of rabid patriotism in the "divine mission" of Japan. A new school history completely condones Japan's aggressive policy from the rape of Manchuria to the attack on Pearl Harbor. The power of local school boards is being reduced and the national Education Ministry is resuming its old authority.

The honest and wholehearted effort of the Allied Powers to improve Japanese education is bound to have some permanent value, but its importance has been greatly exaggerated. Japan is not being educated for democracy. Increasingly she is being conditioned for new military adventures.

With the hot breath of Russia on her neck, Japan feels she can take no other course. She has not yet learned that a democracy can fight wars, that a free and informed public is the nation's best defense. Whenever Japan's militarists have prepared for war they have always begun with a war against their own people. They have lopped off rights, curtailed liberties, discouraged initiative, forbidden freedom of action and even "dangerous thoughts."

The old pattern now begins to be repeated. Japanese schools are likely to be increasingly regimented, centralized, and made a ready tool in the hands of a reviving military dictatorship.

17

THROUGH THE ENCHANTED ISLES

JAPAN'S MEDITERRANEAN which, because of its many isles, is so much more interesting than Europe's comparatively empty sea, is particularly beautiful beyond Hiroshima.

Here the islands have a fairytale unreality. Each is adorned with a legend. Sometimes the nature of the legend is suggested in the name as in the case of the island All-the-Saints-Got-Drunk.

Another seagirt hill is known as Objection Island. "When children object to carrying out their parents' orders," said our passenger, Professor Yamaguchi, "they are told 'If you don't mind, I'll send you to Objection Island.'"

"Have disobedient children ever actually been sent to the island?"

"In a few cases, yes—parents have actually carried out their threat. In fact there is a lawsuit in the courts at present over the ownership of the island; a certain family claims to own it because one of their ancestors was sent there for being a bad boy."

We passed another isle of exile, Okakuma, where during

the war Japanese sailors just back from southern waters were confined until the next sailing. They could not be allowed the freedom of Hiroshima lest they might let slip the truth contradicting the stories of victory issued by the navy.

Enoshima—the word means Picture Island—was a remarkable collection of rock arches and caves crowned with fine trees.

Onasaki was not as charming as its neighbors, for its vegetation had been scorched when powder stored here was exploded by the Allies, searing the island and even shaking Hiroshima many miles away.

We landed on Ninoshima to watch the building of a small ship, for most of the craft used on the Inland Sea are constructed in island shipyards. The builder and his men struck off work to talk to the visitors. We thought they deserved a recess when their chief told us that his eight men worked eleven hours a day and were expected to complete a forty-ton ship in six weeks.

The name of the ship was to be *Niko Maru*, Everyday Fortunate. To make sure that this name would be appropriate the builder would put on board a shrine to the god of ships. No ship is considered safe unless equipped with a shrine dedicated either to the god of ships or the Sea God. Usually an offering of rice, saké and fish is placed in the shrine. The fish must have its head on. It must be complete and perfect.

The god of ships is a very natural god. He likes women, therefore models of women are placed in the shrine. He is also addicted to betting and is provided with money for this purpose. One coin will not do. There must be twelve to conform to the lunar calendar and the movements of the tide. He is also provided with dice but they must be in the lucky position—with the 1 on top, 6 on the bottom, 3 in front, 4 behind, 2 and 5 on the sides.

Every sailor must go out of the ship at the opposite side from the one where he came in, or the god of ships will go out with him.

Every good captain is supposed to have an ear attuned to the voice of the god of ships. When there is to be a storm the god warns the captain. Our own captain believed that he received such messages. He was not conscious of any words being spoken to him, but only of a feeling, an intuition, which he credited to his protecting deity. The men of a Japanese crew have more than ordinary faith in the master of the ship because of their confidence that he is in touch with a higher power.

Queen of the enchanted isles is Miyajima, the most famous island of the Inland Sea and rated by the Japanese as one of Japan's three most beautiful spots, the others being Amanohashidate and Matsushima. Most visitors who have seen all three put Miyajima first.

Miyajima or Shrine Island (*miya* meaning shrine, and *jima*, island) is also called Itsukushima, Beautiful Island.

The island is held sacred and is under the protection of the Shinto-Buddhist shrine, a unique structure built out over the sea in such a way that it seems to be floating on the surface.

But the most unusual sight, known all over the world through the many pictures that have been made of it, is the great red *torii* standing up to its knees in the sea. It was a magnificent sight in the warm glow of the evening sun as we looked up at it from the low deck of the *Kompira*.

Once every half century it must be repaired and repainted. Fortunately for our color camera this operation had just been completed and the torii fairly sang in its coat of brilliant vermilion. In the bay behind it the colorful corridors of the shrine spread out over the water, and behind them rose pagoda-crested hills covered with giant trees, who knows how old, for the ax of the lumberjack has not been allowed to touch a tree on the Sacred Island since the shrine was founded in A.D. 592.

And what a torii! Every Shinto shrine must have the sacred gateway but usually it is of moderate size and consists merely of two uprights supporting two crossbeams. Shinto loves simplicity and Buddhism loves ornament. In those cases where the torii has been adopted by Buddhist temples it has been dramatized and adorned until it looks more like the *p'ailou* of China. The torii of Miyajima is elaborated with four extra columns and a narrow curved roof and stands a good forty feet high. It is built of camphorwood, longlasting and insect-resistant. So unpalatable is camphor to insects that an insecticide is made from it.

The professor had telephoned ahead and we were met by the usual delegation and escorted to an imposing inn on the seafront. From our second-story balcony we enjoyed a magnificent Inland Sea sunset.

Our sleep was badly broken by a party next door. Japanese partitions are so thin that every sound in the next room can be heard. Two men and two girls beguiled the time until two A.M. with saké drinking, loud talk and laughter and quite improper songs in a highly nasal rendering like the wailing of contentious cats. Then would come the squeals and giggles of the preliminary love-making and the girls would run about the room with the men thumping after them, making the floor tremble. At last they subsided between the futons with prolonged whisperings broken by cries of *"Itai!"* (It hurts.)

In the morning light the full glory of Miyajima burst upon us. Against the rich dark background of majestic pines blazed unbelievable shades of red and yellow, for the maples had begun to turn. We wandered up Momijidani, Maple Valley, among hundreds of the graceful trees, each with a color of its own, each singing a different tune, but combining in an unforgettable color symphony.

Quite different from the maples of America, Japanese maples carry small leaves, deeply indented and starlike, and as delicate as a breath. They are so translucent that the sun shines through them as through a tinted skylight. You walk in a mellow glow that changes from tree to tree, now golden, now rosy, now pink, now wine-red.

At the time of the maples, schools all over Japan send their children on pilgrimage to Miyajima and we saw hundreds of them picnicking under the trees along the banks of the mountain stream. They were incredibly well behaved. They left not a scrap of rubbish behind them, and although they adored the leaves they picked none except from the ground.

We moved to the Iwaso, one of the most famous of Japan's inns, overhanging a brook in the heart of Momijidani. From our balcony we drank in a ravishing view up the tumbling brook to the little pink bridge, the whole smothered in lacelike billows of color. Behind them rose

196

rank on rank, up the mountainsides, dark pines and cryptomerias centuries old.

There is a road on the other side of the brook, but no
traffic. For this is one of the few blessed spots on earth
not yet desecrated by the automobile. All wheeled vehicles
are excluded from the sacred island. They might alarm the
sacred deer which wander at will through the groves and
nuzzle into the pockets of visitors. The deer almost disappeared during the war years when the people of Miyajima
became very hungry. Now they are once more beginning
to multiply.

It would not be quite correct to say that not a wheel
turns on Miyajima, for I do recall on a previous visit a
geisha party in which the one delegated to get me drunk
became so drunk herself that I had to roll her home in a
wheelbarrow. And during the Occupation an army jeep
raced about over the mountain trails and through the village streets, much to the distress of the priests. But on this
occasion I did not see even a wheelbarrow, much less a
cart, wagon or car.

I understand that Bermuda has at last surrendered to the
automobile. Will Miyajima finally yield to "progress"?
Probably not, so long as a shrine that combines the conservative traditions of both Shinto and Buddhism rules the
island.

For a thousand years births and deaths were taboo on
Miyajima. Up to eighty years ago the rule was strictly observed. Every expectant mother was sent to the mainland,
and so was every person who because of disease or age
seemed to be approaching death.

Sometimes, of course, Nature got in her innings before

such action could be taken. In that case the mother and child were exiled to the mainland for thirty days, or if death occurred on the island the body was sent for burial to the mainland where the family and chief mourners also must remain for fifty days for ceremonial purification. Then they might return, but must never again walk through the main street of the village, that being peculiarly sacred to the gods.

Now you may be born or die on Miyajima, but the afterbirth must be hurried away to the mainland, and the body of the deceased likewise. There is a convenient cemetery on the mainland just opposite the island, but there is not a tomb on Miyajima.

In spite of the relaxation of these ancient rules, most Miyajimates still contrive to do their childbearing and dying on the opposite shore where a hospital is provided for this purpose.

Although Miyajima has no wagon it does have a horse. It too is sacred and is kept in a booth by the path frequented by pilgrims who buy from the attendant priest small dishes of food to be placed before the horse.

Since white is held sacred by the priests because it is symbolic of stainlessness, the holy horse must be white. As we stood gazing at the snow-white quadruped in the booth, the clerk of the town hall who accompanied us said:

"This horse was bought during the war. It was very dark in color. Now it is white."

We stared. "What made the change?"

"The priests say it changed because it had been made a sacred horse."

198

"Do you believe that?"

The clerk grinned. "Well, I don't know. But it happens every time. You can bring a horse of any color to this island and it will change to white. It takes four or five years." Seeing doubt in our eyes he added, "I vouch for it."

If the town hall vouched for it, who were we to question it?

"It may be because the horse is kept indoors," speculated the clerk. "Or because it does not work like other horses, or perhaps because of its food."

"What food does it have?"

"Sweet potato, beans, wheat straw, rice straw and boiled wheat."

How such foods could turn brown hair white was as great a mystery as how the change could be accomplished by dedicating the horse to the gods. But however it is done it helps to make Miyajima a mecca for pilgrims and tourists.

"We miss the cruise ships," said the clerk. "They used to come through the Inland Sea and stop at Miyajima. Now they just go in to Kobe and out again. That is because the mines dropped by American planes have not all been cleared out."

"But I see quite a few GIs here."

"They come by railroad down the mainland. We don't want GIs. They get drunk and make trouble. We want tourists."

The little clerk is getting his wish for as this is published the cruise ships are once again visiting Miyajima.

But the stream of Japanese pilgrims never ceases. They bow and clap their hands in the great shrine, they try to grasp the meaning of the colorful sacred dances, they climb

199

to the hilltop temples and the old pagodas, they puff and
pant their way up hundreds of stone steps to the top of
Mount Misen where an eternal flame is kept burning, they
feed the holy horse, they tie paper prayers to iron lanterns.

The shrine does a thriving business in prayers. The
procedure is as follows: You shake a box full of bamboo
sticks until one comes out of a small hole at the end of the
box. Your stick bears a number. At the shrine office you
exchange the stick for a prayer paper bearing the same
number. Of course you pay for this service. In some
shrines an automatic machine is used. You put in a coin
and out comes a prayer. But at Miyajima personal service is
still rendered.

The prayer is not to be read and then thrown away. It
must be fixed in a sacred place—hence thousands of them
are tied to the many iron lanterns that adorn the shrine.

We became friendly with one of the white-bloused, blue-
skirted priests of the temple and he offered to accompany
us on a circuit of the island. The trip was made on the
Kompira for there is no road. Except near the shrine village, there was no one to be seen in the seventeen-mile
circuit, no villages, no farms, nothing but magnificent
trees, and mountains upon mountains. However on each
of the "seven shores" there was a small shrine. Stretches of
sandy beach with not a soul to enjoy them alternated with
precipices overhung with pines. Rocky, pine-stuck promontories projected like monsters' heads with hair all awry.
A few birds, most of them kites, soared above the trees.
There were no open stretches—the mighty trees occupied
every inch except the beaches and the precipices. This un-
touched forest wilderness seemed strangely out of place in

200

the heart of one of the world's most crowded countries.

Arriving once more before the shrine, we were about to drop anchor when the priest proposed that we sail through the torii. But wouldn't our masts strike the crossbeam? No, no, insisted the priest, *daijobu*, safe. I was mistrustful, but Wide-Margin-of-Safety got that gleam in his eye.

Under engine power only we impudently putt-putted up to the venerable torii. The ship's nose passed through and all eyes were fixed on the top of the foremast. "*Daijobu, daijobu*," said the priest. But the thirty-foot mast was eight inches too tall to clear the crossbeam. It struck and bent far back with a great cracking sound. The wire cable connecting the peak of the mast with the bowsprit snapped and lashed about, flailing the passengers. A shower of vermilion splinters from the sacred torii sprayed the deck.

Wide-Margin hastily reversed the engine and we backed out.

The mast straightened but it was badly strained and the running gear was broken and tangled. This would have been an appropriate moment for some strong language. Wide-Margin looked a little dark but he said nothing and the priest contented himself with polite regrets. We gathered up the vermilion splinters and put them into the shrine of Kompira at the foot of our foremast.

And so back to the Iwaso, into our yukatas, and off to the bathhouse. The maid informed us that by special arrangement we were to have the great, chin-deep, eight-by-six-foot bath to ourselves. The bathboy showed us how to lock the door to insure privacy.

We entered, locked the door, and divested ourselves of

our yukatas. The bathroom appeared to be solidly walled with brick. Reveling in our seclusion, we proceeded to the soaping operation. Halfway through it we were startled to see the supposedly solid wall open and the bathboy poked his head through the hole to inquire whether the water was *yoroshii.*

"Yes, yes, it's perfect."

He crawled in through the hole. "Would you like to have it a little cooler?"

"No, it's just right."

"Perhaps a little warmer?"

"No thank you."

"Shall I scrub your back?"

"If you like."

He pummeled and thumped, chattering as he worked. "You know, this is a very good *yadoya.* In most inns you couldn't have the bath all to yourselves. But in good times we have many foreign guests. We know how to treat them. We know they like privacy."

We had worms for dinner. They appeared in the soup along with Chinese-style fragmented eggs. The maid said they were not worms, but fish. If appearances mean anything at all I should call them worms and have done with it.

They were white, about an inch and a half long, twisted as if they had died in agony, and each had two small black eyes, a pointed nose, and a tapering tail. They would pass very well as albino earthworms except that they were more slender in the hips.

They tasted surprisingly good—as good as all the rest of the Iwaso dinner which was excellent: rice, beefsteak, butter-broiled fish, a half dozen condiments, soup, tea, huge persimmons and oversized grapes.

18

BIRTH CONTROL AND POPULATION

AFTER LOITERING for several days under the Technicolor maples of Miyajima, we sailed on to an island so extensive that its chief bay seemed as large as New York harbor.

In a bay of this bay was a busy town sending up smoke from a dozen factory chimneys. As soon as Good-Fortune, who was at the tiller, saw it his eyes sparkled and he altered his course to visit it. Since the day was already well spent it was quite evidently his intention that we should spend the night alongside one of its docks.

Driven to desperate action, we spied the shoreline until we spotted a quiet cove some miles short of the town and ordered the ship into its protecting arms for the night.

It was a lovely retreat. A wooded isle adorned with a small shrine and torii shut out the waves of the great bay and on the other side of us was a half circle of hills of all shapes and sizes and a village nestling far back in the valley, the smoke of evening fires rising from it.

Our presence escaped the notice of both peasants and pirates. We slept on deck but had to envelop our heads warmly for it was October now and the nights were a bit cold. Toward morning a sudden gale threatened to wash us up on a lee shore and the men hastily put out a second anchor.

In the morning we visited the town. The officials took us to see—of all things—a birth control clinic.

We were in it before I realized its nature. Then I tried to retire but soon found out that if I did so official feelings would be hurt.

"This is a very important office," I was told.

"I am sure it is important," I replied, "but do I belong here?" I glanced around the outer room where pregnant women silently waited while from behind a closed door came the sound of discussion.

"Why not?" said my guide. "All the members of the committee are men."

The closed door was opened and we were ushered into a room where a terrified little woman sat before a long table behind which four owl-like judges studied her papers.

They at once rose, bowed, and drew breath. We were introduced. They were honored, they said, that their work should interest visitors. They were the members of the local Eugenic Protection Investigation Committee. We sat down, and of course tea was brought in.

I stole a look at the woman, expecting to find her painfully embarrassed by so much masculine scrutiny of her private affairs. But she had brightened up considerably and was chatting amiably with our guide. No women are more modest than the Japanese, but they are modest by rule and rote. A woman who would not uncover the back of her neck on the street will walk nude into a bathroom. The one is improper, the other is proper. The new law had given this woman the right to plead her case before this committee, therefore she felt no embarrassment. But she was worried for fear her application would not be granted.

"We are very poor," she said when the committee chairman asked her reasons for application. "We cannot feed the children we already have. It would not be wise for us to have another."

The chairman fixed his disapproving eye upon her. "Was it wise for you to allow yourself to become pregnant in the first place?"

The woman bowed before she answered. "I assure you we made every effort to prevent it."

"You mean you used a contraceptive device?"

"We did. But it failed."

"So you ask authorization for interruption of pregnancy?"

The woman bowed.

"For economic reasons?"

"For economic reasons."

"The case will be investigated. You may go now."

The woman rose, bowed in turn to every person in the room, and left.

A name was called and another woman in like condition came in. It was hard to convince myself that our presence was not an added trial to the applicants and I suggested to our companion that we would like to see more of his fair city. We retired, the women in the outer room raising their heads dully as we passed.

The term "interruption of pregnancy" as used in the birth control clinics is a polite substitution for the harsher word "abortion." Abortion was made legal in Japan by the

206

Eugenic Protection Law of July, 1948. It may be resorted to if childbirth would endanger a woman's health, if the family is unable to support another child, or if the woman has been made pregnant against her will.

Abortions have always been numerous in Japan, though illegal before passage of this law. For three centuries before the arrival of Commodore Perry in 1853 the population of Japan was stationary at about twenty-six million. It was held stationary by the practice of *mabiki*. It means "thinning out" and was originally applied to the thinning out of a row of vegetables, but was later used to justify the widespread practice of infanticide.

Now mabiki has received official sanction and any woman who can meet the conditions prescribed by the law may have a legal abortion for five dollars, the fee fixed by the government. An illegal abortion may cost as much as seventy dollars. Some unscrupulous doctors oppose the new law because abortions were so lucrative. Other doctors, alarmed at the number of legal abortions (566,000 in 1950), object to the law on moral grounds. Many believe that emphasis should be placed upon the prevention of pregnancy rather than its interruption once it has begun. This opinion was echoed in the press. Said the *Mainichi* in 1951:

"A characteristic feature of birth control this year was that the couples concerned took recourse to abortion rather than to contraception. This drastic measure was taken mainly on account of the fact that (1) organized institutions for dissemination of knowledge concerning contraception are not enough in numbers as well as in their established facilities and (2) trustworthy drugs and devices

207

are not available . . . Of the thirty-five different kinds of drugs for contraception which were permitted to be sold, there was only one that passed the examination as to the effectiveness thereof when such an examination was recently conducted by the Ministry of Welfare."

Contraceptives, most of them ineffective, are sold to the tune of fifteen million a month. The law requires every prefecture to maintain at least one office where free instruction in contraception may be given. Some two hundred of these offices are now functioning. Newspapers and magazines treat the subject quite frankly, illustrating their discussions with anatomical drawings.

Birth control advocates, worried by the unreliability of present devices, have been encouraged by such statements as that of Guy Irving Burch, Director of The Population Reference Bureau, Washington, D.C.:

"There are indications that science is on the threshold of discovering means of controlling the birth rate which are far superior to those now employed and which would be inexpensive and acceptable to all religious groups. So advanced is this undertaking that the head of a large pharmaceutical concern has stated that, given five top scientists and the necessary funds, in three years his company could find a satisfactory and acceptable means of controlling the birth rate."

That the birth rate needs to be controlled is now recognized by all Japanese except those who still cherish the dream of Japanese domination over Asia. And yet very little is being done about it. In spite of the legalizing of abortion and the talk of contraception, each family seems to consider family limitation as the problem of the folks next door. In a land where the veneration of ancestors is considered important, a man must have children to venerate him when he becomes an ancestor. Male children are needed to carry on the family name. Children can help on the farm. Female children are a financial asset, for in times of stress they may be hired out to the cotton mills or sold to a geisha house. If wedded they may bring a good dowry.

Besides, for a solid century now, the Japanese have been taught by their government that they should have plenty of children in order to compete with the West. Commodore Perry started it. When his black ships sailed into Uraga Harbor in 1853 Japan began her struggle to match power with the West. The population grew rapidly. By 1925 it had doubled. For three centuries before Perry Japan had avoided foreign wars. Her new ambition to become one of the world powers made it necessary for her to have more sons to fight Russia, to take over Korea, Formosa and the isles of Micronesia, and to prosecute the "China Incident."

It was patriotic to have many children. The fever of propagation rose to its greatest height just before the attack upon Pearl Harbor and government posters appeared carrying the slogan: "Bear more children and increase the population." A law effective in 1941 offered subsidies to big families, subsidies to men who married before the age of twenty-five and to women who were married at twenty-one when, according to the document, they should have a procreative period of about twenty years. The law declared as its objective an average of five children to each family and the increase of the population of Japan to one hundred million by 1951.

And so the baby mill went into high gear and in 1947 the birth rate reached a peak of 34.8 per thousand—the highest ever recorded in Japan.

By this time the rabid nationalists who had dreamed of overwhelming the world by sheer force of Japanese numbers had been discredited. They were purged, exiled from public office. But they could look on with sly satisfaction as their work was continued by those who had purged them. The Allied Occupation unintentionally contributed more to the overcrowding of Japan than the Japanese militarists had ever been able to do in the same period of time.

Population growth is stimulated either by raising the birth rate or reducing the death rate. The Public Health and Welfare Section of SCAP under the inspired direction of Brigadier-General C. F. Sams launched drastic medical reforms that so improved Japanese health that the death rate was reduced from 29.2 a thousand in 1945 to 10.3 in 1951.

By measures of sanitation and a concerted attack upon endemic diseases the average span of life of the Japanese was prolonged by thirteen years as compared with that in 1935. Millions of babies who would have succumbed during the first ten years were kept alive to become adult and claim a place in the crowded sun.

The achievements of Sams and his devoted assistants deserve nothing but the highest praise.

To eliminate smallpox, every human being in Japan was vaccinated. That meant about eighty million vaccinations, a project never before attempted in medical history.

Japan's tuberculosis death rate has been one of the world's highest. Sams introduced many important changes in treatment and had every Japanese under the age of thirty-five immunized with a new agent known as BCG. Within the immunized group deaths were reduced by eighty-eight percent.

Immunization brought the diphtheria rate down eighty-three percent.

Typhus has been endemic in Japan for decades. When an active epidemic broke out in 1946 nine million persons were vaccinated against typhus and forty-eight million were dusted with DDT. From a peak of 31,147 the number of known cases has been reduced to fifty.

In the summer of 1946 cholera was brought in by repatriates from mainland countries. Prompt action was taken and thirty-four million persons were immunized. No case of cholera has been reported since December, 1946.

Dysentery, formerly very common, has been reduced seventy-nine percent.

Typhoid and paratyphoid have been reduced ninety percent.

Sams reorganized Japanese medical schools, and opened the first nursing schools. He persuaded the Diet to pass a medical service law stipulating minimum standards in hospitals. A child welfare law was enacted. Narcotics were placed under strict regulation. By encouragement of new branches of agriculture, nutrition was improved.

It was a glorious story of unselfish service, though not a new one. The same humanitarian spirit was shown long ago by the British in improving the health of India, by many European nations in their colonies, by America in the Philippines, by the Japanese themselves in the Micronesian islands. But perhaps nowhere and at no time has there been such an outpouring of practical goodwill from the victors to a defeated enemy.

Perhaps "practical" is not precisely the word since it was hardly practical to take measures that would drastically reduce the death rate in an already overpopulated country without at the same time paying attention to the need of reducing the birth rate. General Sams was aware of this problem but was not free to do anything about it. He did not determine Occupation policy. That policy, as demonstrated by General MacArthur, was to promote the health and longevity of the Japanese without assuming any responsibility for the overpopulation resulting from such measures.

That SCAP was unwilling to come to grips with Japan's greatest problem, that of population, was proved when Professor Ackerman was trimmed down to size. Dr. Edward Ackerman of the University of Chicago at the request of SCAP came to Japan and spent two years on a detailed study of Japan's natural resources.

The outcome was a two-volume analysis of Japan's economic condition. Dr. Ackerman's conclusion at the end of his analysis was that overpopulation was Japan's main economic problem. He stated that only by holding population at the present level could the Japanese have any hope for a balanced economy. If Japan did not limit her population the consequence would be a starvation living standard, and increasing reliance upon aid from America or elsewhere.

Some of the first copies of the Ackerman report fell into the hands of American religious workers. A few Protestant opponents of birth control protested to General MacArthur. The American Catholic Women's Clubs of the

Tokyo-Yokohama area challenged him to disavow advocacy of family limitation.

He promptly did so by suppressing the report. Only fifty-seven copies had been distributed. The remaining 2,443 copies were locked in a Tokyo vault. The chief of the Natural Resources Section which had published the report got a sharp reprimand for having "embarrassed" the Supreme Commander. He was ordered to tear out the offending pages, including his foreword which contained the sentence: "Japan is a nation of too many people on too little land, and its most serious economic and social problems stem directly from this condition." All charts and figures representing the need for family limitation were ordered out.

Why this sudden withdrawal of the Supreme Commander's support from a conclusion which he had previously endorsed by releasing it for publication? One of his civilian aides gave me what he believed to be the reason: "Mac didn't want to be caught in the middle." In other words, his rejection of his economic expert's findings was due not to any doubt as to their accuracy but to fear of criticism both from American groups and from militaristic factions in Japan.

For the same reason he refused an entry permit to Dr. Margaret Sanger, birth control advocate, when she was invited to give a series of lectures in Japan under the auspices of Japanese organizations seriously concerned over postwar population increase. She had to wait until after the Occupation. In 1952 she filled her engagement.

MacArthur justified his action on the grounds that population limitation was something for the Japanese to decide for themselves. This excuse had considerable merit. Many of the questions decided by SCAP might better have been left to the Japanese. If they had been, there would not today be such wide-spread rejection of SCAP reforms.

But just why it was proper to impose the will of SCAP upon the Japanese in hundreds of smaller matters but improper even to give advice on Japan's most pressing problem, is not clear.

MacArthur also excused his position with the familiar theory that as a nation industrializes, its population growth slows down. Certainly that has happened in the case of some Western nations. But it takes a century or two when it works, and often it does not work. To trust to this chance rather than to active measures would be like waiting for lightning to do what ought to be done by electricity.

The shakiness of the theory may be illustrated with a single example: The population of China, an unindustrialized nation, remains practically stationary while Japan which has been highly industrialized for half a century has a more rapid population increase than at any time in its history and than any other nation in Asia.

How can Japan afford to wait a hundred years on the bare chance that urbanization will slow her growth, when in only thirty-three years her population will double at the present rate—*a rate more than twice as fast as the increase of the world as a whole!* Japan is becoming less self-sufficient daily as the number of her people grows. She produces food for about sixty-five million people. She has eighty-six million people crowded into an area no larger than the state of Montana. Only sixteen percent of this land is arable.

"No country," writes Professor Edwin Reischauer in *The United States and Japan*, "not even the teeming lands of India, China or Java, can equal Japan's record of almost nineteen hundred members of the purely agricultural population to each square mile of cultivated land. The average Japanese farmer has less than one fifth as much land to cultivate as the average farmer in Belgium, the West's most densely populated country. Include Japan's huge cities, and she has more than thirty-four hundred people per square mile of cultivable land, putting her far above all competitors as the world's most crowded land. She has more than twelve times as many people to feed per square mile of farm land as the United States and approximately one third more people to feed per acre than a thoroughly industrialized and urbanized land like Great Britain."

Emigration is no adequate answer. The Japanese do not want to leave home and could not if they would. While Japan controlled the great fertile expanses of Manchuria, few Japanese could be persuaded to settle in that rich land. They didn't like to leave their friends, they didn't like the Manchurian winters, they couldn't compete with the Chinese peasants already settled in Manchuria. Comparatively few Japanese ever went to Formosa and only a handful to the Japanese Mandated Islands. Since the loss of these territories, their settlers have returned to Japan.

Countries not controlled by Japan do not have a very large welcome mat out for the Japanese. It once looked as if they would gain entry to New Guinea, the Philippines, and other parts of Southeast Asia. But their war upon these lands has made them feared and distrusted. Australia, the emptiest land on the Asiatic side of the world, bars Asiatics. The United States, where Japanese farmers willing to work sixteen hours a day were a serious embarrassment to American farmers who preferred to go at an easier pace, has all but closed the doors.

Japan was delighted when in 1951 Brazil extended an invitation to Japanese emigrants to grow jute in the Amazon valley. Japanese enthusiasm cooled when it was learned how many emigrants were wanted—five thousand. There are more than five thousand babies born in Japan in a single day.

And even if all doors were open, which they are not, and if the Japanese were willing to break home ties and move to strange lands, which they are not, it is incredible that emigration could be organized on such a scale as to offset Japan's population growth of two million a year.

The improvement of Japanese health is one of the brightest chapters in the story of the Occupation. But health measures must be accompanied by a definite plan for caring for the increased numbers. More people require more room. Are we ready to provide the room?

"Every time a Christian housewife in Omaha puts ten cents in the collection plate to help the medical missionaries in Asia," an American in India told James Michener, "she is committing a grave moral sin unless at the same time she is taking steps so that one day we can cede all of Canada to surplus Asiatic populations—or all of the United States west of the Mississippi."

"I shudder to think of the explosiveness of this population growth," said a sober-minded Occupation official in

Japan. "In five years I expect to see them overrunning Asia."

Intelligent Japanese are keenly alive to the danger. Dr. Kageyas W. Amano, a prominent Japanese physician, says, "The rising birth rate will make our country increasingly vulnerable to the communists or militarists."

No nation has a moral right to allow reckless increase that will lead either to the poverty and privation of its people or to seizure of the lands of its neighbors. Expansion leads to aggression, and aggression, as the Japanese well know, leads to disaster.

MacArthur's word was law in Japan. When he threw a wet blanket upon proposals of family limitation and discredited those who had made them, the several Japanese movements on behalf of regulation collapsed. For a time no one dared advocate control.

With the passing of the Occupation, the heretics have come out of hiding, their doctrine is being more widely accepted and "marriage consultation offices" are established by the government. Japan has as yet hardly made a beginning in the solution of her greatest problem, but it is at least encouraging when a large newspaper such as the *Mainichi* publishes and heartily endorses such a statement as the following by Warren Thompson, scholar of population:

"An intelligent and persistent effort to educate the Japanese people in the need to keep their families small will do more to increase the nation's welfare, to raise the general level of living, and to rehabilitate Japan's economy than any other single program that can be undertaken."

19

THE TRAGEDY OF THE FARMS

THUNDER ROARED, lightning blazed, heavy rain driven by a strong wind swept almost horizontally across the deck. All day we had been fighting our way along the coast of Kurahashi Island. We were cold, wet, hungry and annoyed. Night was closing in, and the idea of spending it on board was not inviting.

This would be an opportune moment for a town to put in its appearance, one with a comfortable inn to welcome storm-tossed seafarers. But not even a fishing village interrupted the farmland that checker-boarded the mountain slopes.

Rounding a point, we saw through the gathering gloom and scudding rain a blob of a farmhouse behind a small bay. I looked at Mary.

"Let's try it," she shivered.

We ran into the bay and dropped anchor in the lee of a rocky cape. The captain and his two passengers went ashore in the dinghy. Since the ship could not be left unattended, Good-Fortune and Literature stayed aboard. They would go below and hug the hot motor.

Beaching the boat, we walked a narrow, muddy ridge between sweet potato plots to the house.

"*Komban wa*," called the captain. "Good evening." He did not knock. It is considered discourteous to pound a Japanese door. Only the police ever did it, and they do it no longer.

He had to call twice again before he was heard over the cry of the storm. Then a door slid back and the master of the house peered out.

We explained our predicament and were at once invited to come inside. In the *genkan* or vestibule, we removed our shoes, stepped around the screen that is supposed to prevent evil spirits from entering the house, and padded over the resilient *tatami* into a large room lighted by a single electric bulb. It is hard to find a spot in Japan that electric wires have not penetrated.

The room was bare and poor. Its only decorations were a crude scroll hanging in the sacred alcove, and a small Shinto shrine on the godshelf. The tatami were in bad repair and the paper doors were torn. There were no glass doors outside the paper doors, but there were heavy *amado*, storm doors of solid wood, that more or less successfully kept out the rain and wind. The roof was of thatch supported by smoke-blackened rafters.

The man was perhaps in his fifties. His face was weather brown and work lined and both his shirt and trousers were patched. His feet were bare and as tough and gnarled as oak stumps.

He profusely begged our pardon, as if the storm had been his fault. He did not seem quite to know what to do with us and called his wife.

She came in with many bows and smiles and apologies. She had reached the early old age of the woman who has borne many children without letting it interfere with her work in the fields.

She took one look at our sodden figures, exclaimed, *"Ma! Taihen desu! Chotto matte!"* (Oh! Terrible is! Little wait!) and scurried out to get us a change of clothing.

While we contrived to get out of our wet clothes and into the worn but clean *yukatas*, she made tea and we could hear rattlings that told us the fire was being stirred up under the family tub.

There were no cakes with the tea, but it was strong and hot and sent the blood once more coursing through our dishrag veins. Then, one at a time, we soaked in the near-boiling water of the three-foot-wide and three-foot-deep wooden tub. We returned to the big room, our lobster-red skins glowing with comfort and radiating steam.

Dinner was served. There being no table, it was brought in on trays and set before us as we sat on the floor. The woman apologized deeply because there was no rice. The meal consisted of sweet potatoes, sliced raw fish, and baked fish. There was more tea. It was a profoundly satisfying meal.

Then we talked.

The man's name was Ando. He owned two acres. I wanted to know whether the Occupation's program of land reform had helped him. I had been asking the question of farmers all the way down the Inland Sea. Ando-san's reply was typical.

"Makasa [MacArthur] tried to help us. We are very grateful. Now for the first time in my life I own land."

"You used to be a tenant?"

"Yes, on this same land. For thirty years I farmed it, but it was not mine. Of everything that grew I must give sixty percent to my landlord. Now it is all mine."

His wife sighed. Ando-san reproved her with a look.

"So life is easier for you than it used to be?"

Ando-san smiled a wry smile. "*Sa!*" he exclaimed thoughtfully, with a glance at his wife. He was plainly anxious to avoid giving offense. "It is good to own your own land. It is a very good feeling."

"Everything is harder," broke in his wife. "The taxes. The inflation. The government."

Ando-san was keenly embarrassed. "You will pardon my wife," he entreated. "She mourns the loss of her daughter."

"Your daughter has died?"

Ando-san hesitated. "You must understand that we are very poor. My wife was ill and needed medicines. A man came from Osaka, visiting the islands, looking for girls. He thought our Yuriko good-looking. He offered two thousand yen. We refused, but Yuriko insisted upon going."

Two thousand yen is the equivalent of $5.60. No one said anything for a moment. The storm beat upon the amado. I could not bring myself to inquire what Yuriko was doing in Osaka. Nine out of ten girls recruited in this fashion are destined for the houses of prostitution.

"She was your only child?" I asked.

"Oh no. We had four boys and two girls. Three of our sons were killed in the war. One died of troubles of the chest. Two years ago our elder daughter . . . went to the city. And now Yuriko." He laughed softly in apology for

221

burdening his guests with his troubles. *"Shikata ga nai."* (It can't be helped.)

"But you managed to live on this land for thirty years. And now your income should be much larger since you no longer have to pay sixty percent of your crops to a landlord."

Ando-san nodded gravely. "That is true. Now all that we earn is our own. That is democracy. It is better than the old way. But I am afraid we still have many things to learn before we can do everything in the new fashion. We used to be able to go to our landlord for help when we were in difficulty. We have gone to him twice since the war and he has said, 'Why come to me? My land has been taken away from me and now I am as poor as you. I cannot help you.' He used to own twenty-five acres, and eleven of us tenants farmed his land. He could buy fertilizer and seed in large quantities at a very low price. He could afford to keep an ox and a horse and would let us use them. He had a pump to pump irrigation water to all of the farms. Since the land has been redistributed there is no pump and some of the plots on the slope are not being farmed because the small holders cannot afford to irrigate them. And then the taxes! In the old days the landlord paid the taxes. Now we must pay them, and they are six times as high as they were. And this terrible inflation makes us poorer as fast as we get richer!"

"They have given the women the vote," his wife put in. "But there is no one to vote for who will protect the rights of the farmers. Each party is a landlord party. Our government has no sympathy for the farmers. The good changes the Americans made—little by little they are being changed back. But you must be very tired after your hard journey and here we chatter on and on about our foolish troubles!" She rose briskly, slid open a closet door and began to take out padded futons.

"The most successful experiment of its kind in history," was MacArthur's appraisal of his land reform program. The judgment was perhaps a little premature. It was like declaring a horse the winner the moment it had left the post. Only time will tell whether the experiment will end in success or failure. Strong interests are determined that it shall fail.

Certainly it was a "noble" experiment even though we must wait a while to be sure of its success. Its intentions were the best. The land reform law was passed by the Diet in October 1946 by order of SCAP. Its purpose was stated to be "the wide extension of the ownership of agricultural land, so that cultivators may receive the fruits of their labor, thus promoting stability among farmers, increasing productivity, and fostering democratic tendencies in rural communities."

It ended the autocratic power of the absentee landlord. He must sell his tenant lands, all except two and a half acres, to the government at a sacrificial price, and the government would then resell them on very reasonable terms to individual farmers. These new landowners would be allowed twenty-four years to pay for their land.

Before the law went into effect forty-six percent of Japanese cultivated land was operated by tenants. By December, 1949, only eleven percent was tenant operated.

More than four million acres had been bought by the government and distributed to former tenants.

One third of the total cultivated land of Japan had passed into the hands of three million working cultivators. More than fifty percent of all farm households had purchased land.

For the remaining tenants, rents which had varied from fifty to seventy percent of the crop were placed under a twenty-five percent rent ceiling.

The old-time *nogyokai*, agricultural associations controlled by the government, were replaced by a system of cooperatives controlled by the farmers. By 1949 there were thirty-three thousand such cooperatives, one in almost every village in Japan, with a total membership of eight million.

However, cooperation was not a new thing among the Japanese. Farmers have customarily helped each other through the guidance of the village office. They have planted and harvested each other's crops on a roster system, built each other's houses, and joined in repairing roads or building bridges. Rural Japan was never a place for the rugged individualist. An American farmer a mile or five miles from his nearest neighbor might go it alone, but not the Japanese farmer on a small plot of ground closely surrounded by a thousand others. The new cooperatives did not initiate teamwork, but organized and developed it.

To study the effects of land reform the Natural Resources Section of SCAP conducted in 1947 and 1948 a competent survey of thirteen fairly typical villages.

They found that in these villages forty-one percent of the cultivated land had been transferred to former tenants.

"Most new owners," according to the report of the survey, "found taxes high, delivery quotas heavy, and the continuing inflation burdensome . . . A number in each of the villages were asked if, in the face of these economic problems, each of which has become worse, they would prefer to, or would just as soon, be tenants again. All of them said no; they wanted to hold onto their ownership of the land."

The farmers could hardly believe their good luck. They feared there might be a change of policy in Tokyo. One said he would feel his purchase of land was morally more binding if the former landlord had been paid a more adequate price by the government.

The large landowners (and by a large landowner is meant one who had owned a dozen acres or more) naturally complained of losing their land. To them it meant "that now a son at home would need to find a livelihood elsewhere, or that it would not be possible as planned to give the children an upper secondary education, or that they could not establish for their son or daughter or cousin a separate household as they had hoped."

The new cooperatives were reported by farmers to be a real improvement over the earlier associations. Now the farmer could obtain payment for crops on the day of delivery whereas it sometimes used to take a month, and there was much official red tape.

The expanded school system prescribed by SCAP with nine years of compulsory education instead of six required more money and in 1946 for the first time most farmers were subject to income tax. This was an unhappy event that they had not anticipated. The Western farmer takes his taxes as a matter of course. After paying them he has enough left to live on. But to the Japanese farmer who rarely or never makes enough to feed and clothe his family, a tax is a matter of the gravest concern.

"The problem of inflation was on the tongues of villagers everywhere," runs the report. "Frequent references were made to the phenomenally large amount of yen now needed to purchase a plow, a bicycle, a power-driven thresher or a calf."

The slivering of the holdings of "large" landowners into still smaller fragments had raised serious problems. The plots were too small to farm economically.

This problem was further aggravated by the provision of the new Civil Code that all children and relatives have the right to share in the inheritance of land. This meant that if a farmer died leaving, let us say, a wife and five children, his already tiny farm must be divided six ways so that each survivor might have a share.

This was democracy gone wild. Most of the people of the thirteen villages chose to cling to the old custom by which the eldest son inherits the land while the younger children seek employment in town or city. The sound horse sense of the people nullified the law. Children legally entitled to land refused to exercise their rights. The survey report states:

"The majority of young people interviewed in youth association meetings favored the continuance of the traditional methods of inheritance. Because the elder brother is obligated to take care of the aged parents and look after the welfare of the younger children until they reach maturity, it was only proper, they argued, that he should inherit the family property." And it was the common opinion that any further subdivision of the already pitifully small holdings was impractical.

Village young people are steady. They are not swept about by every breeze from America or Europe as are the young folks of Tokyo. The revised Civil Code allows a young man and girl to marry without the consent of their elders. But the finding of the investigators was: "There is no evidence that the incidence of parental selection has materially declined in the thirteen villages since the Surrender."

As for divorce, "Until the revised Civil Code was promulgated, Japanese women were not able to sue for divorce, and divorce action was considered to be a prerogative of the husband. Under the revised Civil Code, however, wives can sue for divorce on the same grounds as can husbands. Nevertheless, the post-Surrender divorce proceedings recorded in the villages were all initiated by men."

The general conclusion of the investigators was that there has been a change for the better in the thirteen villages, but any claim that there has been a social revolution would be unwarranted.

Among the farmers of Japan as a whole there is considerable disillusionment and reaction. Owners who cannot bear the burden of high taxes and high prices and the responsibilities of ownership are selling their land and once more becoming tenants. In 1950 according to the Japanese Agriculture Ministry one hundred thousand farmers disposed of portions of their property. In 1951 transfers of farm lands were 2.6 times as frequent as in 1950.

"In Tohoku," reports the *Nippon Times*, "the rate of sale has increased to five times compared with 1949, in Kinki twelve times and in Chugoku twenty-eight times."

Large numbers of the farmer-owned cooperatives have gone broke, probably because of lack of experience, and the commercial banks are refusing to lend money.

The farmers are politically impotent since the major parties are opposed to reform.

The "slave market" is the most reliable barometer of rural welfare. Rarely, except in times of national disaster due to earthquakes or famine, have so many farm girls been sold into prostitution.

The Occupation tried to stamp out the practice. Not until 1949 was a case reported. This may have been because there were none to report, or because the newspapers dared not report them. In 1951 four thousand girls from rural communities were sold into prostitution, some for as little as $2.80.

More than half of these girls came from families earning only eleven dollars to fourteen dollars a month for an average family of six.

The girls of such families were sometimes sold for as little as a sack of potatoes or of rice. More usually they brought about eight dollars if purchased as prostitutes. A girl intended for a factory fetched about the same. Highest prices were paid for girls possessing enough beauty and talent to qualify them as "entertainers." They brought an average of forty dollars with a maximum of about two hundred dollars.

Under the law as it stands on the books girls thus sold may renounce their debt at any time and go home. Actually they rarely do so. The pressure of custom and the feeling of obligation are so strong that they stay until they have worked off their debt. The company or house employing them may so manipulate their expenses that they never clear themselves.

The reason why the land reform program, though valuable, falls far short of being "the most successful experiment of its kind in history" is that it does not touch the basic problem.

The basic problem of the Japanese farmer is *too many people on too little land.*

Japan today is one half the size of prewar Japan, 147,000 square miles as against 262,000. Practically all the land that can be cultivated is being cultivated. No farmers in the world work their land so intensively. The Japanese farmer gets roughly triple the yield of the American farmer and double that of the European farmer. In the warmer parts of Japan at least two and sometimes three crops are raised on the same land every year.

Every inch of space is used and some plants that would ordinarily spread along the ground are trained to go up into the air to save room. To turn back to the report of the thirteen villages, "So great is the pressure for land that cucumbers often are tied up on poles, and pumpkin vines may be planted at the foot of a trellis leading to the roof of a farm building." Japanese rice yields are the highest in Asia.

The average size of the Japanese farm is two and a half acres. Compare that with three acres in China, 3.6 in Korea, ten in the United Kingdom, 47 in the United States, and eighty in Canada.

The Japanese who has two and one half acres is lucky. Nearly one third of Japanese farms are one acre or smaller.

Japanese agronomists calculate that the size of the average farm would have to be tripled to give the typical farming family a fair livelihood. Another way of saying this is that there are three times as many people on the farms as there should be.

What is to be done with this surplus population? The Occupation had no answer, and refused to allow its economic experts to offer an answer.

Where people starve, democracy has no chance. Desperate farmers will turn to communism or to militarism. Rural discontent in the thirties was the chief means by which the militarists rose to power. Army officers promised the farmers prosperity and, as a matter of fact, gave it to them. War raised farm prices and drew off the surplus farm population into the army.

This bloody pattern will be repeated, or one dictated by the Soviet will be substituted, unless Japan solves the problem that proved too tough for her teachers.

Japan's population increase must stop. Ways must be found to farm the mountains and to farm the sea. The trend toward smaller farms, accelerated by land reform, should be reversed. Industries must be expanded to employ unneeded farmers. We of the West must open our markets to Japanese goods, keep tariff barriers low. If we do this, our manufacturers will complain that it is done at their expense; if it is not done, we shall have the expense of another war with Japan.

20

ISLANDS THAT TIME FORGOT

HOW MODERN IS the most modern nation in Asia?
As we walked through a village on the island of Kurahashi a woman opened her door and flung some rice into
the street. Then, observing that she had barely escaped
peppering us, she apologized.

"It's no matter," I said. "But why are you throwing
away rice?"

"So the baby can sleep," she replied.

Since rice is not grown in the islands and must be
brought from the mainland, it is costly. It is hardly something to be thrown away. What connection could there be
between the waste of rice and a baby's sleep?

We questioned the woman until we had the story. It
seems that there is an evil spirit that bothers babies. It comes
in the form of a little man wearing a suit of armor and
riding a horse. He can enter any room no matter how
tightly it is closed. He prods babies with his sharp sword
and makes them cry. But he dreads rice. It alone will keep
him away.

"Once when I was nursing my baby," the woman said,
"the door of the room slid open and ten little men came in.

Each was as tall as my finger. They wore armor and rode small horses. They galloped toward us and my baby began to scream. But I always kept a dish of 'throwing rice' handy and I seized it and threw some rice at the little men. They vanished and a little smoke went up. The rice dish was stained with blood."

The woman obviously was not making this up. She really believed that it had happened. She believed it because people for a thousand years have believed it. Anything that has been believed for that long, they calculate, must be true.

A survey conducted by the Education Ministry in 1948 revealed that seven out of ten persons in rural Japan still believe in ancient superstitions.

It was found that seventy-two percent of the farm dwellers and more than half of the city dwellers believe in astrology. Twenty-two percent of the farmers and fifteen percent of those living in cities trust to the magic powers of charms. Half the farmers believe in *yakudoshi* or unlucky years.

Following the survey, the Education Ministry appointed a thirty-man Superstition Investigation Commission to study the causes and cures of superstitious beliefs.

It will be a colossal task. The causes are lost in the mists of prehistory and the cures will be speedy indeed if they are accomplished within the next hundred years.

Even in Tokyo streets palmists, phrenologists, astrologists, soothsayers and necromancers do a thriving business. But it is in the country that one is most strongly reminded that the Japanese are an ancient people. They may flutter back and forth like a leaf on a tree, but they remain attached to the tree.

On the islands that time and the Occupation forgot, the "ten little men" and a host of other phantoms and phantasies still govern daily life.

We were interested spectators at the building of a house. It seemed to us that it ought to face northeast because in this direction the view across the Inland Sea was superb.

"That wouldn't do," the carpenter said. "The devil comes from the northeast. You never put a gate on that side —the devil would use it." He pointed to the ridgepole where a small bow and arrow had been fixed. The arrow pointed to the northeast. "That's to keep off the devil."

The second-best view was to the southwest.

"That wouldn't do either," the carpenter explained. "A gate on that side would be a *byomon*, sickness gate. Many diseases would enter by it. Yes, you have to know what you're about when you build a house. That's why it's wise to have an experienced builder. I've been building houses for thirty years. Now here's another thing you have to look out for—the well. It must be on the south side of the house. That's the prosperity side."

A Japanese who didn't know his directions would be in difficulty. Each point of the compass has its own significance. For example, you must not sleep with your head to the north. That is only for the dead. If you are ill you must go in the correct direction to get your medicine, varying according to the disease. The local sorceress can help you, for she possesses a "disease compass." It is too bad for the local druggist when the medicine needle does not point in his direction. One druggist sought to solve this problem by spotting many small branch depots here and there through the countryside so that no matter where the needle came to rest it would point to his wares.

Another popular practitioner is the "*soroban* doctor" who figures out on the soroban or abacus just what is the matter with you and what treatment is indicated. Some of the medicines are most primitive. Tuberculosis may be treated with an infusion of the dried fetus of a deer. A slip of paper inscribed with sacred characters may be glued to the forehead as a remedy for headache or swallowed for internal pain. Sore eyes may be treated by burning the wrists. Evil spirits are persuaded to leave the body through holes made by acupuncture needles.

All this, in spite of the fact that Japan is more advanced in the practice of modern medicine than any other nation of Asia, and in spite of the educational campaign of the Medical Section of SCAP.

A kindly old lady heard me complain of a nightmare induced by a too-hearty meal of *tempura*, prawns fried in batter.

"You should have a *baku*," she said. "Then you may eat whatever you please and you will have no bad dreams. Wait—I will get you one."

She retired into her house and in a moment brought out a sheet of paper bearing a picture of an extraordinary animal with a pointed head, rhinoceros eyes, a nose like an elephant's but shorter, a tiger's legs, and a cow's tail. Altogether it looked more like a tapir than anything else.

"You put it under your pillow," she said. "It will eat all your dreams and you will have perfect sleep."

The tradition of the baku or dream-eater came from

China probably in the eighth century. The legendary beast is supposed to be able to eat anything including rocks and iron blocks and it especially enjoys feeding upon nightmares.

The mystery of death has naturally inspired many superstitions. Over an island stream we saw a white cloth supported by four stakes. On the shore was a tablet to a departed child, and a ladle. You were supposed to fill the ladle from the stream, repeat a Buddhist prayer, and pour the water through the cloth. The dead soul would remain in a sort of purgatory or state of travail until the cloth was worn through.

And everywhere may be found statues to Jizo, guardian deity of children. You will find his image heaped with pebbles. It is supposed that every child who has gone to the other world is forced by an old hag to pile stones on the bank of the River of Death. The child's labors may be relieved by the living if they will pick up stones from the road and place them upon the head or shoulders or lap of Jizo.

If the members of a family cannot resolve a family problem they consult a dead father or grandfather through an *ichiko* or medium. The spirit of the dead enters the body of the ichiko and speaks through his mouth.

In the household shrine are the *ihai* or mortuary tablets of the family dead. The ihai is regarded as something almost alive, or something that may become alive if the dead person it represents needs to return to earth. Then it becomes flesh and blood. If a child cries for its dead mother, she may thus return to suckle it. A wife may come back to comfort her bereaved husband or even to bear him a child. A servant may come back to aid his former master. An enemy may return to take revenge. After the errand of vengeance or mercy has been performed, the living dead becomes once more only a tablet.

The older folk of the islands still believe in reincarnation. Children are warned that if they are not good they will come into the next life as hideous animals or insects. An old widow lavished great attention upon her cat. The neighbors speculated that the cat was really her departed husband in his new incarnation.

Names are lucky or unlucky according to the number of strokes and dots in the ideographs which form the name. There are professionals in this art who will recommend names for infants or suggest a new name for an adult who fancies that his name is responsible for his bad luck. Stories are told of one who was ill and was cured by a change of name, another whom a new name made successful in business, another who had a serious accident because his ideograph had too many dots and too few strokes.

Agriculture and industry suffer severely because of the superstitions that cluster around the old lunar calendar. According to the Education Ministry survey, lucky and unlucky days are still observed by seven out of ten persons in the country and six out of ten in the cities. What effect such notions have upon the daily work may be imagined. In one village when a child is born the men of the family must not go fishing for three days. In another, the superstitious refuse to leave the village on the seventh, seventeenth, twenty-fifth and twenty-seventh of the month or to return on the fifth, fifteenth and twenty-fifth.

In planting crops, most farmers follow the signs of the

zodiac. Rice must not be planted on the day of the monkey because the rice god and the monkey god are enemies. Sugar potato ought to be planted on the day of the cow so that it will grow large like the cow's head.

Every day has its fortune, good or bad. There is a day for weddings, and a day for funerals. A new business may not be opened until the proper day arrives, and there is a right day to start on a journey. There is a day when things are stolen, and a day when people are killed. There are days when one should be completely inactive, for anything done on those days is bound to end in failure.

Such beliefs have for the past several hundred years been gradually wearing away. But there has been no recent sudden change. Tokyo has changed, and is changing, but even there the grip of tradition is strong. Having lived in Japan before the war and visited it after six years of Occupation, I see nothing that could justifiably be called "a social convulsion unparalleled in the history of the world." The "spiritual revolution" which according to General MacArthur "almost overnight tore asunder a theory and practice of life built upon two thousand years of history and tradition and legend" was about ten percent fact, ninety percent fantasy. The normal and orderly progress of Japan is not helped, nor our understanding of the Japanese promoted, by such grandiloquent exaggeration.

21

RUSSIA TURNS THE KEY

MAKING ANOTHER TRANSIT of the Inland Sea, we arrived at Matsuyama, a city that was in 1941, was not in 1945, and now once more is. Bombed to bits and burned to the ground, it has been completely rebuilt and is the home of 160,000 people. No city better represents the remarkable Japanese ability to bounce back out of disaster.

The city put us up in one of the inns of the famous Dogo spa, the oldest spa in Japan with a history of more than 2500 years—and still the boiling water pours up out of the earth without a sign of abatement. Of course we took the baths. Men and women did not bathe in the same room, which would seem to be a triumph for propriety. But comely young women in shorts were provided to scrub the backs of the men, and men in shorter shorts were available to accommodate women bathers.

The proprietor of the inn kindly offered us a room with a western bed. It was a bit narrow for two persons, and springless. We expressed a preference for a Japanese room and were conducted to one next door. There we slept comfortably on the floor.

During the night we heard much creaking from the foreign bed beyond the partition, and sometime after midnight a terrific thump followed by groans. Twice again we heard the bump and the groans. The next morning upon going out into the corridor we found our captain, looking a little haggard from loss of sleep. There had been only two rooms unoccupied—since we had taken the Japanese room, Wide-Margin had been forced to accept the foreign bed, and had fallen out three times.

"I don't know how you manage to stay on top of the thing," he said wearily. "It's worse than a ship in a storm."

I was taken at noon to a Rotary meeting of Matsuyama bankers and business men who limit their luncheon cost to nineteen cents. They had become used to such strict economy during the hard days of the desolation and rebuilding of their city. From a Rotary song book they sang familiar western melodies with Japanese words. Then they seriously ate their *oyakodombri*—a bowl of chicken, egg and rice without any side dishes of soup, pickles or dessert.

They were very sober fellows. They discussed serious problems. There was no tomfoolery, no Tail Twister. But they do have an annual party and in preparation for it they had called in the president of the Geisha Guild, an elderly lady of charming demeanor who gravely apprised them as to how many geisha they should have and what songs and dances should be featured.

We spent a day and night with a remarkable American, Dr. Clarence Gillett, principal of a large secondary school for girls. His teaching staff was made up of intelligent young Japanese, full of energy and ideas.

Their greatest worry was communism.

"That's the real danger in Japan," said Teacher Kinny

239

Honami. "A group of students in this school recently held a meeting to discuss the relative merits of communism and Christianity—as if they were two comparable religions, both seeking human betterment. Communism has more appeal because it has a definite program of things that people can do whereas Christianity, as it is generally practiced, has not."

"Are many of your teachers communists?"

"Not in this school. Since it is a private institution, salaries are adequate. But in the government schools where salaries are at a starvation level a great number of teachers have turned to communism, thinking it may offer relief. The same is true of priests and pastors whose salaries are desperately low. Would you believe it?—a majority of the Methodist pastors in this ken are communists."

In the schools of the Inland Sea, as well as in the city schools and universities we were to visit during our later months in Japan, communism is creeping with the speed and deadliness of blood poisoning.

It makes a special appeal to immature minds. It thrives upon ignorance and confusion. The young people of Japan are a sadly bewildered lot. They are upset by war and reconstruction, by the dictation of foreign powers, by the bright promise of democracy that faded, by the hot-and-cold policy which for a while taught them that Japan was to be "the Switzerland of the Far East" and then that Japan must rearm and prepare for new and bloodier adventures.

They look for a way out, any way out. They take seriously the Soviet promise of a better world, lacking sufficient international experience to know that wherever Russian communism has been applied it has meant a worse world.

Communism is making a determined effort to capture Japan. Stalin called Japan the key to Asia. He said, "A union of the Japanese people with the people of the Soviet Union would be invincible."

With a high sense of strategy the Soviet is making its primary attack upon children and young people. Great numbers of communist clubs for children have been organized under such pleasant names as Smiling Children's Club, Friendly Children's Club, Happy Children's Club. The children are entertained by amusing games, plays, songs and stories. At first there is very little about the communist philosophy but gradually it creeps in and the children begin to hear about "capitalist exploitation, the pernicious ambitions of America to rule the world."

The schools and colleges are a hotbed of communism. The number of actual Party members is probably small but the number of students sympathizing with the communist program is said to be no less than forty percent. Many teachers and professors follow the communist line. When they are discharged the students go on strike. Communist students persuade non-communists to join them in such protests. They have much to say about "freedom of thought"—something not allowed in Russia.

"We want to study all isms and make our own judgments," said a law student at Chuo University. "I am not a communist but we were given freedom of thought under the Constitution. The actual situation is far from what is described in the Constitution. If we want to hold a meeting, we have to get permission from the Metropolitan Police Board. That is not freedom."

The student who uses this argument does not think far enough into the problem to realize that his thought is not free if it is bent and twisted into a certain channel by a teacher who himself does not exercise freedom of thought and expression but says only what he has been told to say by a subversive foreign power.

When certain professors sympathetic to the communist cause were disqualified in 1950, student agitators launched a nation-wide campaign of protest, picketed campuses, boycotted examinations, and destroyed school property. A quarter of a million members of a left-wing students' organization created such disturbances that normal educational activities were interrupted throughout Japan.

In what the Kyodo News Service described as "the worst scandal in the history of the student movement" pitched battles took place between the police and the students and large numbers of the latter went to the hospital or to jail.

Again in 1951 students were on the rampage, this time protesting against the conclusion of a peace treaty without the participation of the Soviet Union and the Chinese People's Republic.

The success of Soviet propaganda in Japan is all the more surprising since Russia is Japan's traditional enemy. No nation is more hated and feared by the majority of Japanese. Partially it is the fear of the Soviet and the feeling of helplessness that makes so many Japanese ready to follow the communist line. The Japanese like to think of themselves as realists. Once they had surrendered they submitted completely to Allied control because further struggle would have been inexpedient. The same reasoning leads many opportunistic Japanese to feel that now their only hope of escaping destruction at the hands of the Soviet lies in embracing Soviet philosophy.

Fear is but one of the factors. Economic conditions in Japan, says former U.S. Ambassador to Japan Joseph C. Grew, "are working in favor of the communist cause." He sees Japan "standing at the crossroads between democracy and the deceitfully easy road to communism and totalitarianism" and lists the economic factors which draw the Japanese toward the left as "the inflation of currency, the shortage of consumer goods, the lack of appreciable foreign trade, the housing shortage, the destruction of national ideals and the disorganization of society."

He believes there is still a chance to reverse the trend because "the average Japanese still is malleable."

His sober view of the communist menace contrasted sharply with General MacArthur's opinion as of May 3, 1950 that communism was beaten and nothing remained of it but "shattered remnants."

The postwar furore over democracy has caused many Japanese to adopt communism because, they say, it is a further development of the democratic way of life. Why stop half way when you can go all the way? It is hard to convince these people that Soviet communism is not democracy plus, but is a road leading in the opposite direction.

Other Japanese realize quite well that the Soviet brand of communism is neither communism nor democracy, but a particularly effective kind of totalitarianism. This makes it attractive to militarists who long for a return of the absolute power they once exercised. Dictatorship by the few is a form of government the Japanese understand. The Russian practice of placing all power in the hands of a few

243

leaders and denying the common people any voice in the government is quite in the traditional Japanese pattern. In Japan as in Russia the state has been everything and the individual has had no rights except the right to serve the state.

That communism can appeal to some people because they think of it as a super-democracy and to others because it is a super-despotism illustrates the consummate guile of the propagandists who make communism all things to all men. They make duplicity a fine art. On the islands we found them advocating high prices for farm products; in the cities they promise low prices. In the labor unions they stand for high wages and when trying to win businessmen they favor low wages. They are for big taxes or small taxes, depending upon their audience.

The communists are indifferent to politics. True, in the 1949 election they piled up a popular vote of almost three million and won thirty-five seats in the Diet. But they have since paid little attention to political maneuvering and prefer to burrow beneath the surface.

They appear in the most unexpected places. For example, they have worked their way into the hospitals through membership in the boards of trustees. This puts them in an admirable position to win friends and influence people. They see to it that those who embrace communism enjoy a reduction of hospital fees. Also they arrange that in every ward under their control there is a professional communist who will carry on "educational" work among the patients. In the same way they impregnate many other institutions— schools, jails, tax committees, farmers' cooperatives.

Red publications that have been banned as subversive

still continue to go through the mails, but under various disguises. Many are concealed within legitimate publications. Others put on an innocent front.

One entitled *How to Raise Flower Bulbs* outlines tactics for organized violence against the Japanese police. It declares, "We must commence preparations for armament and action." It reveals the ominous fact that Japanese communism is now entering a military phase. It gives the details of the organization of a corps for the instigation of riots and disturbances. It directs corps members to steal arms "from hostile armed agencies" including the American security forces. In addition to modern weapons, such implements as bamboo spears, spikes for puncturing automobile tires, carpenter's tools and farm implements useful as weapons should be obtained.

"Have these weapons ready for action!" it directs. "One thing that must be made very clear is that the members of the corps are to risk their own lives for the liberation of our race, for democratic revolution and to fight against American imperialists and traitors. It must be made clear to them that they must never betray the corps and must keep secrets for the cause of the revolution.

"The organization of the corps should be such as to enable their quick action. They should be organized into units in factories, rural communities, towns and schools as bases with not more than ten persons in one unit. As the number of members increases, two or three platoons may be made into one company, and two or three companies into one battalion. All units must be able to take concerted action. Each platoon must be organized so as to be able to take military action independently."

245

The "shattered remnants" of communism must be doing fairly well if communist leaders are now ready to consider the possibility of armed insurrection.

Weapons are not the only things to be stolen from "the enemy." The corps will require funds "and in this case too the general rule is to get it from the American forces. At such bases as Sasebo and Yokota our laborers have been carrying out various enemy war materials such as metals and have sold them for cash."

Continuing its instructions on how to raise flower bulbs, this amazing secret document goes on to outline in detail the organization of the underground army, methods of "morale and political education" for training the armed forces, and "tactics and action" covering methods of guerrilla warfare and sabotage. Repeatedly the document refers to both the Japanese and the Allied powers as "the enemy."

If there were any human being on this planet still in doubt as to the sinister purposes of the U.S.S.R., the document *How to Raise Flower Bulbs* would dispel his doubt at once. Many other documents discovered by Japanese government investigators tell the same story.

The communist world is preparing to fight to win Japan with propaganda if possible, with violence if need be. Formerly violence was considered as a last resort. Under the new policy, first place is given to plans for armed revolt.

This revolt may come independent of world events. More likely, insurrection from within Japan will be synchronized with Soviet attack from without. Such an attack, of course, would mean world war. Whether this will be the outcome depends upon the strength and unity of the noncommunist world.

246

In the meantime acts of mass violence are steadily increasing. In 1949 there were forty-three cases of violence believed to have been communist inspired; in 1952, seventy-four cases. In a May Day demonstration of communists in 1952 sixteen hundred policemen battled for two and a half hours with ten thousand Reds. The day's toll was two dead, 1,454 injured, 131 of them critically.

Again on the last day of May which the communists had designated as "Martyr's Day," it took twenty-five thousand police to smash demonstrations staged by communist agitators armed with sulphuric acid bombs and flaming oil bombs. The riots were staged simultaneously in sixty-two of Japan's large cities.

Again in the following month a thousand communist demonstrators armed with Molotov cocktails battled Japanese police in Fuita near the U.S. Itami Air Base in an anti-American demonstration. Among the injured was an American general.

Month by month the disturbances continue, the Reds steadily improving in their guerrilla tactics. A small minority, as the police well know, can cause a great deal of trouble. There are about 350,000 communists in Japan of whom 100,000 are card holders. But there are several million fellow travelers. There are 600,000 Koreans in Japan of whom 500,000 belong to associations which have pledged allegiance to North Korea. Red agents are continually being smuggled into the country. Small fishing boats bring them across the straits from Korea in nine hours.

The hard fighting core of the communist insurrectionists is made up of former Japanese soldiers taken prisoner by the Russians and thoroughly indoctrinated with communist ideas before being returned to Japan. Most of the half million repatriates were unaffected by communism or rejected it after return to their own country, but it is estimated that at least 100,000 are in the communist ranks. Being already trained for warfare, they are invaluable in the new Soviet program of military action.

The Communist Party thrives on discontent. "We can use the people's discontent," says the communist leader, Sanzo Nozaka. The farmers, dissatisfied with the results of land reform, are being lured by the usual communist promises. Of 3,629 known communist cells, 2,750 were in the farm districts.

Labor discontent is a fertile field for the communists. Already communists dominate unions representing more than half of Japan's 5,600,000 unionized workers. In nearly all labor unions Young Peoples Action Corps have been organized, made up entirely of communists. They meet under portraits of Lenin and Stalin, wave red flags, sing the *Internationale*, and vow their readiness to "brave death for the Cause" as did the suicidal kamikaze pilots of the Pacific war.

That poor peasants and underpaid workers should turn wishfully to communism is understandable, but it is astonishing to see important industrialists and businessmen turn in the same direction. These men are not interested in communist ideology. They simply want to trade with Communist China. Therefore they curry favor with the Japanese Communist Party, knowing that the Chinese communists will be most inclined to trade with those whom the Japanese communists recommend.

Sanzo Nozaka sets himself up as an intermediary. "Many

businessmen have approached me in this matter," he says. But he does not pass them easily. "They must meet our character test."

So we have Osaka businessmen attending classes and studying Marxist doctrine. An even better "character test" than a knowledge of communist philosophy is the ability to contribute to communist coffers. Large contributions have been received from Japanese capitalists. Just as Germany's industrialists tried to keep on the good side of Hitler, so Japan's industrialists are trying to butter up Mao Tse-tung and Malenkov.

By 1949 the Communist Party had become the wealthiest party in Japan with contributions for the year totaling 113,000,000 yen—three times the financial backing of the dominant Liberal Party, and twice as much as all other major political parties of Japan combined.

Said industrialist Aikawa, "No matter whether you agree with the political ideas and principles of the Peiping communist regime, it is a plain fact that practically all materials indispensable for Japanese industry are in continental China under Mao Tse-tung's control. Nobody can deny this basic fact which has almost decisive significance for Japan's survival."

And unfortunately, he is right. A large proportion of Japan's exports formerly went to China. Japan used to get from the mainland 83 percent of her imports of coking coal, 31 percent of her iron ore imports, 78 percent of soy beans, 92 percent of peanut oil and 43 percent of her salt imports.

When the Chinese communists entered the Korean war in 1950, trade relations were broken. However, such trade was so natural and so inevitable that most of it was continued by smuggling.

More recently this trade has been coming out into the open. Even conservative Premier Yoshida recognizes its necessity:

"Red or white, China remains our next-door neighbor. Economic laws will, I believe, prevail in the long run over any ideological differences."

It is felt that Japan faces a dilemma: either she must trade with China, or she must receive aid from the United States. The latter expedient is distasteful to the Japanese. They quite naturally wish to go their own way on their own power. And they prefer to get their raw materials more cheaply than they can be had from America.

They are susceptible to such arguments as those used by the Russian trade representative in a meeting with Japanese Diet members: "It pains us to see Japan import coal from the United States at $30 a ton when it can easily be imported from Sakhalin at $10 a ton."

Iron ore from the United States costs $25 a ton; from China, $8 a ton.

The great and growing danger is that if Japan depends upon communist countries for her trade, she will wind up, sooner or later, in the Russian orbit. Particularly if communist control should spread over Southeast Asia, Japan would be forced to accept Russia's economic and political terms.

It is one of the bitter ironies of history that the Soviet plot for the conquest of Japan was unwittingly aided by our Occupation.

How this happened is ruefully described in *Contempo-*

rary Japan, the important review edited by the brilliant Helen Uno and always most friendly and fair toward America and Britain. It is related how the Ocupation authorities, shortly after the Surrender, ordered the release of all communist leaders from prison and declared freedom of thought, press and association. Promptly the Japan Communist Party was organized as a legal body and ten days after political prisoners were freed the communist newspaper *Akahata* (Red Flag) put in its appearance. Sanzo Nozaka, communist leader, who was in China collaborating with Chinese and Russian communists, was brought back to Japan by an American military plane. He was set free to conduct subversive activities as the tool of a hostile foreign power.

"While most of the Japanese were in rags and lacked food," continues the statement in *Contemporary Japan*, "they saw communist leaders dressed in new American suits, wearing new shoes and riding in American cars. Those communist leaders were constant visitors at the Occupation headquarters . . . The Japanese witnessed these developments with their own eyes and wondered why the Occupation authorities were taking measures that resulted in encouraging communism in the country."

Certainly it was not communism that the Occupation wished to encourage, but freedom of expression. The leniency toward communists was altogether benevolent and idealistic. It was part of the general effort to teach the virtues of democracy. Instead of accomplishing that result, it taught the Japanese to be wary of the sentimentality that under the guise of democracy allows thieves the same freedom as honest men.

The communists did not show proper gratitude toward their American benefactors. They grew in numbers and in violence until SCAP thought it necessary to make an exception to its policy of goodwill toward all, forget freedom of the press long enough to suppress *Akahata*, and order wholesale arrests of communists. It was then that General MacArthur announced communism beaten and nothing left but the "shattered remnants." The remnants were quickly reunited and today the communist conspiracy in Japan is the most sinister and formidable that the country has yet known. And, ungratefully, it does not hesitate to make anti-Americanism the high note in its appeal to the Japanese people.

It may be taken for granted that the Soviet will spare no effort to win Japan. Stalin might well say that control of Japan would make international communism invincible. The reason is simple—Japan is the industrial heart of Asia. With its millions of skilled workers and its great industrial plants turning out armaments, ships and planes for the Soviet Union, the domination of all Asia would be practically assured. A Russia backed by the industrial power of Japan, the manpower of China, and the natural resources of Southeast Asia, would be ready to strike with overwhelming force against the West.

Japan is the key. Russia is turning the key.

22

TYPHOON RUTH

"THE WORST TYPHOON in twenty years"—so the weather bureau classified it when it was all over—caught us between Matsuyama and Beppu.

There had been advance warnings but we had lightly disregarded them. So had most of the other shipping of the Inland Sea, for what ships could suspend operations on the basis of the vague report that "Typhoon Ruth" was proceeding north from the Philippines and might or might not strike Japan?

The western Pacific experiences some twenty typhoons a year. But not more than two or three of them are likely to strike any given spot. They pursue highly erratic courses. Because they are so changeable and unpredictable the waggish meteorologists give them women's names. Whether or not the imputation is fair to the ladies, it certainly fits the typhoons. One can never be sure when they will come, where they will go, what they will do.

"Typhoon Margie" which struck Japan shortly before the beginning of our sea trip raised a tidal wave that battered the west coast of Kagoshima Prefecture, destroyed villages, tore away embankments, caused damage exceeding

253

five million yen. Torrential rains accompanying the typhoon created floods that inundated thousands of acres of farmland, and carried off houses.

So whimsical was the storm that while one area was being well-nigh ruined by it, a nearby prefecture which had been desperately suffering from drought and praying for rain received not a drop.

Ruth might choose to ignore the Inland Sea entirely, or at least the part of it under our keel. With this happy thought we set out on the long reach across the Iyo Nada. *Nada* means open sea, and *iyo* means strange, queer, fantastic, grotesque. There is reason for the name since the waters of this portion of the Inland Sea play curious tricks. Tides rush in from the Pacific Ocean on the south, the Japan Sea on the northwest, and the northeastern part of the Inland Sea, and the three surges meet to raise a ruckus that is particularly trying to small craft.

We were bowled along by huge waves that broke on the poop, making the overhanging box untenable.

Each wave struck us a quartering blow that raised the bow and screwed it to port. Then the bow dropped and screwed to starboard. So our bowsprit went round and round counterclockwise as if we were trying to bore a hole in the western horizon. Six hours of this extraordinary spiraling was a little trying on the head, though it fortunately did not affect our stomachs.

For the night we pulled into a tiny village harbor and tied up alongside a cargo boat loaded with lumber. Its captain was suffering from the pain of two badly mashed fingers that had been caught between the logs. When Mary expressed sympathy he asked if we had any medicines. We had, and Mary flinchingly applied them, and since they hurt like the devil the captain was confident that his fingers would get well. With the characteristic Japanese inability to take anything without giving, the captain reappeared an hour later with a basket of sweet potatoes for Mary.

We slept on deck and pulled out early, hoping to complete the long jump to Beppu before the arrival of the reported typhoon. Leaving port, we sailed into a vast, horizon-bounded sea. This is, in effect, the ocean, for although it is part of the Inland Sea it is open to the Pacific through a wide strait.

The *Kompira* rolled giddily in the big waves. At each roll the deck took on water, now from one side and then from the other. There was an uneasiness in the air, and it got into our nerves. I put the cameras and films into their tin boxes, taped the boxes watertight, and buried them in the hold.

The water was suddenly ironed smooth by the tide welling up from underneath. These ironed-out stretches alternated with tiderips where the waves stood up like knife edges. All the waves were crested with white like snow-capped mountains.

Now we came into a region of whirlpools, set spinning by the counter action of incoming and outgoing tidal currents. To steer precisely along the ridges between whirlpools was like walking a tightrope. Good-Fortune was a skilful helmsman, but our bow was frequently caught by the clutching waters and round and round we went until the whirlpool died or until the combined strength of motor and sail pulled us free.

In one of the whirls we saw a large tiger shark going

round and round, apparently enjoying his ride. He must have been a visitor from the nearby ocean since sharks are not common in the Inland Sea. His presence did not make us feel any more comfortable in our careening craft.

Ahead we saw a most curious formation. It looked like a circular racetrack about a mile in diameter with hundreds of white horses running around its circumference. We tried to avoid it but it came our way and presently engulfed us.

Then we were in really rough water. The ship pitched and rolled like a crazy thing. The leverage of the heavy mainmast threatened to turn us over. Fortunately the mast was stepped in a hinge and so could be laid flat on the deck. It was lowered and lashed tight.

This was no sooner done than the reason for doing it disappeared. The wind dropped, the welling from beneath dispelled the white horses, and we floated on a surface as smooth as a pond. The air was oppressively hot. It lay against the face like a suffocating blanket. The sun was fogged and the blue sky disappeared behind a ghastly white pall, the typical "typhoon sky." A spiritless drizzle of rain began to fall. It was a sort of hot steam rather than rain.

The captain stuck his oil-spotted face up out of the engine hole. He looked at sea and sky and then at me. His manner was apologetic as if this were all his fault.

"Typhoon Ruth!" he said unhappily.

"Do you think we can make Beppu?"

He peered ahead and shrugged. He might well shrug for there was nothing to be seen ahead. Even the horizon had been blotted out. Every moment the sky was growing darker. One could have believed that the time was twilight instead of mid-morning.

I studied the chart and the poor little compass. We could rely only on the motor. The sails were useless without wind. With wind we might be even worse off for it would not be the sort of wind a sailor would choose.

"Better put back," I suggested.

Good-Fortune-in-Autumn pushed the tiller hard over and we turned toward the shore we had left. It was some two miles away. We could not hope to get back to the port where we had spent the night. No other ports were indicated on the chart. We should simply have to take a chance of finding a protecting bay in the savage precipitous coast.

Still we were smothered in the breathless calm disturbed only by our own motion. The darkness thickened.

"There it comes!" cried Literature-Pursuing-Sixth-Son, staring to starboard.

A smooth, rounded wave was coming our way. There was no crest on it. Not a ripple disturbed its surface. Not a breath of wind accompanied it. It swept under the *Kompira* and the ship rolled heavily.

Then came another wave, as smooth and windless as the first, but larger. Then another, still larger. Three, the usual number. They are the silent heralds of the storm. They roll from the scene of commotion into the region of ominous calm. Nature had given us fair warning; now she allowed us a moment for silent prayer before the first blast.

We were ready, or hoped we were. The sails were tight furled and the mainmast down. The dinghy had been double lashed to the deck and so had the oil barrels. A protective loop of rope had even been thrown over the *benjo*.

257

We could dimly make out a dent in the shoreline, a small bay backed by rocky precipices. A schooner was already huddled within its protecting arms. A few minutes more, and we would make it.

Vain hope. We were still half a mile out when Ruth struck. She came aboard all in a rush, spitting, shrieking, ripping up the calm surface into steep waves as if the sea had been dynamited. The wind fell upon us like a stone wall. We flattened ourselves upon the deck and clung to the ringbolts.

Technically, we should have headed into the wind. We did not, for that would have meant giving up hope of reaching land. Good-Fortune grimly clung to his tiller and held his course. We heeled far over with our lee rail awash. We clung to the deck as if to the roof of a house, a roof becoming more steeply pitched every minute.

A junk does not have a deep enough keel to hold it steady in a broadside attack. A little more of this and the *Kompira* would certainly roll bottomside up.

Now Ruth had changed into a terrier with the *Kompira* in her teeth and was shaking it as if she meant to tear it plank from plank. The wind was drumming and vibrating like a taut wire. It seemed that all the joints in the ship were rattling loose. Our jaws rattled, our brains rattled.

Then the wind tried new tactics. It thumped down upon us vertically, then came from ahead, then burst in upon us from the rear, as if trying to catch us unaware and unprepared. All this time Good-Fortune stuck to the tiller, his cap blown away, his hair standing out stiffly, his eyes slitted down against the wind.

Suddenly the gale dropped to a breeze. This was not because the typhoon was diminishing, but we were getting into the shelter of the mountain range. The deck leveled out and we made better time.

We slid into the bay and were relieved and greatly disappointed. Relieved, because it was a haven of rest, free of waves and wind. The mountain range towering beside us cut off the storm, which screamed across the peaks far above us and out to the sea we had just left.

But we were disappointed because the bay had no curving horns to serve as breakwaters. It was wide open to the sea. This did not matter in the least so long as the wind was offshore.

But the one thing that was predictable about unpredictable Ruth was that she would change. I had been in typhoons before and of course they were an old story to our crew. I understood their concern as they studied our exposed position and the savage rocks along the shore.

Yasuhiro gazed at me sadly. *"Ikemasen!"* (It won't do!)

The captain of the schooner hailed us. The merits of the anchorage were argued between ships. There was a sharp difference of opinion. The schooner's crew was afraid of the sea, Yasuhiro was afraid of the bay. (I was afraid of both.)

"They don't understand how a typhoon works," our captain said bitterly when he had failed to convince them of the danger of staying in the bay.

A typhoon is a revolving storm. It is like a whirlpool, but a gigantic one, often a hundred miles in diameter. The wind circles counterclockwise in the northern hemisphere, clockwise below the equator. This wind may have a velocity of 150 miles an hour. The entire whirl moves forward, but slowly, at the rate of about twelve miles an hour.

Cyclone and hurricane are but different names for the same phenomenon. The tornado is a smaller version of the same. A still smaller edition is the ordinary "twister," the column of whirling dust that wanders over our fields. No matter what the name the principle is the same—a whirling at great speed, and a slow movement forward.

The wind over our bay was from the south. But since it was a circling wind and the circle was moving forward, we were quite likely some hours later to get the same wind from the north. Then it would mean great waves in our unprotected bay and almost certain destruction on the rocks.

The captain came to us with a proposition.

"You go ashore. I'll take the ship out. When the storm is over I'll come back for you."

He grinned when we refused. He had never really expected us to desert him but now his conscience was clear. If we sank it was our own stubborn fault.

For three more hours we waited while the wind howled steadily overhead. The air about us was as still and hot and damp as that of a steam bath. It was noon now, but so dark that it seemed early evening.

The wind was no longer a continuous scream—it was broken by stutters and gasps. That was a sign of coming change. It was time to go. We must be well out in the Inland Sea before the south wind became a north wind. The idea of escaping a storm by facing it was a bit wild, and to the schooner captain it seemed downright ridiculous.

As he saw us preparing to depart he summed up his opinion of our captain in one roaring word.

"*Baka!*" (Fool!)

It is the strongest expletive in Japanese, the nearest thing to a curse that this polite language knows.

With it ringing in our ears and in our consciences—for he might be right at that!—we powered out of the bay. As we left the shelter of the range the wind began to reach down to us, first in gentle puffs, then more and more violently, but always in bursts and gusts as if it did not know its own mind. Soon these spasms became terrific and we were flat on the deck, whipped by the wind, deafened by its roar, drenched with spray, and thinking regretfully of the peace we had just left.

But the wind explosions were growing fewer now, the pauses longer. Once for a good ten seconds there was no blast. The captain shouted:

"Almost!"

We were almost in the center. A few more blasts, and the wind died away. It could be heard roaring, but at a distance. We were in the "eye" of the storm. It circled around us like a great merry-go-round. Here the air hardly moved.

But the commotion of the sea was greater than ever! The waves did not move in orderly fashion in one direction. They came from every direction, met each other head on, blew up in jets and geysers like the spouting of a thousand whales. But what whales!—for these spouts went forty or fifty feet high.

The reason for the indescribable chaos was that, since the storm was all about us, the waves were rolling into the center from all points of the compass. And without a wind to take their heads off and keep them down, they leaped out of all control.

The *Kompira* leaped with them. She seemed to have gone insane. Now was the time for her sea god to come to her rescue.

There were others beside ourselves clinging to the dancing ship. Hundreds of birds blown into the center by the circling winds milled about in the sky, clutched the rigging, or landed on deck only to be thrown off by the leaping ship. Insects by the thousands plastered our wet clothes or blundered over our faces. Many of them were hornets, bees and wasps, and if one tried to beat them off the neurotic creatures were quite likely to sink their stingers into the nearest soft surface.

On all sides of us moved the black storm but above us the sky was incredibly blue, an opening in the typhoon like the hole in a doughnut. The noonday sun poured down upon us, obscured only by birds and insects. One was tempted to believe that the worst was over.

But our crew, knowing much more about storms than about navigation, came forward with lines and proceeded to lash Mary to the foremast. I tied up to the lowered mainmast, Literature looped himself to the deck, Good-Fortune to the tiller, while the captain went below to coax every ounce of power from the engine.

A few more hushed, breathless moments—then it came with a crash. The spouting waves were decapitated as if by a magic sword. Instead of plunging and bucking in all directions they all began to move with the wind.

The pressure of the air squeezed the breath out of us.

262

It was necessary to turn one's face away from the wind to breathe and even then it was difficult, for the air currents moving past the head on both sides made a vacuum about the nose. The spray was blown back in the form of flying needles that cut into exposed flesh. The birds and insects were gone. The blue sky and sun were gone and we were wrapped in dark blankets.

It was soon plain that this bout was to be worse than the first. I had never known such a wind. It was later reported to have varied between one hundred and two hundred miles an hour. On the Beaufort scale it registered a reading of twelve. The force of the average strong gale is six. Now one could understand the derivation of the word typhoon—from the Chinese *taifung*, Great Wind.

The engine and rudder kept the ship's nose in the wind, but we were being relentlessly pushed back toward the shore we had left. It was still several miles off. But if this continued we might just as well have stayed in the bay and gone to the devil all at once rather than by degrees.

Between here and there, anything might happen. The wind might turn. Typhoons were changeable—pray God this one would be.

Back, back we went. Now I could see the bay. Where was the schooner? For a time I could not make her out. Then when the wrack lifted momentarily she stood out clearly.

She was upside down on the rocks with her two masts stuck out akimbo and tons upon tons of water thundering over her hull. Already half the strakes were torn off her counter. With good luck, the crew should have escaped to shore, but their ship would never ride again.

263

It gave us no satisfaction to see the wreck, for were we not hellbent to the same fate? Ruthless Ruth, have pity! Remember that typhoons are never consistent. Sea god, come out and command your unruly waters! The shrine at the foot of the foremast was half blown away. Had *Kompira* gone too?

Now, to add to our woes, came rain. Not rain, but a sea from the sky. It came down in solid masses, unbelievable weights of water pounding like pile drivers upon our shoulders. Typhoon Ruth delivered more rain in a day than Japan had received all the rest of the year.

The rain cut off all view of the shore. We were completely shut in. Our only guide was the wind and Uncle kept the ship's nose pointed into it.

When the wrack cleared for a moment Good-Fortune shouted with joy. I opened my wind-sealed eyes and looked for the shore. It was not where it had been. Instead of lying behind us it was now on our port beam.

The shore had not changed but the wind had. The typhoon had crazily altered its path. Now the gale was coming to us straight out of the great bay of Beppu, our destination. If the wind pushed us backward it did not matter too much—there was plenty of sea room behind us.

But the heavy rain seemed to have shaken the wind's confidence. It still blew fiercely but we managed for an hour to hold our own against it, and then to make some headway. As we neared Beppu the mountains behind the city gradually cut the force of the wind. Five more toilsome hours, and we pulled into the harbor lined by the hotels of this famous hot spring resort.

The two uncles stayed aboard to baby the ship through

a bad night, the captain went to a Japanese inn, and we repaired to the home of the Shavers, American missionaries, in the nearby town of Oita. The storm again changed its course, descended with full fury upon Oita and Beppu, shook the big two-story frame house and gave the anxious missionaries not one wink of sleep all night. I am ashamed to say that we slept solidly through to late morning.

In bright sunshine we rode back to Beppu. The shore road, a magnificent stretch of cement highway and stone seawall, had been ripped up in a hundred or more places by the force of the waves. Power poles were at all angles. Many houses had been battered to bits by the waves or carried away by the wind.

In Beppu the streets near the waterfront were full of debris. Even whole roofs barred the way. About the ruins the indefatigable Japanese were as busy as ants, already rebuilding. By afternoon the streets were cleared so that traffic could get through everywhere. The process of reconstructing hundreds of ruined homes was already under way.

The damage at sea was great. Shipping schedules were entirely demoralized. Not only were hundreds of light craft destroyed, but the *Hakuryu Maru*, 3,181 tons, and the *Kinsei Maru* 2300 tons, went aground while a 16,500-ton Panamanian tanker was sending off SOS signals from the vicinity of Amami Oshima Island.

The worst typhoon in twenty years had inundated a thousand houses in Yamazaki, taken a toll of forty-two lives in Kagoshima, started floods and landslides in Kyushu, produced three major whirlwinds in Miyazaki Prefecture killing twenty-one persons and destroying thirty houses and twenty-nine fishing boats. A high tidal wave inundated the waiting room of the Kansai Steamship Company in Kobe and put twenty shops of the port of Osaka under water. Rice and orange crops were hard hit throughout Japan.

But in this land of earthquakes, fires, typhoons and bombings, disasters that would floor an ordinary people are taken with a perverse amiability. The Japanese grin at the ruins, say, "What of it?," and begin again.

23

CITY OF A HUNDRED HELLS

BEPPU, full of devils, is one of the most delightful cities of Japan. Its six hundred hotels and the homes of its hundred thousand people are built upon the roof of the infernal regions. Stamp too hard and your foot may go through the thin crust and come out parboiled.

The city lies on a mountainside skirting Beppu Bay. Approached by sea, the mountain slopes appears to be stuck with scores of erect white feathers waving in the breeze. These are geysers of steam from the volcanic fires beneath.

For this is the city where every house has boiling hot water every minute of the day and night without the cost of a penny for heating, where taps may be left running continually without waste, where bathtubs overflow twelve hours a day and meals are cooked without fuel.

The boiling, grumbling, ever-flowing solfataras of Japan's greatest hot spring resort cover twenty square miles. Hot springs even bubble up through the floor of the bay and have a unique effect upon the fish population. The Black Current which washes the eastern shore of Japan comes from the equator loaded with tropical fish, but most of them soon die in the chilly northern waters. The fortunate ones that happen to be carried into Beppu Bay make themselves quite at home and the waters here are filled with brilliantly-colored immigrants from the South Seas. Floating like gray islands among the technicolor fish are huge South Sea turtles covered with barnacles and looking like rocks—and sometimes as dangerous as rocks to fragile craft that happen to collide with them. Fishermen never molest them since Buddhism honors the turtle as the sacred symbol of long life.

Even without its hot springs Beppu would qualify as the Japanese Riviera, thanks to a lucky break in climate. It is cool in summer because of the trade wind. It is warm in winter because during that season there is no trade wind.

The monkeys that swarm on Monkey Mountain are also evidence of the salubrious climate, for monkeys do not like cold weather. The townspeople do not kill them because, who knows, they might be reincarnated ancestors. So they are politely tolerated even when they enter houses in search of food. This is particularly trying since the monkeys never travel alone but in groups of twenty or thirty. Each group has a leader and any member who does not obey him is severely punished by the other members of the group. It is well authenticated that these clever monkeys come down to the sea, dive in, and catch fish—a very unmonkeylike procedure. To make sure that they eat well, food is regularly placed in feeding troughs on the mountainside.

The fiery fountains of Beppu were first reported in a Japanese history of the sixth century and they still show no sign of failing. On the contrary, as new vents are opened the spectacle becomes even more thrilling.

No wonder these growling, rumbling, hissing or

screaming outbursts from the jaws of the earth are called *jigoku*, hells, and each has its presiding devil.

Many are the stories that are told of the caprices of these evil spirits and the innocent bystanders they have hypnotized, lured over the brink and devoured. Their reputation is not improved by the fact that they are, next to the volcanoes, the scene of most of Japan's suicides. Perhaps to the suicidal mind there is something satisfyingly conclusive about diving into the blazing bowels of the earth from which rescue is impossible.

As one would expect near the doors of Satan, the region of the hells is the happy home of many serpents and of hideous toads weighing a pound and measuring eight inches across the back. Actually both snakes and toads are harmless and are here to enjoy the warmth.

We visited the more important hells. Bloody Pond Hell is a lake of almost blood-red water throwing up jets of iron sulphide and great clouds of steam. Its floor evidently rises and falls, once being located at a depth of one hundred feet and at another time at 540 feet. In 1927 it spouted three hundred feet high.

Thunder Hell has at times caused so much damage that it is now placated by the statues of two gods. The Fire God, Fudo, stands in the swirling steam, and the Wind God with a bag of wind on his shoulder is sheltered in a small pavilion because the image is made of perishable wood and is already four hundred years old.

White Pond Hell is a vivid blue pool six hundred feet deep continually bubbling with natrium chloride said to be good for diseases of the digestive organs.

A statue of a great dragon, hollowed within to make a

passage for steam which spouts most realistically from its nostrils, is the guardian deity of Gold Dragon Garden Hell, a boiling hot mineral salt spring recommended for rheumatism. Of course no one descends into the pool itself, but the water is diverted into baths. Statues of the apostles of Buddha stand about the pool, clouds of steam rising around their heads. In the home of the caretakers we saw women cooking by the eternal steam, and in an outdoor exhibit the same steam generated electricity to send a toy train speeding around a circular track.

Devil's Mountain Hell is far enough below the boiling point to be comfortable for alligators and crocodiles which are bred in this hot water because it greatly speeds their growth. When they reach full size they are shot and their skins are used to make shoes, jackets and trunks.

Green Lake, also called Sea Hell, is impregnated with alum and daily pours out 800,000 gallons of blue-green water. Picnickers are provided with a basket at the end of a long pole so that they may boil their own eggs in the bubbling waters.

Devil's Stone Monk's Hell is guarded by an ugly-looking demon armed with a club and standing in the middle of the pool, breathing steam.

A unique waterfall of hot water drops ten feet upon the shoulders of nude bathers, relaxes tight muscles and massages away rheumatism. Above the riverbed some of the same water is diverted into a pool occupied at the time of our visit by a bevy of pretty girls innocent of bathing suits and unafraid of our camera. For those who want their sulphur, iron and carbon neither in pool nor in waterfall there is still a third device—a cave full of steam.

If one strays from the paths hereabout he is quite likely to break through the thin shell and find himself in decidedly hot water. We saw a nomadic pilgrim happily boiling his rice over a hole he had punched in the ground.

The chemical content of the baths is bewildering in its variety. There are eight general groups, classified by diseases treated. Old folks with no ailment other than sluggish circulation lie in the comforting hot water for weeks at a stretch, head raised on a support, a large stone on the stomach to keep them from floating away. They eat and sleep without leaving the bath. The sulphur and iron turn their hair a rusty red and prolonged immersion mottles and crumples their skin until they look like wrinkled lepers. The dearest wish of some ageing Japanese is to retire under a rock in an ever-flowing Beppu bath.

Then there are the famous "sand baths" on the Beppu beach. You go first into the bathhouse to pay your fee and remove your clothing. Then out to the beach where an old woman with a shovel digs a grave for you. Water seeps into the bottom of it. It looks innocent enough, but when you lie in it you jump out with a cry of pain for the water is boiling hot.

All over the beach, heads are turned your way. Nothing but heads, for the bodies are buried. Your pain causes general amusement.

"These foreigners—" you think people are saying, "they can't stand much." The old woman cries shame upon you. She pulls and pushes you down into the steaming grave and then proceeds to shovel sand over you. When a neat burial mound has been raised and nothing remains visible but your red-hot face, she knocks the breath out of you

271

by giving the mound a final whack with the flat of her shovel.

You are quite sure you cannot stand this for more than five minutes. But the pain merges into blissful comfort, muscles and nerves untie their knots, time becomes of no importance, and you are sorry after three hours to see the old woman coming with her shovel to disinter you.

At the lovely Suginoi Yadoya (or, in English, The-Well-by-the-Cedar-Tree Inn) far up on the mountainside we had a charmingly unfurnished cottage to ourselves, its central attraction being a great tile bath full of crystal-clear hot water welling up out of the earth and continually running over.

The same luxury is afforded to all dwellers in Beppu, whether in mansions or in hovels, in schools, hospitals or jails. Hot water is available for all purposes. It is used to irrigate the rice fields. In greenhouses it maintains a perpetual summer and makes possible swiftly matured muskmelons, watermelons, green peas, cucumbers and tomatoes in midwinter. Here muskmelons ripen in thirty or forty days. A system of pipes carries hot water through twenty greenhouses. The temperature of the water as it enters the system is 180° F. After circulating through the twenty conservatories it still has a temperature of 150° F.

The experiments of engineers in using volcanic steam to generate electricity have led to ambitious plans financed by the government to make use, here and elsewhere in Japan, of the volcanic boiler upon which Japan rests. By the use of underground steam it is hoped to cut Japan's coal bill in half.

The first powerhouse using natural steam is being estab-

272

lished by the Kyushu Electric Power Company. It will initially generate three thousand kilowatts and eventually reach an output of 150,000 kilowatts. Forty other such power plants are on the books.

When the program is fully worked out it is expected that the total output of electricity from volcano-powered turbines will be four billion kilowatts per year. To generate this amount of electricity it is now necessary to burn four million tons of coal.

One of the many surprising sights of Beppu is the mighty statue of Buddha, the largest in Japan. It stands eighty feet high, far outstripping the forty-seven-foot Daibutsu of Kamakura.

It is chiefly remarkable, not for its size, but for its composition. It is made of concrete, human bones, hair, and ashes. The remains of a million people who had no relatives to mourn their souls have here found a magnificent if bizarre resting place. The bones and ashes are those of prisoners, fugitives, orphans, suicides, and the dead of the Russo-Japanese War and the Japan-China War. The money to build the statue was collected by a priest of the Zen sect of Buddhism. Every year on April 8th the priests hold a ceremony before it and the faithful come with ladders, buckets and brooms and give it a thorough scrubbing from top to bottom as an act of penitence and devotion.

This must be no small job, as the statistics of the statue will indicate. Its head is adorned with 1,008 concrete curls. The length of the face is twenty-four feet. The nose is four feet long. Each eye is more than six feet wide and the mouth spans seven feet. One year a donor contributed a wreath of flowers to be placed on one of the great thumbs.

He was mortified to learn that his wreath was too small. The thumb is seven feet in circumference.

We journeyed back of Beppu four hours by train to visit the greatest hell of all. Mighty Aso Volcano boasts the largest crater in the world, fifteen miles long and ten wide, with a circumference of nearly forty miles. Most of the crater is dormant and seventy-five thousand people cultivate its rich soil.

Rising from the crater floor are five volcanic cones, four of them extinct and one decidedly active. The latter is highly temperamental. It may smoke quietly today and send up screeching fountains of hot stones and ashes tomorrow. Its more recent violent eruptions have occurred in 1884, 1889, 1894, 1904, 1929, 1933 and 1950.

It stands a mile high, and after leaving the train at Bochu we must bump in a bus for an hour and a half up and up over a trail strewn with chunks of lava; a road that would be considered impassable in America or Europe, even on the level, and here they climb it!

The motor must be kept continually in low to climb the steep grades. The roaring and fuming are terrific. The bus lurches from side to side, much to the peril of busses passing in the opposite direction. At these moments when a driver most needs two hands on the wheel, the polite Japanese chauffeur drives with one hand only—because he must salute with the other.

At the end of the bus line there is still a long climb on foot. Here not a thing grows. The mountaniside is strewn with scoria and volcanic detritus and the path clambers over immense lava boulders and across jagged volcanic sword points never meant for human feet. The wind is icy cold and so strong that everyone must tie on his or her hat with a scarf or handkerchief knotted under the chin. One's ears ache with the cold.

We reach the crest and stand at the edge of the pit. The wind pulls and pushes as if determined to throw us in. Our backs ache with cold while a cooking heat strikes us in the face. Everyone gets out still another handkerchief, this one to be tied across the nose to keep out the stench of brimstone.

The roar of a titanic blast furnace rises from the pit. Clouds of snow-white steam alternate with billows of pitch black smoke. Hundreds of feet down are boiling, thundering pools of sulphurous mud sending up geysers of fire. These are like red clutching fingers that barely reach us as we peer over the edge.

They have a dreadful fascination. We can understand why this is a favorite suicide resort. There is no fence or barrier along the edge. It would be so easy for the discouraged student or the lovelorn pair to yield to the roaring invitation and the shoving wind and slip over the edge into oblivion. In fact it is surprising that so many visitors keep their senses in this mind-addling turmoil of sight and sound.

Songs, recitations and stories beguile the down-trip in the bus. For the bus girl at a Japanese resort must be able to do more than collect tickets. She stands behind the driver, facing her fares, and performs steadily for an hour or more at a time, relating stories, reciting poems, and singing ballads, all having to do with the wonders we have just seen or are about to see.

The train waits at Bochu. The nature of this mighty

amphitheater, the world's largest crater, becomes evident when it takes our train a full hour to climb slowly to the crater wall, through which it plunges by way of a mile-long tunnel. Then we slide smoothly through lovely forests of cryptomeria, cedar and bamboo down to Beppu.

24

THE FINAL DASH

ONCE MORE we crossed the Inland Sea, this time at its widest point. Except for the Kunisaki Peninsula on our port side, we were circled by the landless horizon. And the peninsula would be of no use to us in rough weather, for it offered no ports of refuge. Fortunately the sea was glassy smooth.

Rounding the point, we saw the U.S.A. At least the village by that name has found mistaken identity highly profitable. It turns out a variety of products for sale the world over and on each it prints neatly "Made in USA." This expedient makes possible a higher price than could be asked for goods labeled "Made in Japan."

Now all five of us searched the west. As yet nothing was to be seen in that direction except sea and sky. But just below that horizon lay the end of our trip. We were eager to reach our goal, sorry to part company. Our three pirates had worked themselves well into our affections.

Wide-Margin-of-Safety had proved a skilful and resourceful captain. His inexperience in navigation was more than balanced by his courage in emergencies and his desire to please. Bit by bit, his character had unfolded. He was strictly honest. His face was not the shut face of some Japanese, but open and frank. He made no promises that he could not keep. He commanded his uncles with none of the friction that might have been expected between a twenty-six-year-old chief and elders twice his age. He usually responded to our requests with a cheerful "Oh yes!"— the only English he knew.

Not that he was always sweetness and light. He was jealous of his prerogatives as captain. We took great care not to question his sovereignty but since there were certain points that we wished to visit and others that we preferred to skip it was sometimes necessary to cross swords with him. Then he would do as told, but moodily. When he ceased to say "Oh yes!" we knew that we had hurt his feelings. Then a casually dropped compliment would restore him to sparkling good humor.

He disliked slowing the engine, and hated like sin to stop it so that a picture might be taken—and with good reason, for it took about ten minutes to start it again. But full-speed vibration is fatal to pictures and even a slow engine does them no good.

He quite wisely favored a safe and noisy harbor as a stopping place for the night, while we preferred a quiet bay. He had never in his life stopped in so many fine inns and was inclined to work the free-entertainment racket for all it was worth. We enjoyed the inns and appreciated the hospitality, but with a love of night air that the Japanese cannot understand we should have been glad to spend more nights on deck. As it was, the captain won hands down. Of forty-three nights we spent thirty-three in the inns, ten on the *Kompira*.

Yasuhiro was most at home below decks with his beloved engine. He kept the awkward oil-burner in perfect condition and faultlessly clean, evidently transferring all of its surplus oil and grease to his own clothing. He habitually looked like a white leopard with black spots.

He was a born mechanic, had been in the tank division during the war, and owned a small store in Kanonji selling engine parts. He would have preferred to run the engine all the time and had ill-disguised scorn for the old-fashioned lug sails. He was annoyed when we preferred the smooth glide of the ship under sail to its frenzied vibration under power.

The sails were the province of Uncle Good-Fortune-in-Autumn. He was wise in the ways of the wind and handled the great thirty-foot batwings with skill. As fond of the tiller as Yasuhiro of the engine, he was always nervous when it was in the hands of anyone else. He was prognathous and we never saw him with his mouth closed. He had a fine display of gold in his prominent teeth. His face was wrinkled and eyes squinted with long looking up to the sails against a sunlit sky.

Uncle Literature-Pursuing-Sixth-Son was fifty but moved about as if he were seventy. He was the one appointed to go up in the bow and throw the line ashore or step ashore with it if there was no one to throw it to. But Literature moved so slowly that the chance often had passed before he could act. It might not be his fault but that of Good-Fortune who steered too wide of the pier, or Wide-Margin who did not stop the engine in time. At home they never pulled up to a pier but just anchored in the inlet, so they had had little practice in this art. Usually in attempting to come alongside the dock we had to circle two or three times like a dog trying to find a place to lie down.

The man with the literary name looked the part best when picking his teeth. Then he had an air of deep contemplation. His gaze traveled over sea and land as if drawing deep draughts of inspiration. His teeth were huge and to pick them was no light matter.

He never had much to say. He spent most of his time patiently doing nothing, for he was neither a sail-man nor an engine-man. He was quite competent at breaking up kindling, laying it in the shichirin on top of an oily rag, adding charcoal, lighting the fire, and fanning it until it was in condition to cook rice.

He pursued literature only as far as the comics and the cheap magazines and then drew back the starboard corner of his open mouth and wrinkled his forehead as if comprehension were almost too much for him.

The dispositions of both uncles were pluperfect. We never heard from either of them an impatient word, much less an angry one. They never swore and I am sure would not have done so even if their language had allowed it. They drank but were never drunk. That they got along so well with the captain was due more to their placidity than to his tact. At the least provocation their wrinkles would spread into a grin. They kept religiously out of their passengers' way, but just the lift of a finger would bring them running. They could never do enough for us. And we learned early never to insult them with tips. Presents, yes, but not tips—and for every present they received they gave one in return.

The western end of the Inland Sea remained obstinately below the horizon but toward evening we raised the north shore and crept into the harbor of Mitajiri for the night.

It was not inspiring. On one side was a great and ugly saké factory and on the other a row of noisy docks and the tenements of factory workers. The *Kompira* was headed for the docks.

We intervened just in time and persuaded Literature to drop anchor in the bay well removed from the town—too far out for a midnight conversation between ship and shore.

Here it was better. Two green mountains as shapely as Fuji were silhouetted against the evening sky. The saké factory became glamorous as the darkness softened its outlines and its windows were lighted. A few miles back of the coast rose the jagged ranges of Honshu. That is really all Japan is—a narrow band of arable soil along the coast girdling a vast core of impossible mountains.

The water was like black glass. It reflected the lights of the town and of the saké factory where work still went on regardless of night. A half moon was mirrored in the sea. But even without benefit of reflection the sea glowed with the ghostly light of thousands of phosphorescent organisms. It was a cold quiet night, comfortable within the futons.

The next morning we continued west over a glassy sea. Except for the shore of Honshu to starboard there was no sign of land. The water was as blue as bluing and the sails as white as if they had been blued.

The age of sail finished? We counted the sails visible at one time—there were twenty-eight. No doubt every one of these boats also had an engine. Thus Japan combines new and old.

We had planned to spend the night at Ube—then finish the trip the next day at Moji. But we made Ube earlier than expected, and anyhow its huge smoke-belching cement plants did not make it attractive. So we changed our objective to Tanoura on the Kyushu side.

Suddenly the captain began to dance and shout. "End of the Seto Naikai!" (Inland Sea). Ahead of us were what looked like two low-lying clouds. They were not clouds. They were the mountainous tails of Kyushu and Honshu, their ranges overlapping to hide the narrow Straits of Shimonoseki.

It was still early afternoon when we approached Tanoura where we had intended to stop for the night. "But how long would it take to get to Moji?" I asked. The captain jumped as if electrified. "You want to go?" And without giving me a chance to reply he ordered Good-Fortune to steer for Moji. None of us wanted the trip finished, yet the final goal drew us like a magnet.

Mary and I feverishly packed as we passed through the tide rips of the Straits of Shimonoseki. We landed in a jam of shipping in smoky Moji.

The trip is finished. It has taken six weeks and has covered eleven hundred and twenty miles.

That is nothing in the sagas of the sea, but something in our own understanding of "the heart of Japan"—something too for our treasure chest of memories. Never can we hope to look upon a more beautiful world than the sea of the three thousand isles. And at the mayor's dinner party that consumes half the night we find ourselves about to weep into our sea urchin's eggs as we think of parting with

Wide-Margin-of-Safety, Good-Fortune-in-Autumn, and Literature-Pursuing-Sixth-Son.

Tomorrow they will set sail for their pirate stronghold, while we, shorn of our thirty-foot wings, prosily continue on train, bus and foot to explore backcountry Japan.

25

JAPAN IN FACT AND FANCY

STOP THE "MAN ON THE STREET" and ask him what he thinks of our foreign policy since the war.

He may be full of gripes about Korea, China, Iran, Germany, France, but he is likely to say:

"Well, anyway, we did a great job in Japan."

Self-satisfaction with our job in Japan and elevation of General MacArthur to a sort of sainthood are perfectly natural in view of the circumstances. For six years we were consistently misinformed.

We derive our opinions from press and radio, which in turn depend for their news of Japan upon foreign correspondents in that country. During the period of the Occupation the newsmen in Japan were under strict military control. They entered Japan only under a special military permit. Once in, they remained only on sufferance. They were subject to prompt dismissal if they became "poor security risks"—that is, if they unfavorably represented the works of the Occupation or dared to criticize the Supreme Commander or his aides. If having fallen from grace they left the country they found it difficult or impossible to return.

284

The newsman caught in this predicament was quite likely to lose his job, his assignment being transferred to a man more adept in treading thin ice. Any newspaper that refused to make this compromise faced the loss of its representation in Japan.

By such methods of intolerance and intimidation, both the individual correspondents and the newspapers behind them were whipped into line.

Only a few powerful journals resisted the pressure. *Time,* which had for years endured the ban of Argentina's Perón rather than lick the boots of that dictator, was equally frank about SCAP. It gave generous space to the achievements of the Occupation but did not mince words in discussing its faults. It found one of the chief of these faults to be the suppression of news:

"U.S. correspondents who have written dispatches critical of the commander or of Occupation policies have soon learned what it is like to be unpopular. Some got the deep-freeze from MacArthur's staff. Others who left Tokyo on visits, or assignments in the Far East, had to wait weeks and slice through endless snarls of red tape before they were allowed to return to Japan."

The distinguished military analyst, Hanson W. Baldwin, was allowed to speak frankly in *The New York Times.* Concerning the Occupation he commented, "What it needs most, but can tolerate least, is criticism."

The Christian Science Monitor dared the thunderbolts with statements such as the following:

"Many of the repressive or regulatory techniques favored by the Japanese have been applied at Occupation headquarters in the treatment of American and other foreign correspondents . . . While practising censorship, Occupation spokesmen blandly talk of 'freedom of the press' and point out that it is guaranteed in the new constitution—which most Japanese know was written primarily by Americans."

In another article the *Monitor* reported that "the Japanese complain that the MacArthur supervision of newspapers, books, radio and movies is worse than Tojo's."

"Every American newsman and magazine writer in Japan," declared *Look*, "knows the consequences if he sends to this country facts that displease General MacArthur or the all-powerful members of the high command. He will find all official avenues closed tight against him. Besides that, he will very shortly be forced by some means to leave the Far East, with no possibility of returning." General MacArthur, said the magazine, "has misled the American people."

Frank Hawley, a noted Japanese classic scholar and correspondent for the London *Times*, was expelled from Japan in June, 1950. The memorandum of expulsion signed by General MacArthur declared that Hawley was no longer welcome in Japan and ordered his immediate departure. Hawley had incurred official wrath by his statement that SCAP's ban on public demonstrations was a violation of the new, American-written Japanese constitution which declares, "Freedom of assembly and association, as well as speech, press and all other forms of expression are guaranteed."

The correspondent of *Newsweek*, charged by SCAP with associating "with the wrong kind of Japanese" was barred from Japan for almost a year.

Tiltman of the London *Daily Herald*, Bill Costello of CBS, Jessup of McGraw Hill, had difficulties.

Dozens of such incidents led to an open revolt of the Tokyo press corps. The correspondents drew up a manifesto charging that men who merely reported facts were subjected to persecution by SCAP. They requested that the American Society of Newspaper Editors investigate "intimidation, coercion, and censorship in Japan."

When a committee of correspondents complained to SCAP's press relations officer he warned them: "Every time [you] have pressed for a clarification of policy, the policy has grown tighter."

No wonder Senator Knowland, after a personal investigation of the situation, charged that MacArthur was setting up an "iron curtain" to ward off all criticism of the Occupation.

"Ever since the Surrender," wrote *Fortune*, "Americans have had the comfortable illusion that while the rest of the world was in a fearful mess, this Occupation was just about an unqualified success. Yet on the briefest investigation this belief turns out to be moonshine, and each deeper probe merely confirms and darkens the bad news."

But these were voices crying in the wilderness. Ninety-nine percent of the American press was uncritical of the Occupation or, like the Hearst papers, gave it incessant and overwhelming praise. Hundreds of press handouts from SCAP headquarters were printed verbatim. General MacArthur's personal reports and directives got page one every time and their ringing eloquence convinced millions that we were truly accomplishing in Japan "the greatest reformation of a people ever attempted."

Even more amazing than this mesmerism of the outside world was the fact that the Japanese themselves did not know what was going on in Japan.

They read and rejoiced in MacArthur's announcement made at the beginning of the Occupation that a "free, uncontrolled and unfettered press" was being established in Japan. On the basis of this solemn declaration they had a right to believe that what they now read in their papers or heard over the radio was the truth.

Japanese editors who took seriously the promise of an "unfettered press" were soon disillusioned. They ran into snags of censorship at every turn. No slightest criticism of the Occupation nor of any of its personnel was allowed. Criticism of the new constitution was banned. It was a constitution for the Japanese and it might have been supposed that the Japanese had a right to discuss it—but no. Nor was any comment other than favorable permitted of the Land Reform Bill. Any suggestion that the industrial trusts had not been fully abolished was blue-pencilled by the censors.

No mention must be made of past offenses of statesmen approved by SCAP for a place in the new government. There must be no reflection upon the emperor. The fact that the militarists were still active underground was not to be printed. It might disturb the people's faith that Japan was now and forever more a democracy. The golden age of labor had supposedly been ushered in by SCAP and news of labor unrest, strikes, wage demands, were suppressed. Nothing but glowing words might be written about the United States. Lord Bryce's *Modern Democracy* was edited to retain his praise of America but omit his criticism of

American politics. Parts of Leo Tolstoy's *War and Peace* were deleted. Even a volume of Hans Christian Andersen's *Fairy Tales* was banned because of its description of a naval fight.

Papers were encouraged to extol democracy and condemn the sort of emperor-worship and hero-worship that had proved so injurious to Japan in the past. The ban on hero-worship was subject to one exception. When the people chose to make General MacArthur their hero, no objection was raised. Reading nothing but praise of the general, and having no way of knowing that the chorus of approval was not spontaneous, the people gave themselves up to an adulation that became fanatical.

This worried the wise editor of a great Japanese paper. Knowing that hero-worship and democracy were not compatible, he assumed that SCAP would approve his effort to check it. He wrote:

"Japan used to abound in ardent Hitler worshippers. . . . When the Japanese-American war started they switched their worship to General Tojo, and, after the Surrender, to General MacArthur. Japanese teachers have traditionally been bent on inspiring the children with this habit of blind worship for the ruler . . . a tendency constituting the worst enemy of democracy. . . .

"It must be emphasized that unless and until the Japanese are cleansed of this servile concept, democracy in Japan will make no progress. . . . The proper way for the Japanese to repay General MacArthur's sincere efforts to democratize this country and his wise administration is not to worship him, but to rid themselves of subservience and strive, with high self-esteem, to assume the actual authority of government by themselves. Only then will the Supreme Commander be assured that the object of the Occupation has been achieved."

It might be supposed that SCAP's reaction to this editorial would be a profound "Amen." Instead, when one of the first copies of the papers reached headquarters, the presses were ordered stopped and the papers already printed were pulled from the delivery trucks and destroyed. General Willoughby, speaking for SCAP said, "The article is in bad taste." Some felt that the bad taste lay not in the article but in the suppression of it.

There was a similar personal reaction when the Japanese news service *Kyodo* received dispatches from the United States reporting the formation and activities of anti-MacArthur-for-President clubs at the University of California, Harvard, and University of Wisconsin. SCAP killed this news as "of controversial conjecture" and unsuitable for publication in Japan. A Japanese businessman visiting the United States was astounded to find that, contrary to the impression in Japan, the entire American public was not solidly back of MacArthur for President.

The maze of taboos became so bewildering that Japanese editors mustered up the courage to protest. They were delighted when SCAP in 1948 announced the end of censorship—but bewildered anew when censorship before publication was replaced with censorship after publication.

Now the editors were left to themselves to figure out what was fit to print. If they guessed wrong, they were likely to have their publications suspended. An editor was sent to prison for two years for making such a mistake. Editors felt it necessary to step more cautiously than ever before. The new system, instead of liberating the press, completed its suffocation.

All of this, we are willing to suppose, was motivated by the highest purposes on the part of the Supreme Commander. He sincerely desired to transform Japan into a democracy and believed that the way to do it was through thought control. The Japanese were to have only the highest thoughts, see nothing of the seamy side of life or of the Occupation.

In a way, it worked. The unremitting flood of good news kept the people quiet, made them acquiescent and obedient. This pliancy was interpreted by MacArthur to be the birth of a new spirit in Japan.

It was not a new spirit, but a rebirth of the age-old spirit of subservience to dictatorship. Seen from a distance as MacArthur saw it—for he never permitted himself to mingle with the people—it looked like democracy.

But the Army, necessarily autocratic from top to bottom, is hardly the best teacher of democracy. People cannot be pushed or herded into democracy. Democracy is not achieved by putting blinders on citizens so that they can see neither to the right nor to the left.

At first the word "democracy" had a tremendous vogue in Japan. No one knew what it meant, everyone had his own idea.

A schoolteacher thought it meant equality and that meant that boys and girls in the sixth grade should be examined together by the instructor in hygiene.

"But they will be stripped naked," the instructor objected.

"We have been living in a world of false modesty," said the teacher. "This is the age of the equality of the sexes."

The children were stripped and examined. Infuriated fathers and mothers called a meeting of the PTA and the teacher was dismissed. He believes he is a martyr to democracy.

A girl joined a group to study freedom and democracy. She came upon Patrick Henry's inspiring line, "Give me liberty or give me death!" Greatly moved, she wrote a will declaring her purpose to die "so that democracy might live," then drowned herself in Tokyo Bay.

To many young people, democracy meant freedom to do anything they pleased regardless of others and regardless of consequences.

Every newspaper, every magazine, every radio station extolled the beauties of democracy, but carefully ignored its faults and difficulties. The picture of it was too highly colored, too devoid of tone and shadow. People became hysterical about it.

But one extreme invites the other. The curve of devotion to democracy was up during 1945 and 1946, fairly level during 1947, then descended ever more steeply and plunged abruptly after the end of the Occupation in 1952.

In the beginning, every political party sought to be known as democratic. The Socialists renamed themselves the Social Democrats. The middle-of-the-road party called itself the Democrats. The rightists became the Democratic Liberals. The Communists did not change their name but they also claimed to be the chief champions of democracy.

By 1952 the democratic label was no longer an asset.

The Social Democrats were once more Socialists. The Democrats now called themselves the Progressives. The Democratic Liberals were now just Liberals.

In 1946 books on democratic institutions were in great demand. For the right to translate and publish such books, Japanese publishers paid royalties fifty percent higher than the average. By 1949 the reaction had set in and, as reported in *The New York Times,* "a noted professor, an established author on such subjects, reported that his publisher had told him the sale of anything favorable to the United States was doubtful, but if he would venture some criticism of democracy or say a few kind words for the Communists public acceptance was certain."

This does not mean that democracy is done in Japan. Far from it. It means that the Japanese have found it is not something that can be thrown on like a coat. It must grow from the inside. It has been growing in Japan, with occasional setbacks, for the past hundred years. We can only hope that it has not been retarded more than it has been advanced by the effort to impose it by force.

The Japanese were carried away by MacArthur's manifest idealism, by the contagion of his overoptimism, and the surprising goodwill of the occupying forces. Now they have come back to earth. They are counting their gains and losses.

Certainly their form of government is more subject to popular control than it was. Japan owes a lasting debt to the able General Courtney Whitney and brilliant Frank Rizzo, chiefs of the Government Section of SCAP, who were instrumental in the extension of the suffrage, the writing of a new constitution, and the elevation of the Diet to a position at least theoretically superior to that of the Cabinet, premier, or emperor.

Some of this must remain, despite present efforts to minimize the Diet and restore the power of premier and emperor. The truth is that the Japanese governing classes have never had much faith in the wisdom of the common people. To them, government by the people seems dangerously close to mob rule. Nor do the people have much confidence in themselves. In every case, the free elections have returned ultraconservative leaders. There is no sign of the emergence of a people's party.

Half of the members of the present cabinet are men who were purged for wartime activities, now depurged and restored to favor. The premier, Shigeru Yoshida, acts without consulting the Diet or waiting for its decisions. He does not defer even to his own party. He summarily hires and fires state ministers. Fifty-seven of them have come and gone at the will of the premier, without consultation between him and the leaders of the Liberal Party. He now proposes a Special Maintenance Law which would give the premier nothing less than autocratic wartime control over Japanese society.

The Occupation believed in states' rights. The states or *ken* and the cities were given a large measure of self-government. The trend is now back toward centralized control.

It is quite possible that the self-government idea was carried too far. It may be proper for Texas and New York to conduct most of their own affairs without dictation from Washington. But why the government of a nation smaller than California should be distributed among units no larger than California's counties is not clear. Public dissatisfaction with this system is now turned to advantage by the premier who concentrates power in his own hands rather than in the Diet where it belongs.

Another reform that nullified itself by being carried too far was the decentralization of the police force. Formerly all police were controlled from Tokyo and were a dangerous tool in the hands of the military. To correct this situation MacArthur ordered the national police abolished, leaving every town and village to establish its own police force. The result was complete inability to handle any national crisis such as a strike or a communist riot. Also the expense of maintenance of separate forces was too great and in 1952 there was a return to the prewar police system.

The national government used to reach into every village through the *tonari-gumi*, neighborhood association. This was an association of villagers for mutual help, but because it was used to kill self-government in the village and enforce the will of Tokyo, it was abolished by the Occupation. However, it seems that nothing adequate was put in its place, for when a public opinion poll was taken in 1951 it was found that sixty-five percent of the villagers questioned favored the lifting of the ban upon the neighborhood association, while only eighteen percent were opposed. These groups are now being revived.

With the passing of the Occupation, all its reforms are to be critically studied. An Ordinance Review Committee appointed by the Yoshida Cabinet is examining, with an eye to repeal or amendment, laws originally adopted in accordance with SCAP directives. Many have been abolished and others modified.

"It's all going back," a missionary told me sorrowfully.

"Back to the old ways of nationalism and emperor-worship." Comments the London *Times*, "The forces of old Japan are again gathering." While the progressive *Nippon Times* sadly remarks, "Signs of Japan returning to where she was before the Occupation began and the eventual undoing of many of the postwar reforms are very much in evidence these days."

The worst of it is that the people are indifferent. Reforms which they did not fight to gain they will not fight to hold. The postwar Japanese government was not, as promised in the Potsdam Proclamation, "established in accordance with the freely expressed will of the Japanese people." The people merely submitted to reforms imposed by alien authority.

I asked the famous Tokyo teacher and editor, Florence Wells, "Will the changes stick?" Her reply was significant: "Those that return Japan to what she was will stick."

Japan in the twenties was moving steadily toward democracy. The trend was reversed by the conquest of Manchuria beginning in 1931 and the ensuing wars in China and the Pacific. In so far as the Occupation helped to restore Japan to the pattern of pre-aggression days, the changes will stick. But American ways of life imposed upon Japan by Washington can no more be expected to endure than would Japanese ways dictated to citizens of the United States by Tokyo.

A healthy appreciation of this fundamental truth was shown by General Ridgway when he inherited MacArthur's job in Japan. A memorandum from GHQ to all members of the Occupation laid down a radically new policy:

296

"Many of the social customs and manners that you observe in Japan today were already old a thousand years before Columbus discovered America. So don't come barging into Japan with any idea of revolutionizing their customs, or of remolding their daily lives into a carbon copy of your own. In the first place, it can't be done. In the second place, Japanese customs and social mores are adapted to the kind of life the Japanese must live."

Here at last was sound common sense. That this policy was to guide American conduct not merely in Japan, but the world over, was promised in the fourth of the nine principles stated by President Eisenhower in his inaugural address in January, 1953:

"Honoring the identity and heritage of each nation of the world, we shall never use our strength to try to impress upon another people our own cherished political and economic institutions."

When democracy develops in Japan we may be sure it will not be the democracy of Britain and America. It may be inferior to our brand in some ways, better in others. It will take account of Japanese traditions two thousand years old. It will be based upon cooperation rather than competition. The Japanese do not like our individualism. They regard it as selfish and antisocial. They cannot understand the principle of "Every man for himself." A Japanese will never act alone if he can help it. He prefers group action. He calls in his friends, his neighbors, even his rivals, to advise him and work with him.

Who shall say that this philosophy is a poorer basis for democracy than the principle of devil take the hindmost?

Besides objecting to an egocentric society on moral

grounds, the Japanese consider it too expensive. It may be feasible in a land of great natural resources such as the United States for each man to go his own way, but Japan, they believe, is too poor to afford it.

In Western society great stress is laid upon happiness. The Japanese regard the pursuit of happiness as unworthy. They consider it even immoral, and as a goal of life it is not likely to enter into the Japanese conception of democracy. They place the emphasis on duty. If happiness comes to them in the performance of their duty, they accept it gladly. But it is a byproduct, not an end in itself.

Of paramount importance in the Japanese democracy will be *on*. Perhaps the closest English equivalent of the word is obligation. A Japanese feels acutely any debt of gratitude he owes to anyone who has helped him and will not rest until it is paid off. Even then he is not satisfied until he has placed his former benefactor in his own debt. He finds his greatest enjoyment in giving. He does not understand our conception of sacrifice, for he has no feeling of sacrifice when he gives. Nor does his religion promise him any reward or merit for giving. He does not do unto others in order that they shall do the same or a little better unto him. His democracy, when it comes, will be a democracy of mutual helpfulness.

It will be slow in coming, for feudal traditions are still strong. Probably no people change so quickly on the surface and so slowly beneath as the Japanese. They adopt the new without rejecting the old. Isolated from the continent, with a remarkably homogeneous people who all think alike, Japan is deeply conscious of its own history. Its religions, language, drama, arts, have persisted through centuries.

Equally persistent has been the subjection to autocratic control—in early days to that of the emperor; later, to that of the shogun speaking for the emperor; in modern times, to that of the militarists manipulating the emperor. For two thousand years the Japanese subject has not dared to call his soul his own. It belonged to his emperor, or to anyone strong enough to usurp the power of the emperor. The inbred docility of the Japanese made them like rubber in the hands of the Occupation.

Like rubber, not clay. Clay can be molded and will hold its form. Rubber can be pressed into shape but will spring back when the pressure is removed. The Japanese have largely reverted to their historic character, and have resumed their painfully slow progress toward a democracy of their own making. Even this snaillike advance will often be interrupted, as it seems now about to be interrupted by the resurgence of militarism in Japan.

26

WAR NEVERMORE

THE CROWNING ABSURDITY of the Occupation was the promise exacted of the Japanese that they would never again go to war.

Tongue in cheek, the Japanese made the pledge as ordered by the Supreme Commander. It was embodied in the new constitution written by SCAP and adopted under compulsion by the Japanese government.

Every visitor to Japan has heard the classic witticism: One Japanese asks another, "Have you read the new constitution?" The other replies, "No, I can't read English."

The constitution is, of course, in Japanese, but, having been translated from English its conceptions and phraseologies are so alien that its foreign origin is painfully apparent.

Article 9 of the constitution under the heading, Renunciation of War, runs as follows:

"Aspiring sincerely to an international peace based on justice and order, the Japanese people forever renounce war as a sovereign right of the nation and the threat or use of force as means of settling international disputes.

"In order to accomplish the aim of the preceding paragraph, land, sea and air forces, as well as other war potential, will never be maintained. The right of belligerency of the state will not be recognized."

Anyone familiar with the writings of General MacArthur cannot fail to recognize here the fine sweep of his imagination and his customary use of such words as "forever" and "never."

In this case, "forever" and "never" had a short life, since Japan is now actively preparing for war.

This is, of course, a great pity. All peoples, including the Japanese, long desperately for an age of unbroken peace. But it would be hard to find a schoolboy so naïve as to suppose that any nation would keep a pledge to abjure the right to maintain land, sea and air forces during these troubled years—let alone forever!

The constitution of a nation is something almost sacred. So at least we regard our own constitution. We respect it because it has worked. Those who framed it were highly idealistic but practical as well and put into it nothing that would not work. The Japanese have a constitution which they cannot respect since it obviously will not work. It invites circumvention and fraud. Japanese legal authorities are now busily reinterpreting the Renunciation of War to mean just about the opposite of what it obviously does mean. They say it does not preclude "defensive" war. This interpretation, of course, opens the gate wide since any sort of war can be called defensive. Japanese militarists claim that their attack upon Pearl Harbor was defensive.

Having found a way around one article of the constitution, apologists are working to undermine other articles. Once the worms get in, they are hard to stop. The responsibility for this corruption and chicanery goes back to those who compelled the acceptance of a document so unrealistic that it made evasion necessary.

By 1951 the Occupation had reversed itself on the question of rearmament. Japan was urged to rearm and America would help her. Japan was to be made ready for her role as one of the Allies in the event of a war with the Soviet. This change of heart is expressed in Article 5 of the Peace Treaty:

"The Allied Powers recognize that Japan as a sovereign nation possesses the inherent right of individual or collective self-defense . . ."

As we have already noted, any aggression is excused as self-defense by those who commit it.

While the effort to disarm Japan for all time was merely ridiculous, the pressure to rearm Japan in a hurry is positively dangerous.

That she will rearm to some extent is inevitable, but the process should not be speeded nor financed by us. Overemphasis on militarism in Japan will inevitably make her a menace, not merely to Russia, but to her present friends, and to herself.

The common people, with their native wisdom, realize this. They have been through a war too recently to want another. They have suffered too severely at the hands of their own militarists to wish to see them restored to power. Yet every day the new militarism of Japan takes on more of the color and character of the old.

Some seventy thousand purged nationalists and militarists have been restored to full citizenship rights. War criminals sit in the Diet, the Cabinet, and the imperial court. War criminals are revising textbooks, running newspapers, producing moving pictures, operating radio stations. Japan's war guilt is denied and Tojo is made a hero.

Under the guise of a National Police Reserve, a new army is in the making. It is organized into regular military units, with engineer, artillery, medical, and supply divisions, and receives basic field training. Purged Japanese officers and officers of the United States Army serve as advisers. The new soldiers use United States Army-type equipment. They train with mortars, bazookas, machine guns, anti-aircraft guns, howitzers and U.S. Pershing tanks. The United States is supplying most of the arms until the Japanese munitions industry gets into full swing. The goal for the next few years is a 300,000-man army of fifteen divisions, a 1500-plane Air Force and a 300,000-ton Navy. To start the navy the United States has transferred fifty landing craft and eighteen frigates to Japan's Coastal Safety Force. Concerning this transfer *Time* remarks:

"The news created hardly a ripple in either country, though in 1942 any U.S. serviceman in the Pacific would have been laughed down had he predicted such a turn of events in one decade."

Japan begins the manufacture of aircraft with a monthly output of seventy-five twin-engine and twenty-five four-engine planes. The first postwar warplane, the Tachihi R-52 is in production. Ever since the Korean war began Japan's prewar munitions makers have been turning out armament for the American forces and are therefore fully prepared to make them for Japan's own use.

Japan is now spending two hundred billion yen a year for defense, *one quarter of the national budget!*

Some nations might afford it. Japan cannot. The people are already burdened by unprecedented taxes. Rearmament will still further lower their living standards. This must lead to unrest, and once again Japan will be tempted to resort to a policy of expansion and aggression.

Already expansionist ambitions are emerging. The tremendous revival of Japanese export trade calls for markets. The markets most desired, outside of China, are Indonesia, the Philippines, Malaya, Thailand and Indo-China. If obstacles are placed in the way of Japan's trade—and this is already happening—Japan will be strongly inclined to use force. The militarists and the big industrialists will join hands as they did before Pearl Harbor. There will be a new attempt to make Asia a "co-prosperity sphere" under Japan.

The seeds of the new fanaticism are already being sown. Voices are demanding the return of Japan's far-flung territories. State Shinto with its slogan of "All the world under one roof" is being revived. The Rescript on Education of the Emperor Meiji which declares that the Way of the gods is "infallible for all ages and true in all places" and which was used by the ultra-nationalists as proof that the power of the emperor should be extended to "all places" is still read and venerated in the schools. The constitution of a new political party, the Working Masses Party, declares, "The emperor is the source of all," and "Let the universe be a single house ruled by the emperor."

The emperor, at the behest of SCAP, gave out in 1946 a statement disavowing divinity. This was publicized throughout the world and was hailed by the American public who supposed that it would mean a complete change in the thinking of the Japanese people.

For very simple reasons, this did not happen. The Japanese suspected that the statement had been ordered by SCAP. In the second place, the statement as it appeared in Japanese was worded rather ambiguously and could easily be misinterpreted. In the third place, the fact that the emperor would belittle his own worth was taken as proof of his modesty and further endeared him to his people.

Proof that their emperor was "sacred and inviolable" was the fact that the invaders had not dared to lay hand on him. War criminals were arrested while the emperor not only went free but was accorded the most profound respect. Great care was taken in the war guilt trials not to involve the emperor—and this in spite of the fact that everyone was perfectly well aware of the responsibility of the emperor for the war. As commander-in-chief he was responsible for the acts of his subordinates. He had been fully informed of all war plans and, although he did not approve of the war, he did not use his extraordinary powers to prevent it. If he had publicly warned his people of the plot of the militarists the people would have risen in protest and there would have been no war.

Weak-kneed apologists say, "But that would have cost him his throne, or even his life." It is true that it might have meant abdication, even assassination. But was that too great a price for a man to pay if by paying it he could save the lives of hundreds of thousands of his countrymen?

The Japanese themselves were generously willing to excuse their emperor on the grounds that he had been "misled," but they were astounded to see the respect if not awe and reverence accorded to their monarch by the Western barbarians.

This had never happened before. Never before had an emperor of Japan been revered by other nations. In olden times the emperor of China had exacted obedience and tribute from other lands, including Japan. Now that old humiliation was wiped out and the conquerors of Japan, representing most of the great and small nations of the earth, were bowing to the unconquered emperor!

What greater sign could be given, said the fanatical, of the approach of the day when all men everywhere would be brought under the benign rule of the Son of Heaven?

The deference of foreign powers to the emperor strengthened the emperor institution as nothing in Japanese history had ever done. Nothing could have given greater pleasure to the militarists. For two thousand years it had been the custom of the military to use the emperor to convey their orders to the people. Therefore the purged warmakers desired above all the careful preservation of the dynasty so that they might use it again at some later date. In the meantime, instead of striking out on a truly democratic path, the visiting armies were making use of the imperial voice of authority just as it had been used by Japanese armies for ages past.

A correspondent, Darrell Berrigan, asked an officer in GHQ to permit him to see a certain report.

The officer objected. "The report contains the draft of a suggested Imperial Rescript and it might be a little too early to let the Japanese people know that the emperor doesn't see his rescripts until he signs them. SCAP policy is to use the emperor as long as we possibly can."

"How are you ever going to eliminate the people's dependence on the emperor myth," the correspondent pro-

306

tested, "if you continue to discourage it with one hand and encourage it with the other?"

Typical of the Japanese attitude toward the emperor is the suggested morals code drawn up by the Education Minister, Teiyu Amano, in 1952. It states that the emperor "as the symbol of state is the moral center of the nation."

Someone asked whether this declaration would be valid "even if we had a morally degenerate emperor?"

Dr. Amano considered that he explained away this objection when he said, "When I say that the emperor is the moral center of the nation, I mean that from him emanate all faith and love. I am only saying that he is the center of all love."

A Buddhist priest in Kyoto explains why the Allied Powers did obeisance to the emperor and why he should be venerated throughout the world. It is because he is the head of the Japanese people and because "the Japanese are the only race on earth directly descended from the gods!"

"Let's face the facts," said W. K. Bunce, the Occupation's chief adviser on religion, two years after the emperor had disclaimed divinity, "the Japanese people still worship the emperor."

I asked a very modern young woman, "Now that the emperor is one of you, do you ever use his name?"

The young woman blushed deeply as if I had said something unspeakably vile. "We call him *Tennō*," she whispered.

Tennō means King of Heaven.

In the theological seminary of Doshisha, a Christian university, we listened to a lecture by Dr. Edmund Soper. His audience was made up of Japanese Christian ministers. A

307

Christian preacher interpreted for him. Dr. Soper in his lecture used the name, Hirohito. The interpreter, who had been translating the address faithfully word for word, avoided the name, using Tennō instead. And this before Christian theological students!

In the question period an American professor on the Doshisha staff rose to ask, "Can a Christian also be a Shintoist? Some of the Christian professors of Doshisha go three or four times a week to a Shinto shrine and clap three times. When I ask them about it, they say they are Shinto first, then Christian."

Doshisha is certainly not given to emperor-worship, but even this stronghold of western ideology cannot keep it out. At the time of our visit a week's conference was being held in an auditorium on the Doshisha grounds. Perhaps the university would not have rented out the hall if it had been known in advance what use was to be made of it. It had been hired by a Shinto group, and three thousand people a night attended to hear lectures on behalf of emperor-worship.

One can well imagine the power that resides in the hands of any clique who control an emperor whose every word is sacred law to millions. Ostensibly, the emperor's political power is gone—it was transferred to the Diet by the new constitution. Actually, the emperor is more powerful than at any time in history. But he is powerful, not in his own right, but as the spokesman of the ruling groups.

And the emperor's son, Akihito? What will happen when he comes to power? That able and charming book, *Windows for the Crown Prince*, by the American tutor of the boy of destiny, gives a fine picture of the inculcation of democratic ideals in the mind of a future ruler. To some readers it may have given the impression that Japan will be different under a democratic monarch.

But in the Japanese scheme of things the personal preferences of the emperor are not important. No ruler could be more democratic in spirit than the present emperor of Japan. No ruler could be a more fervent champion of peace. And yet his reign has seen the most ruthless aggression in the long story of Japan. Any emperor, no matter what the bent of his own mind, will be forced by the pressure of Japanese custom to follow the pattern of two millenniums.

So as the Japanese war machine now begins to roll again, the soldiers can rely upon the dynasty. So far they have also been able to rely upon Uncle Sam for active financial and material aid in their rearmament program. Japanese militarists want the United States not as their overlord but as their underwriter.

We cannot tell Japan to stop rearming. But we do not need to stimulate the process. If we spend millions to help Japan develop an overwhelming military establishment, the ensuing events are likely to follow this design.

In the event of war with the Soviet, Japan will play a large part as our ally. With the war over and victory won, Japan will once more be the dominant power in Asia. In that case she will be less than human if she is not tempted once again to bend Asia to her own uses. In pursuit of that goal, she is bound to come once more into collision with the United States and any other great powers having interests in the Far East. Then, another world war.

To save ourselves, as well as to save Japan, from such a calamity, what can we do?

Very little, perhaps, at this late date. There are too many things already done that cannot be undone.

However, we can leave Japan alone. We can refrain from spending millions to build a boomerang that is quite likely in the course of events to fly back.

We can avoid by every means in our power the conflict with the Soviet that would involve Japan as our ally. We can strive for a world settlement that will make great armament programs unnecessary.

Another war between Japan and the West would, considering the resources on both sides, doubtless end as this one has ended—in disaster for Japan. Therefore it is to the interest of the Japanese people to curb militarism—and, most particularly, to control population and so decrease the terrific pressure that drives the nation to dreams of expansion.

Immigration of Japanese to empty regions, such as the great Amazon watershed as large as the United States and with a present population of only one half man to the square mile, should be facilitated.

Tariff barriers blocking Japanese goods should be lowered—because Japan must either sell or fight. It will be cheaper for us to let her sell.

Finally, the goodwill, which was the noblest bequest of a stumbling, naïve, but right-hearted Occupation, should be zealously fostered between Japan and the West. In the long run, it means more than money, arms, or directives.

INDEX

INDEX

Ackerman, Dr. Edward, 212
Agriculture, 81, 220 ff., 272
Akahata, 251-2
Area of Japan, 229
Army of Japan, 303
Army of Occupation, 129 ff.
Aso, Mt., 140, 274
Atom bomb, 178 ff.
Attitude toward Americans, 48, 66-7, 93, 130
Awaji Island, 23

Bath, 72 ff., 201-2, 272
Bed, 77-8
Benjo, 35-7
Beppu, 262 ff.
Buddhism, 128, 148-9, 273
Besshi Copper Mine, 151 ff.
Birth control, 204 ff.

Castles, 106
Cave of Devils, 84 ff.
Censorship, 132, 134, 140, 212, 284 ff.

Charts of Inland Sea, 40
China, 249-50
Christian Science Monitor, 160, 285
Christianity, 128, 191, 308
Civil Code, 119, 123, 226 ff.
Communists, 21, 239 ff.
Constitution, 12, 122, 188, 241, 300
Contemporary Japan, 251
Cooperatives, 224-5
Cressey, George, 14
Customs, 48, 298

Deconcentration Law, 158-9
Democracy, 71, 119, 243, 291 ff.
Descent into the Maelstrom, 56
Diet (parliament) of Japan, 117, 244, 293-4
Divorce, 119, 227
Doshisha University, 307-8
Dress, 120-1